SOUNDS FROM THE BELL JAR

Gordon Claridge is a Fellow of Magdalen College, Oxford, and University Lecturer in Abnormal Psychology. He was previously Reader in Clinical Psychology in the Department of Psychological Medicine at the University of Glasgow. His publications include *Origins of Mental Illness* (also published by Malor), *Personality Differences and Biological Variations* (with S. Canter and W. Hume), *Drugs and Human Behaviour*, and *Personality and Arousal*.

Ruth Pryor has held teaching and research posts at the University of California, Los Angeles; the University of Washington, Seattle; Lady Margaret Hall, Oxford; and the University of Wales. She is the editor of *Letters to Vernon Watkins* and *The Collected Poems of Vernon Watkins*.

Gwen Watkins taught at the University of Washington and the Extra-Mural Department of the University College of Swansea. Her publications include *Portrait of a Friend*, about Dylan Thomas and Vernon Watkins, *and Dickens in Search of Himself.*

SOUNDS
FROM THE
BELL JAR

TEN PSYCHOTIC AUTHORS

by
Gordon Claridge
Ruth Pryor
Gwen Watkins

MALOR
BOOKS

This is a Malor Book
Published by ISHK

P.O. Box 391069, Cambridge, MA 02238-1069

© 1990, 1998 Gordon Claridge,
Ruth Pryor and Gwen Watkins

First published by The Macmillan Press Ltd., 1990
Second edition published by ISHK, 1998

Claridge, Gordon.
Sounds from the bell jar: ten psychotic authors /
by Gordon Claridge, Ruth Pryor, Gwen Watkins.
      p.   cm.
Originally published: New York : St. Martin's Press, 1990.
Includes bibliographical references (p. 248-257) and index.
ISBN 1-883536-15-4 (pbk.)
1. English literature--History and criticism. 2. Psychoanalysis and
literature--Great Britain. 3. Literature and mental illness--Great
Britain. 4. Authors, English--Psychology. 5. Psychoses--Great
Britain. I. Pryor, Ruth. II. Watkins, Gwen. III. Title.
PR149.P78C55   1998
820.9'920824--dc21   98-23264
                                                            CIP

For Tristan

Contents

Acknowledgements

The authors are grateful to the following for their help: The Archives Department of the Bethlem Royal Hospital and Maudsley Hospital and the Archivist, Miss Patricia Allderidge; Susan Chitty; Lyndall Hopkinson; Ted Hughes and the Sylvia Plath Estate; the Librarian, English Faculty Library, Oxford; the Master and Fellows of Magdalene College, Cambridge, and the Pepys Librarian, Dr Richard Luckett; the Librarian, Swarthmore College, Pennsylvania; the Librarian, Trinity College, Cambridge; Dr David Newsome; Mrs Alice Russell, Trustee of the Benson Deposit, and the Bodleian Library, Oxford; Marion Schulman; Drs R. L. Spitzer and J. Endicott, New York State Psychiatric Institute; Dr Kerith Trick, St Andrew's Hospital, Northampton; Karina Williamson; Dr Pamela Clemit; Rachel Norris; and, finally, their publisher's Editor, Sarah Roberts-West.

Preface

Even a cursory glance at the contents of this book will reveal that it falls outside the usual attempts to combine psychological and literary analysis and, having been asked by my co-authors to write the Preface, it rests upon me to explain the purpose of the book and how three people of such disparate professional backgrounds – a mediaevalist, a critic of Victorian literature and an academic/clinical psychologist – have appeared in print together.

My own involvement is easily explained, the germ of such a book being sown many years ago when I was a Sixth Form pupil at school. In preparation for the Oxford Entrance Examination (which I never took) I was asked by my English teacher to write an essay on the subject of the Dryden quotation, part of which forms the title to our first chapter here. I have no idea what I wrote and I cannot imagine that I reached any sensible conclusion about whether or not great wits and madness really are 'near ally'd'. All I remember is that, either to deter me from reading English at University or to encourage me into my future profession, the teacher wrote across the bottom of the essay: 'You should become a psychologist!' And so it turned out, though it is almost a career later – coinciding with my eventual, much more recent arrival in Oxford – that I, for my part, have had the opportunity to try writing the essay again.

The chance to do so arose through a fortuitous meeting with my co-authors, Gwen Watkins and Ruth Pryor, who, I discovered, also had an interest in the topic of creativity and madness, albeit from the different perspective of the literary scholar. A year of incubation (and some trepidation on both sides about whether it would work) and the idea was born for a jointly authored book which drew upon our three respective fields of expertise.

Even so it may be asked what is unique about the book, given that a considerable amount has already been written about creativity and madness generally and about their specific association in literature. The answer, we believe, does indeed lie in the fact that there have been no previous attempts to address the topic in quite the way we have here – by combining a detailed knowledge of literature and literary figures with ideas that can be distilled from contemporary thinking in psychology and psychiatry. As my co-authors have frequently pointed out to me, literary experts who 'psychologise' about their subject matter are mostly ignorant of psychology. On the other hand, professional clinicians writing on the topic have tended to do so from a very particular point of view. In both cases the most favoured approach has been psychoanalytic. We do not wish to decry the importance of psychoanalytic ideas (indeed we occasionally draw upon them in our book) and we recognise the affinity that has traditionally existed between Art and psychoanalysis, which appears to offer attractive concepts and a natural language for understanding and describing creativity and the creative person. However, by concentrating exclusively (either through choice or through unfamiliarity) on one narrow psychological approach, much has been missed from other branches of psychology and psychiatry which can also inform our understanding. This is especially true of the possible connection between creativity and psychosis. As shown in the opening chapters of this book, we can actually bring to bear on the topic a good deal of empirical evidence and theory from genetics, experimental abnormal and clinical psychology, personality research, and descriptive psychiatry. These sources have never been discussed before in one place; yet taken together we believe they add an entirely new dimension to an old debate.

Having said that, we should make it clear that it is not our main intention to try to prove whether John Dryden (or others who have written in a similar vein) were right or not; but rather to use the conclusions we reach in the first two chapters as a background against which to examine a particular set of authors whose insanity we will demonstrate is not in doubt. A large part of the book is taken up with a detailed discussion of these authors, whose lives and works stand in their own right as examples of the co-existence of serious mental illness and originality of thought. From a literary viewpoint they are of interest because of what a knowledge of their psychopathology can tell us about them as people and about their writings. To the psychologist they are interesting because of the insights they give us into the nature of insanity, some currently popular conceptions of which have, in our view, become grossly oversimplified. Indeed, if we were to try to convey a single message with the book it would be this: that the individuals we discuss (among many others we might have chosen) should give pause for thought to anybody who too readily dismisses as 'merely mad' those, however uncelebrated, whom psychiatry has diagnosed as psychotic. In other words, tragic though insanity is, we believe our conclusions here signal some hope for those who are likely to suffer it, rather than the total despair with which it is now usually associated.

Being given the opportunity to write this Preface unencumbered by my co-authors has one advantage: it allows me to place on record my personal appreciation of them. When I entered our collaboration I felt as though I was drifting in a sea of ignorance about their subject matter, a sensation heightened by an awareness of their own encyclopaedic knowledge of it. As time went on the sea became deeper and wider and I was saved from drowning only by their lessons in how to remain afloat. Their tuition in English Literature, always gentle and never mocking of their uncultured colleague, was an educative experience I value greatly. Beyond that, however, I also wish to thank them as friends for their warmth, hospitality and determined encouragement to continue when they detected in me some moment of doubt.

I would also like to thank The Nuffield Foundation for a grant that enabled me to be freed of my tutorial duties for one term at Magdalen College in order to start work on the book.

Gordon Claridge

If we saved Dr Claridge from drowning (an idea deriving more from his innate modesty than from reality), he saved us from high-flying, always the occupational disease of the literary critic. He caught hold of our airy assumptions that a knowledge of literature included a knowledge of psychology (and more or less everything else) and tethered them to the firm ground of his own discipline.

Ruth Pryor
Gwen Watkins

Oxford

1

Great Wits and Madness

Among its several distinguishing features the human mind has two that most clearly define its uniqueness. One is the capacity to take great leaps of imagination; the other is its susceptibility to the wild aberrations of insane thought. The possibility of an inextricable connection between these qualities has long been debated, with sharp differences of opinion. For some the conjunction has seemed obvious, for others itself a sign of fancy stretched beyond the bounds of credibility. On the face of it the latter view certainly seems the more rational, since the two states in question appear to contain elements that are inherently irreconcilable. One, with its morbid traits of personalised delusion, chaotic thinking, and bizarre affect, is so self-destructive that it frequently reduces the sufferer to psychological incompetence. The other demands talents beyond – in the case of the most creative far beyond – the average, the ability to have insights or craft exquisite objects which, by common consent, we judge of great scientific value or aesthetic worth. Contrasted in this way it seems improbable that madness and creativity could spring from the same source.

Yet from the earliest times it has been suggested that in the insane there is indeed a hint of genius and, by the same token, that originality demands a degree of lunacy. *'Nullum magnum ingenium sine mixtura dementiae'* (no great imaginative power without a dash of madness), wrote Seneca. He was quoting Aristotle, who had drawn the same conclusion three centuries before, and Plato's view of the poet as one possessed by a 'divine madness'. Ever since, numerous writers have paraphrased these sentiments, either in their fiction or through their own self-scrutiny. For Shakespeare, as for Plato, the poet and the lunatic (and indeed the lover) were considered 'of imagination all compact'. 'How near is madness to genius', said Diderot; while Dr Johnson, confessing that he himself had often been nearly insane, commented that 'all power of fancy over reason is a degree of madness'. Swift put it more pungently, enumerating the brilliant thinkers who would 'in this our undistinguished age incur manifest danger of Phlebotomy, and Whips,

1

and Chains, and Dark Chambers, and Straw'. Even Wordsworth, seemingly the most sober of men, was driven to write:

> We poets in our youth begin in gladness
> But thereof come in the end despondency and madness.

Judged on purely intuitive grounds, therefore, an association between creativity and madness can, with equal certainty, be enthusiastically embraced or vigorously rejected, depending upon one's perspective. Which of these apparently contradictory views is nearer to the truth? Is a trace of insanity a necessary prerequisite for originality? Or is the idea merely a piece of folklore belief, sustained over the centuries by an inexact understanding of the quality of lunacy and destined to go the way of other popular myths, such as phrenology, astrology, and Mesmerism?

We should state at the outset that it is not the purpose, nor within the scope, of this book to try to answer such questions in their entirety. This is partly because, for reasons to be discussed later, we shall be confining ourselves to a certain class of creative person, *viz* authors: it would therefore be presumptuous of us to extrapolate from our conclusions to other forms of originality. Our scope is also even further limited by the set of authors on whom we have chosen to concentrate. They were selected because it is clear that, judged by current psychiatric criteria, they all *did* suffer from episodes of psychosis – to introduce a technical term to be defined more precisely as we proceed through this and the following chapter, but which for the moment can be taken as synonymous with the layperson's conception of mental illness as it occurs in its most disintegrative form and which especially refers to serious disorders, like schizophrenia. Being *both* eminent authors *and* psychotic persons our sample is scarcely representative, either of writers or of the mentally ill and therefore cannot, by itself, stand as evidence for the supposed connection between creativity and insanity.

Our interest in these authors, and our reason for choosing them in particular, were also dictated by the fact that their writings contain abundant evidence of their psychological disorder, which they themselves often described in great detail. The main intention of our book, therefore, is to re-examine their lives and works in a manner not previously attempted, combining the expertise of the literary critic and the professional psychologist, in order to show

how their creativity and their tendency to psychosis shaped and influenced each other. We should stress that we shall not be attempting either complete biographies or conventional literary criticism of our chosen authors, most, if not all, of whom have already received considerable attention from both those points of view. Instead our aim is to show how, through joint literary and psychological analysis, new insights can be achieved into the artistic and personal qualities of the authors in question. This will prove to be true, not only in considering the authors individually, but also in demonstrating some common patterns of behaviour, personality, and creative expression among writers subject to pathological mental states.

Despite focusing on some rather special examples where creativity and psychosis co-existed in the same individuals, our analysis will inevitably lead us to consider whether in these particular persons their tendency to madness and their capacity for unusual originality of thought were indeed, in some fundamental sense, intimately connected. This, in turn, will cause us to address the broader issue of whether there is, in a more general sense, a genuine, causal association between insanity and at least some forms of creativity; and, if that is so, what it can tell us about the underlying qualities of psychosis and of the creative process.

As a background, we shall start by considering the evidence and arguments in the creativity/madness debate. This discussion will be spread over two chapters and it should be noted here that, for clarity of presentation, it will sometimes be necessary to introduce very briefly in this chapter certain ideas which will then be discussed more fully in the next. For, as we shall see, the topic we are about to review has many different strands, having been the subject of extensive and increasingly systematic enquiry from several different points of view that have taken it well beyond the realm of intuitive speculation from which it began. For that reason it will be useful to summarise the main themes that will run through our account. This will provide some guidelines for those readers unfamiliar with the area and also help to clear away in advance some misconceptions which, even among those knowledgeable of it, have sometimes obscured the debate.

The first point to be made echoes a remark in the opening paragraph of this chapter; namely that effective creative production and an ongoing state of serious mental illness seem quite incompatible. We cannot emphasise too strongly here that we would not disagree with that conclusion. As we shall see in more detail in the next chapter, there are many features of such conditions that make them quite obviously inimical to the creative act. These include not only chaotic disruption of thinking (and perception) upon which originality ultimately depends; but also disturbances of mood, motor response, and volition that secondarily prevent the individual from organising his or her mental processes into the orderly sequence required for creative work. Or, as Sylvia Plath, one of the writers to be considered in this book, put it, with more feeling:

> When you are insane you are busy being insane – all the time . . .
> When I was crazy that was *all* I was.[38]

We can therefore anticipate – and this brings us to our second theme – that the answers we seek actually lie elsewhere than in a simple equation between creative and mad thought. That is to say, if creativity and psychosis *are* found to be connected then this is more likely to be revealed, not as a function of the psychotic state itself, but in more subtle ways – for example, through certain modes or forms of thinking and perception which the *tendencies* to psychosis and creativity might prove to have in common. Some space will be devoted later to this question, drawing on various lines of research and some current theories about the causes and underlying mechanisms of psychosis. Suffice it to say here that the centrepiece of that part of our discussion will be the idea that normality and psychosis are essentially continuous with each other and that healthy varieties in thinking style and the disposition to psychotic breakdown substantially overlap, indeed may be identical. Viewed in this way some part, at least, of the supposed connection between creativity and madness will then be seen to be entirely comprehensible. In particular it will help to resolve the deep paradox that has already surfaced in this book and will continue to do so: how it is that the same features of individuality can be expressed in such totally disparate forms.

Our third theme will, however, sound several notes of caution. One will be a reminder that, even if the above conclusions are correct, it does not follow that creativity and psychosis (or the tendency to it) are entirely synonymous. The ability to formulate original thoughts, as well as the opportunity to put these into effect, both demand several other qualities, personal as well as situational, that may be partially or completely independent of those that might be ascribable to 'psychotic' modes of thinking. In other words, in considering a possible connection between the creative and the mad it is the differences, as well as the similarities, between them that need to be understood. Furthermore, we also need to keep in sight the fact that 'creativity' is itself an ambiguous concept, having been given various meanings and judged according to differing criteria depending on the context in which it has been studied. How far, for example, is it simply a sign of high intelligence? And is mere eminence a good yardstick? It is unlikely that a single explanation can fully account for a human activity that has been defined in such varied ways. Even if an agreed definition can be arrived at and some core features identified, it need not be the case that all forms of creative expression demand precisely the same set of mental operations or depend equally upon the same intellectual qualities.

Finally, although covered in more detail in the next chapter, a brief word needs to be inserted here about some psychiatric terminology that will be encountered in what follows. This is necessary in order to clarify certain observations that some authors have made about the precise aspects or forms of psychosis to which creativity might be especially connected. As intimated earlier, the general term 'psychosis' refers to serious disruption of the person's mental and emotional life. As used here, it is also confined to a type of disorder that is normally described as 'functional'. That is to say, it has no obvious or gross organic cause, such as a brain lesion, a fact which sets it apart from the truly neurological conditions – like, for example, Alzheimer's disease or epilepsy. But even functional psychosis can vary in symptomatology and psychiatrists generally distinguish between two main forms. In one – schizophrenia – the emphasis is on bizarreness of thinking, hallucinations, and impaired social behaviour. In the other – affective disorder – the predominant feature, as the name implies, is profound emotional change: either serious depression, or more classically, the wild mood swings of manic-depressive psychosis. Although psychiatrists have traditionally preferred to regard these two varieties of psychosis as distinctly separable 'diseases', it now seems more probable – as we shall have occasion to state several times in this book – that that is not so. For one thing, each can occur in a mild or 'borderline' form. Furthermore, the symptoms of even full-blown affective psychosis and schizophrenia overlap considerably, suggesting that they simply represent different ways in which a common tendency to insanity can manifest itself. However, for the purpose of discussion in this chapter it will be more appropriate to preserve the distinction between them.

Bearing these points in mind, let us now start to consider the question of creativity and madness in more detail. A complete review of what is now a vast, varied – and sometimes idiosyncratic – literature would take us well beyond our available space and our aim here will be to summarise the main approaches to the topic, in order to try to disentangle some arguments in the debate and draw some general conclusions from it. In doing so we shall concentrate in this chapter on lines of research that address the general issue of whether psychosis and creativity are in fact connected. Then, in the next chapter, after elaborating further on the features of psychosis itself, we shall return to examine how explanations of it might also give an account of certain aspects of the creative process.

The oldest, and what might be termed the 'classic', approach to the systematic study of creativity and madness is biographical. Traceable to the early part of the nineteenth century, this consisted of retrospective psychiatric analyses of famous historical figures who, because of their accomplishments, can be judged outstandingly creative. The seminal work of such type was that carried out by the Italian psychiatrist, Lombroso, who set out to demonstrate the pathological nature of genius, quoting examples as varied as Julius Caesar, Mohammed, Newton, Rousseau, and Schopenhauer.[22] Writing, as he did, in an era before medicine had even begun to construct its modern classification of psychiatric disorder, Lombroso included among his subjects many who would now be considered to have suffered from brain diseases of organic origin (Julius Caesar, for example, was epileptic). In contemporary terms, therefore, his diagnoses were too inexact to stand as definitive evidence for (or against) a connection between creativity and madness, as we would now construe it. Added to which Lombroso – more famous for his theory about the physiognomic stigmata of criminality – interpreted his observations on genius in a similarly negative fashion, viewing social deviance and the propensity to creativity as alternative expressions of biological degeneracy.

These early pathographic analyses nevertheless started a wave of interest in the topic and subsequently stimulated many other medical writers to apply their diagnostic acumen to the problem. Although mostly not accepting Lombroso's explanation of it, they were virtually unanimous in their opinion that genius is indeed often accompanied by madness, even allowing for cases that could be ascribed to gross disease of the nervous system. Thus, Becker, in his historical survey of the numerous monographs published on the subject in the hundred years up to 1950, notes that the vast majority had reached that conclusion; though he also comments on the many different interpretations that were placed on the evidence.[7] These range from the notion that creativeness reflects the same warring psychological tendencies that are responsible for insanity to the intriguing, though question-begging, idea that some mad people are simply labelled as geniuses because of their apparently mystical and divinely inspired qualities of thought.

A notable exception to this consensus in the early literature that madness and creativeness are frequently connected is a study carried out at the beginning of the century by Havelock Ellis.[15] He conducted a survey of 'British genius', examining the psychological, physical, and other characteristics of 1020 eminent people listed in the *Dictionary of National Biography*. Ellis found only a moderate rate (about 4 per cent) of frank insanity among his subjects; a figure, incidentally, that included some examples of brain disease. Bowerman, in a less well-known but identical investigation of American geniuses, reported the same result.[9]

Two points need to be made about these studies, however. First, although rejecting the explanation of creativity that prevailed among medical writers at that time, both Ellis and Bowerman did consider that there was some connection with psychological morbidity, in a more general sense. 'The prevailing temperament of men of genius', Ellis said (and Bowerman agreed with him), 'is one of great nervous sensitivity and irritability', a tendency to melancholy, and what he called a 'germinal nervous instability'.

The second point to note about the Ellis and Bowerman surveys is that neither was concerned with cases of really outstanding creativity, of the kind that have been the subject of individual biographical analyses. The persons surveyed were certainly eminent, but mostly people (even politicians!) whose achievements were rarely so enduring as to place them in the class apart to which we would assign the truly original thinkers in history. It could be argued that if a connection with florid madness is to be revealed in biographical data this is most likely to be found in a conjunction among extreme cases: the very creative on whom most of the detailed accounts have concentrated. More recent reviewers of the biographical evidence about the latter have certainly continued to comment on the remarkable frequency with which serious mental disorder occurs among outstandingly creative people. For example, Prentky, in his book *Creativity and Psychopathology*, tabulates the probable psychiatric diagnoses that could be applied to certain eminent writers, artists, scientists and composers.[29] Among writers alone – and even excluding those discussed in the present volume – he concludes that all of the following were either schizophrenic or suffered from an affective psychosis: Strindberg, Baudelaire, Kant, Swift, Shelley, Johnson, Hölderlin, Donizetti, Conrad, Kafka, Coleridge, Schopenhauer, Barrie, Schiller, Crane, Chatterton, Rousseau, Tasso, Maupassant, Balzac, and Boswell. In addition, Prentky notes, there were many others who showed signs of 'borderline psychosis'.

A similar exercise has been undertaken by Karlsson whose work we shall refer to again because of the interesting comments he has made about his observations from a genetics viewpoint.[20] To the list of writers who developed psychoses Karlsson adds, among others, Hugo, Scott, Tolstoi, Pope, and Poe and puts the overall incidence of such disorders among the individuals he surveyed at around 30 per cent; a staggeringly high figure, given that, taken together, non-organic forms of psychosis are usually quoted as carrying a lifetime risk of about 5 per cent.

Of course, from a strictly scientific viewpoint these individual biographical studies can be criticised on the grounds that they are biased towards rather special cases; added to which, as Becker points out, such accounts were usually written by clinicians whose professional interest in the abnormal inevitably caused them to focus on signs of pathology. In contrast, some contemporary clinicians who have discussed the topic have been much less enthusiastic about connecting creativity to psychosis. This is especially true of certain psychiatric writers who, drawing on the concepts of psychodynamic psychology, have devoted considerable attention to the nature of the creative process and, in the course of doing so, have expressed an opinion about the idea. Mostly they have been ambivalent, admitting on the one hand that both creativity and psychosis probably share similar underlying psychic mechanisms – unconscious motivation, involvement of 'primary process' thinking (fantasy), ideational styles and so on; yet, on the other hand, unwilling to bring the two states together in any causal sense. Thus, Storr acknowledges that a certain kind of original genius is inseparable from the schizoid (i.e. schizophrenic-like) personality structure, quoting Kafka, among writers, as a particular example.[36] However, he draws back from incorporating this into a general theory about creativity, preferring instead to emphasise the more superficial differences between the psychotic and the creative person: that the former is overwhelmed by and the latter in control of his or her 'original' thoughts.

Rothenberg, another psychiatrist to consider the question, reacts with similar equivocation.[33] He vacillates between describing the connection between creativity and psychosis as 'folk-loristic' and 'clearly exaggerated', and confessing to be puzzled that it has been documented so often. Finally, he comes to the conclusion that psychopathology plays no causative role in creativity, except in the choice of subject matter, and that where it does exist it stems from social causes; for example the stress that the person of original mind experiences in being at odds with society. Somewhat like Storr he suggests that it is only in overcoming such psychopathology that effective creating can occur – an uncontroversial conclusion but one that scarcely illuminates our understanding.

Arieti, an expert on both creativity and schizophrenia – and therefore the most qualified among these contemporary psychiatric writers to comment – is equally disappointing in the light he throws on the issue.[5] Admittedly he is more explicit than the other two in detailing traits, such as unusual forms of thinking, which seem responsible for both psychotic symptomatology and creative production. He even underlines the similarity by noting that such traits can be either adaptive or detrimental – i.e. lead to illness – depending on whether or not they are modified by other, more positive, qualities. However, he then fails to follow through his rather important point to the logical conclusion of considering how it might at least explain those many instances where outstanding originality and insanity have been found to co-exist. In fact Arieti's coverage of the latter is very cursory and he swiftly shifts to a discussion of examples of, to use Pickering's term, 'creative malady'; such as Proust's asthma and Darwin's psychosomatic palpitations – examples that are interesting in themselves but largely irrelevant to the creativity/psychosis debate.[28]

In short, although all three of these psychiatric authors offer some fascinating insights into the depth psychology of creativity, we find little in their writings that helps to resolve the question of its possible connection with psychosis. When the issue is addressed it is skirted around, it seems to us, by the unwillingness of all three of the authors concerned – understandable perhaps because of their daily closeness to the victims of mental illness – to see beyond the pathology of the psychotic state itself; their failure to appreciate our – or rather Sylvia Plath's – point made earlier: that when insane the psychotic individual is too preoccupied struggling against overpersonalised or idiosyncratic thoughts to create effectively. Consequently, they never really probe the significance of what those two activities might have in common. As for the results from individual biographical studies, they seem most comfortable with an explanation that simply appeals to the idea of 'special cases'.

An even more negative view of such studies has been taken in academic psychology. Indeed, in some quarters the whole subject matter of creativity and psychosis has been ignored completely. For example, a quite recent book of advanced readings, entitled *The Nature of Creativity*, edited by a very prominent cognitive psychologist, and intended for researchers in the area, makes absolutely no reference to the topic![35] Where interest has been shown it has tended to be critical of the idea of connecting creativity to madness. The reason for this can be traced historically to the fact that research on creativity in academic psychology has formed a quite separate strand of enquiry from that originating in the early pathographic analyses carried out by medical writers. In contrast to the latter, academic psychologists have concentrated more on creativity as a normal cognitive trait and with problems like its psychometric measurement, development, and correlations with other – mostly 'desirable' – characteristics. This work has its origins in the early intelligence test movement and, later, in a specific concern with creativeness as a possibly separable aspect of intellectual functioning. Much of that research has, in turn, been inspired by an attempt, especially among American psychologists, to understand and predict 'giftedness': as such, in seeking reasons for differences in creativity, their preference has naturally been to look for evidence of the latter's association with excellence, superiority, and health rather than with maladjustment or psychological deviance. The pioneering example here is a mammoth longitudinal study undertaken and described in a six volume work by Terman and his colleagues who, beginning in 1921, selected a large group of so-called gifted children and then followed their progress over a period of thirty-five years. We shall refer again to this investigation but there is one aspect of it which it is appropriate to comment upon at this point.

In what was in effect a digression from the main study, Cox, a colleague of Terman, conducted a 'historiometric' analysis of the mental traits of 301 carefully selected individuals, living between 1450 and 1850, who could be recognised as of outstanding genius.[13] In addition to retrospective estimates of IQ, Cox also constructed 'psychographic' profiles of character and personality for each of her subjects, rating them on the basis of biographical data for a range of social and emotional traits. Since Cox confined herself to the truly great, her sample – unlike, say, Ellis' and Bowerman's – naturally contained the names of many individuals whom others have quoted as evidence for the connection between creativity and psychosis; including, incidentally, one (Cowper) who appears in this book. Yet her own conclusions are strikingly different.

The picture that Cox paints of the prevailing personality of these 'heroes of the past', as she calls them, is glossed in the most adulatory terms, emphasising their extraordinariness in every respect: their single-mindedness, their '. . . persistence of motive and effort, confidence in their abilities, and great strength or force of character.' Furthermore, she notes:

> The rare and striking personality of genius was, in the case of our subjects as a whole, manifested even in early youth by behaviour that deviated from that of average individuals so pronouncedly that the record of its appearance was preserved in documentary form. The remarkable traits of youth were indicative of future greatness. The dynamic quality which, developing, raised performance to so high a level and won for the character it invigorated so large a sphere of influence was present and recognised even in childhood. And even in his earliest years the personality of the genius was something more than the sum of its extraordinary parts.

How do we reconcile Cox's impression of genius as superior, adjustive mental health with that which the medical biographers give, remembering that both are referring to a similar set of individuals? The difference is partly due, we suspect, to Cox's own bias in the selection and interpretation of her data; a bias just as strong as – though, of course, in the opposite direction from – that of which the pathographers have been accused. Indeed, it is rather illuminating to discover that within the first few pages of her book – and before she has even introduced her own work – she peremptorily dismisses the idea that genius is akin to madness. Notably, she reserves her criticism for Lombroso – not by any means, at the time she was writing, the only person to have made the connection – remarking that his method was merely one of 'heaping up instances which support his thesis'.

Even if this is taken as a fair comment on the general scientific validity of the biographical approach to the topic, the preconceptions which Cox brought to her own analysis are also much in evidence. A considerable part of her book is devoted to quite detailed synopses of the lives of the 300-odd geniuses whom she evaluated. Careful scrutiny of these accounts reveals that in almost no instance does she give any hint that there were signs of mental illness in any of her subjects – even among those where this is known to have occurred. For example – chosen, as it happens, from science rather than literature – take the case of Isaac Newton.

It is well-established that Newton had a most difficult personality, revealed on occasions in outright insanity; so much so that his name routinely appears on lists, such as those compiled by Prentky and Karlsson, of psychosis among the outstandingly creative. Even Storr, someone who, as we have seen, is by no means convinced of a general causal connection between psychosis and creativity, writes as follows about Newton, choosing him as another of his examples of 'schizoid' genius:

> Newton's quarrels with other scientists were famous, and need not detain us here. His disputes with Hooke, with Flamsteed and with Leibniz are amply documented. But there was a period in his life at which his suspicion and hostility to others overstepped the bounds of sanity. The details of this illness remain obscure, but in 1693 Newton became sufficiently disturbed in mind for rumours of his insanity to gain widespread acceptance. In September of that year he wrote to Pepys, Locke and other friends accusing them of being atheists or Catholics, and of trying to embroil him with women. Various factors may have contributed to this 'paranoid episode', as we should now label it.[36]

Yet no indication of this appears in Cox's account of Newton. True, her book is devoted mostly to the *early* characteristics of her subjects, the brief biographies she provides for them ending in their mid-twenties. But even here her reporting bias is evident. Newton, for example, she merely refers to as 'a sober, silent, thinking lad', a description that contrasts markedly with Storr's:

> In early youth, Newton was anxious, insecure, hypochondriacal and self-disparaging. Indeed, depressive traits are more in evidence than paranoid tendencies. It was only in middle life that he ceased self-denigration and began to accuse others of the faults of which he had previously found himself guilty.

Cox's preference for understating – or perhaps not looking for – early signs of pathology, even in those of her subjects who later showed it, is understandable if one recalls the origins of her study. As noted earlier, the survey formed part of a larger programme of research into giftedness initiated by the American psychologist, Terman. In the main investigation more than 1500 children were selected – on the basis of their very high IQs – and followed through into adulthood. Periodic evaluations of their physical and mental health, personalities, and intellectual achievements showed that they maintained their superiority in all of these domains, including a relative freedom from insanity and other indications of psychological maladjustment.[37]

Taken in conjunction with Cox's findings, these results are frequently quoted, even in the recent literature, as strong evidence, not merely against the idea that creativity and psychosis are connected, but actually in support of a quite contrary view: that high ability somehow militates against serious mental disorder.[1] As we shall eventually see, it so happens that the latter point is probably correct, but it is not a conclusion that follows directly from the results of the Terman project, for the following reasons.

As Richards has recently indicated, the Cox survey and the longitudinal study are not as mutually supportive as they seem at first sight.[30] The reasons essentially have to do with the relevance of IQ to creativity and are exposed when we compare both the similarities and the differences between Cox's historical figures and Terman's gifted children. Both, it can be agreed, showed very high IQ, the latter well into the superior range, averaging around 150, and in some cases running up to 200. Cox, of course, had to make retrospective IQ estimates for her subjects but these are probably fairly accurate and average about 160, with a range overlapping considerably with that actually found in the gifted children.

Yet the outcome in the two groups is quite different. Cox's subjects were, by any definition, outstandingly creative, to the point of being almost qualitatively distinguishable from their fellow men. This could not be said, however, for any of the gifted children: although many showed talents in various fields and carried these through into adult accomplishments, none achieved the very highest level of creativity seen in Cox's subjects. Admitting this, Terman and Oden comment as follows:

> Several possessing superior talent in music and art are heading university departments in these fields and have produced some excellent original work, but none seems likely to achieve a truly great piece of creative work. There are a number of competent and highly successful writers among the subjects but not more than three or four with a high order of creativity.[37]

The above comparison articulates two, related, conclusions that can be drawn from the evidence reviewed so far. The first is that the question of what constitutes great creativity, at least, is still left open to debate. The second is that IQ, as measured by conventional intelligence tests, does not seem a sufficient explanation of it; even though it might be a necessary accompaniment – and indeed might help entirely to account for some other forms of high intellectual achievement. The latter point has of course long been recognised in academic psychology and from the 1950s onwards considerable effort was expended attempting to identify the unique features of creativity. This work took two directions. One was concerned with the measurement of other intellectual abilities, apart from those revealed in standard IQ tests, that might explain differences in originality. Another concentrated more on non-intellectual factors – such as personality traits – which it was thought might distinguish the highly creative individual.

The first of these lines of research led to the development of so-called creativity tests in which the subject has a free hand to generate his or her own responses to a given problem. In other words, the test situation is open-ended – unlike the usual intelligence test, where the person is required to reach a single (correct) solution. A typical example would be: How many uses can you think of for a brick (or a paper clip)? While much maligned – some might think justifiably – as trivialising what real-life creativity is about, the use of such procedures has in fact helped, to some extent, to clarify our understanding of what is involved in original thinking. For example, research has shown that performance on these tests is unrelated to intelligence, at least above a certain minimum level of IQ, suggesting that they do tap something different. An important explanatory concept has been that of 'divergent thinking'; or what de Bono in a different context has called 'lateral' thinking.[14] This pursuing of tangential trains of thought in order to arrive at novel ideas has been seen to contrast with the 'convergent' thinking demanded by the items in normal IQ tests.

Of course, the ability to think divergently does not guarantee creativity, any more than does a high IQ. Both convergent *and* divergent modes of thought are necessary for a creative act to occur: the writer must actually arrange his freely associated ideas into organised prose or the scientist finally home in on the solution to a problem. So it is the capacity to mobilise both of these resources and switch smoothly between them that seems to be the hallmark of effective creative production. When discussing unexpected failures for this to occur, academic psychologists have generally concentrated on the case where, despite high intelligence (and therefore presumably superior ability to think convergently) individuals are nevertheless relatively uncreative, either in real-life or in their performance on divergent thinking tests. Clinicians, however, have long been aware that the opposite can also be found: an excessive tendency to divergent thinking – though they have usually called it something else – which the person has difficulty in translating into focused thought. Arieti makes these points well:

> ... intelligence, which we have mentioned several times as important for life and creativity, may actually handicap creativity if not accompanied by originality and if used for a too-strict self-criticism and inhibition. On the other hand, originality may lead us astray if not corrected by self-criticism. *Divergent thinking may even bring us to psychosis, if not matched by logical processes.*[5]
> (Italics ours)

Although Arieti himself fails properly to follow it through, his observation underpins an important theme in our understanding of creativity as it relates to psychosis, and we shall have occasion to refer to it again. First, however, it is necessary to consider the second line of research on creativity pursued in academic psychology.

As mentioned earlier, the failure to predict creativity from a narrow view of individual differences based on IQ also led to work focusing more on its personality correlates. This was, in a sense a natural extension of a broadening perspective on intellectual ability, enclosing the idea that psychological qualities such as creativity might be as much a personality trait as a cognitive characteristic. Among other research it led to a series of studies – mostly carried out in the 1950s and 1960s – of the personalities of very creative people. The method adopted differed in important ways from the earlier biographical approach discussed so far. It concentrated instead on living examples of people who were judged highly creative, thereby making it possible to evaluate them at first-hand on objective personality tests or similar assessment procedures. Use of this strategy partly reflected an increasing shift of emphasis among academic psychologists – though continuing the tradition set by Terman – towards redefining creativity as giftedness or eminence. And it meant sampling a more 'dilute' domain of creativity, few of the individuals studied entering the ranks of the great innovators (though they, in any case, are rarely recognised as such during their lifetimes). However, the method does have the obvious advantage of avoiding the pitfalls of retrospective analysis, especially the impressionistic biases that certainly coloured many of the earlier biographical accounts of famous figures.

These personality studies usually proceeded by selecting, on the basis of peer evaluation or similar criteria, highly accomplished professionals in various branches of the arts and sciences.[10, 23, 32] The personalities of the individuals concerned were then examined using one or other of a number of procedures, ranging from objective personality inventories to depth analysis methods, such as the Rorschach ink-blot test. The results of these studies are too numerous to detail here, but it turns out that the investigators concerned all reached fairly consistent conclusions about the personality traits that typified their subjects. Although differences were to be found – especially comparing the arts and sciences – the highly creative were frequently described in similar terms as:

sceptical, aloof, radical, self-sufficient, independent, bohemian, often introverted and usually more open to experience.

To the untutored eye, this picture of the personality of the creative individual might seem far distant from that of the psychotic; it is certainly often cited as evidence against the two being connected. Again, however, we must be careful not to reach a too hasty conclusion. Thus, research carried out over the past few years indicates that the traits described above actually overlap considerably with those found in so-called 'schizotypal' individuals, i.e. people whose temperamental make-up seems similar to that underlying schizophrenia, continuous with it in the personality domain but without any obvious signs of psychotic illness.[11] The description 'schizotypal' is really just a modern equivalent of the older one, 'schizoid', which has long been recognised as having an affinity with schizophrenia. Furthermore – and in a more general sense than the 'special cases' quoted by Storr – it has also been regarded as having some association with creativity. Here it is instructive to read the description by Manfred Bleuler (whose father coined the term 'schizophrenia') on some characteristic features of the person of schizoid character.[8] Noting that many qualities are deviant and undesirable Bleuler also writes of others that are positive:

> His behaviour is aloof and devoid of human warmth; yet he does have a rich inner life. In this sense he is introverted ... the schizoid is also capable of pursuing his own thoughts and following his own interests and drives .... He is autistic. The better side of this autism reveals a sturdiness of character, and inflexibility of purpose, an independence, and a predisposition to creativity.

It therefore seems probable that what the early personality studies of living creative subjects had revealed was their tendency to the schizoidness of which Bleuler writes, and which would now be referred to as 'schizotypy'. One particular finding from the original studies supports that conclusion.[6] There, writers were evaluated on the comprehensive personality questionnaire, the Minnesota Multiphasic Personality Inventory (MMPI): the test provides scores on a number of scales, each of which has as its reference point a particular clinical syndrome (depression, psychopathy, schizophrenia and so on) and is labelled accordingly. On average the subjects scored highly on these scales, including that labelled 'schizophrenia'. This does not of course mean that the subjects concerned were psychotic, in a clinical sense. Indeed an even more striking feature of the results was that the individuals examined were especially high on a measure of 'ego strength', indicating a greater than average *resistance* to mental breakdown: the finding is particularly interesting because the latter is usually very *low* in subjects who deviate markedly on the clinical scales of tests like the MMPI. We seem here to have further evidence of the apparent paradox about creativity and psychosis to which we have referred several times.

The final studies to be reviewed in this chapter help, we believe, to take us a little nearer understanding that paradox, as well as offering more convincing evidence than that considered so far that the connection between creativity and psychosis is indeed genuine. The work to be discussed, some of it quite recent, has generally lain outside both academic psychology and clinical psychiatry, mostly being carried out by experimental researchers from neighbouring disciplines with an interest in the topic. The studies themselves have taken various forms, some directly addressing the issue of creativity and psychosis, others reporting results that bear indirectly on it. All, however, can be gathered together under a common theme: that concerned with the genetics of psychosis.

One of the few established facts about psychotic illness is that it runs in families and only the most stubborn social theorist could now deny that one reason for this is that the disposition to it, at least, is partly inherited. However, like many genetically determined characteristics – some of which indeed may be responsible for illness or deviance – such dispositions may not be expressed, or, if they are, expressed in incomplete form, or even revealed in qualities which at first sight seem distant from, even unconnected with, the pathology for which they are otherwise responsible.[11] It is this perspective on the genetics of psychosis that provides an entry-point into our understanding of the latter's probable association with creativity.

A geneticist who has done much to articulate the above view is Karlsson, whose observations about the high frequency of psychosis among the outstandingly creative we have already noted. What Karlsson proposes essentially is that the genes responsible for the disposition to schizophrenia (he confines himself to this form of psychosis) also code for creative ability. Several lines of evidence do support this theory, including the results of one investigation, a large pedigree study, reported by Karlsson himself.[19] He conducted a retrospective survey of the professional status of the first-degree relatives of psychiatric patients admitted to hospital in his native Iceland between the years 1851 and 1940. Using this same period as a basis for comparison with the general population and examining available records (including the Icelandic *Who's Who*), he was able to show that the relatives concerned significantly more often entered creative occupations. Interestingly, authors appeared in this group with a frequency more than twice that found in the population at large.

Other investigations, using different research designs, point to the same conclusion, and have further demonstrated that the association is probably, as Karlsson suggests, largely genetic in origin. These have concentrated on individuals adopted shortly after birth, making it possible to disentangle genetic from environmental effects. One study, for example, has shown that children separated early on from their schizophrenic mothers are not only more likely than control children to become schizophrenic themselves but also show greater artistic and musical talent.[18] Another investigation, looking at the problem as it were from the opposite direction, compared adoptees selected for later estimates of their *creativity* and then examined incidences of mental illness.[26] Among the adoptees themselves the most highly creative showed an excessive rate of mental illness – as much as 30 per cent. A figure not far short of this was also found in the biological parents from whom they had been separated, though not in their *adoptive* relatives, in whom the incidence was much lower.

It should be noted that the study just described did not focus especially on schizophrenia, the kinds of mental illness observed in the individuals surveyed covering a number of diagnostic categories, albeit mostly ones related in one or another to psychosis and probably reflecting a similar underlying disposition. However, this does raise an important point of debate in contemporary discussions about the relationship between madness and creativity. Thus some investigators have argued that the association is one, not with schizophrenia, but with affective psychosis. As we have already mentioned, and as we shall reiterate in the next chapter, the distinction between these two forms of insanity is probably more a matter of psychiatric convenience than aetiological reality.

Nevertheless they do represent different ways in which psychotic vulnerability can manifest itself and reference to them helps to provide some clues as to which of its aspects might mediate any association that exists with creativity.

One investigator who has put weight on the relationship with affective, rather than schizophrenic, disorder is the American psychiatrist, Andreasen, whose work, also carried out within a partly genetics context, is of particular interest here because it has mainly been concerned with writers.[2] The individuals concerned were all members of the University of Iowa Writers' Workshop, a group which, as Andreasen herself points out, is the oldest and most widely recognised creative teaching programme in the United States, having spawned such eminent authors as Robert Lowell, Kurt Vonnegut and Philip Roth.

In a long study, spanning some fifteen years, Andreasen evaluated members of the Iowa Workshop and their families, comparing them with a carefully selected group of control subjects on indicators of psychopathology. Her findings were that both the writers themselves and their families had a substantially raised incidence of mental illness, but especially of affective psychosis, including depression and forms of the disorder characterised by severe mood swings. The diagnosis of 'schizophrenia', on the other hand, was not very frequent in her samples. On the intellectual side all of the writers, not surprisingly, showed a high tested IQ, though not more so than non-writers, thus confirming other published evidence, discussed earlier, that intelligence as such is not a sufficient prerequisite of creative performance. Finally, complementing these results Andreasen demonstrated that the relatives of her chosen authors also showed unusual creative talent, though over a wider sphere than the literary, including art, music, dance, and mathematics. She concludes from her study that 'the families of the writers were riddled with both creativity and mental illness', the two intertwining to an extent which would make it difficult to deny their real association.

A substantially similar conclusion was reached from another very recent study which again specifically focused on the possible relationship between creativity and the affective features of psychosis.[31] The aims were similar to Andreasen's, but the investigators used a different research design. Rather than creative individuals being taken as the starting-point, the individuals targetted initially were people who had been diagnosed as having had a mental illness, either a severe (manic-depressive) form of affective disorder or the milder, but aetiologically related, mood swings of 'cyclothymia'. These subjects, and their relatives, were then assessed for creativeness, as judged by a comprehensive set of 'Lifetime Creativity Scales'. Although somewhat less in individuals who suffered from full-blown manic-depressive psychosis, creativity was found to be significantly raised in both patients and relatives who were rated as cyclothymic. The interpretation put on these results was that the latter may have an optimum level which facilitates creativeness; though beyond that point – as seen in the seriously psychotic – it may hamper creativity.

If, as the above evidence suggests and as Karlsson has argued, sufferers from psychosis – whether we call it schizophrenia or affective disorder – and the highly creative do in fact share the same genes, then it may be asked: what, in psychological terms, is inherited? One view is that it has something to do with the energy, drive and willingness to take risks associated (in the 'up' phase, at least) with traits underlying manic-depression. Although such characteristics probably do play some secondary role, we find this interpretation unconvincing and suspect that it stems from a need to make a connection with what are perceived as the relatively more 'attractive' features of psychosis, rather than with those emphasised in descriptions of schizophrenia, a concept that has taken on almost entirely negative connotations. The explanation is implausible for two reasons. First, it is too general: several other personality traits, such as anxiety – not specifically related to psychosis, though carrying risks for different forms of psycho-pathology – could equally well be said to generate the motivation necessary for creative production, and often do. Secondly, although certainly important, the current preference by some writers to relate creativity to the affective forms of psychosis should not divert us from the fact that it is actually *schizophrenia* which has inspired most of the theorising – and generated a good deal of the empirical evidence – about how psychotic and creative traits might be related to each other.

It is more likely that what connects creativity to madness is some aspect of the thought styles which psychotic and original forms of thinking have in common and which, in the psychiatric domain, can be observed across the arbitrary diagnostic categories of psychosis. Here, of course, we are referring especially to the capacity for divergent thinking, discussed earlier. Although academic psychologists have been reluctant to use this notion to cross the boundary between the normal and the abnormal, clinicians have for many years used a similar concept. Their preferred description of it has been *overinclusive* thinking which has frequently been used to explain certain forms of thought disorder seen in psychotic patients, such as the tendency to cognitive 'slippage', loosely associated ideation, and difficulty in maintaining a tight boundary for abstract concepts.[27] The term itself was coined in the 1930s and arose originally from studies of schizophrenia, though it has since proved equally (if not more) applicable to psychotics with other diagnoses, notably mania.

It is no coincidence that the clinical tests for overinclusive thinking are not all that different from those devised by academic psychologists as measures of divergent, or 'creative', thinking. Although naturally designed more to draw out signs of abnormality, they nevertheless demand similar mental operations, being open-ended procedures in which, for example, subjects are required to interpret proverbs or sort everyday objects in any way they prefer. Such tests are rarely used nowadays, possibly because the concepts of overinclusive and divergent thinking *are* so similar and, in themselves, have little diagnostic value for differentiating the mad from the merely original. Illustrating the point, a colleague of one of the present authors once administered a battery of overinclusion (thought disorder) tests to a group of local artists. Several emerged as patently psychotic! They were not, of course, in a clinical sense.

This difficulty in distinguishing the cognitive style of the highly creative from that of the psychotic has also often been noted by others. For example, Andreasen and her colleagues asked a large group of psychiatrists to compare the written productions of two creative writers, including James Joyce, with those of psychotics and, without being given any other information, to try to reach a diagnosis.[4] A high proportion of the clinicians diagnosed the writers as psychotic, including 42 per cent who suspected Joyce of being schizophrenic (he did, of course, have a schizophrenic daughter). Turning the comparison round the other way, another recent study examined the performance of schizophrenics on two standard 'creativity' tests.[21] Apart from those with persecutory delusions, the schizophrenics achieved much higher scores than other groups, including normals, with whom they were compared. The authors concluded that creativity and psychotic symptomatology do indeed reflect equivalent forms of cognitive processing. It is also very probable that the cognitive style which overinclusive and divergent thinking have in common is strongly inherited. Part of the evidence here comes from genetic analyses (e.g. twin comparisons) of normal subjects' performance on 'creativity' tests.[12] Other investigations have addressed the same question in a clinical context. Thus, McConaghy and his colleagues carried out a series of experiments on what they call 'allusive thinking', a concept similar to overinclusive thinking and actually measured by them with a clinical 'thought disorder' test.[24, 25] They reported that the healthy relatives of schizophrenic patients show high degrees of allusive thinking; as indeed do the relatives of mentally healthy subjects who themselves have high scores on their allusive thinking test. These results, in turn, confirm a large body of other findings that 'psychotic' characteristics – temperamental as well as cognitive – tend to cluster in families where one of the members is diagnosable as mentally ill.[34, 39]

From a genetics point of view, therefore, a crucial psychological feature connecting creativity to psychosis would seem to be the distinctive cognitive style responsible for both. Certainly Karlsson is clear on this point and, in commenting, also helps to unravel some of the mystery surrounding their apparently unlikely conjunction:

Although there appears to remain little doubt that carriers of the schizophrenia gene indeed differ in thought patterns from noncarriers, no scientific support exists for the view that the deviation is toward inferior thinking. In fact, it may well be in the opposite direction. If one defines 'normality' as the characteristics exhibited by the majority and equates the term with 'superiority', any deviation is by definition abnormal and undesirable. However, if a minority with a different thought pattern can be established scientifically to reason more precisely, despite that way being deviant, it seems unwise to condemn their mode of thinking as automatically somehow inferior. Scholars should not forget that a schizophrenic explained the nature of gravity, which had puzzled 'normal' people for centuries.[20]

What Karlsson does not explain here, of course, is how some apparently psychotic individuals manage to achieve effective creativity – albeit in some cases only in between periods of illness –

whereas others, probably the majority, fail entirely to do so. Or, more critical perhaps, why – if evidence reviewed earlier is to be believed – many creative individuals even seem to have enhanced resistance to the mental illnesses to which, according to the theory outlined, their dispositions should make them more than usually susceptible. Another problem that remains unresolved is the generality of the connection between psychosis and creativity. In other words, can *all* creativity be explained in this way? Or are we indeed, as some writers quoted previously would argue, merely dealing with certain special cases? We believe that at least partial answers to these questions will emerge later in this book – we shall certainly return to them – but a few brief comments are worth setting down before closing the present chapter.

The first two questions posed above are probably related. Even if the essence of originality lies in certain modes of psychotic thought, the ability to harness this in effective creative work – and by the same token the capacity to resist the psychopathology which it implies – must depend on other factors being present. These *might* be intrinsic to the very temperamental make-up which itself predisposes to psychosis: here it is instructive to recall Manfred Bleuler's description, cited earlier, of the schizoid personality, with its overtones of hard-edged indifference to others, a quality that many will recognise in the highly creative. Another important factor is certainly intelligence. Although difficult, psychometrically, to disentangle from creativity, intelligence, as measured by IQ at least, certainly seems to represent a distinguishable feature of cognitive performance and, to the extent that it is genetically determined, is probably separately inherited. Almost all outstandingly creative people are high in assessed IQ, a fact which must surely protect them to some extent from mental breakdown, both directly and indirectly, in the first case, by providing them with more flexible psychological resources to cope with stress and, in the second, by enabling them to make socially valued contributions that strengthen self-esteem. In any given individual the balance between these various influences is no doubt a delicate one, and in some instances precarious, depending on numerous casual and pervasive situational factors.

Turning to our third question, whether the undoubted connection with psychosis offers an all-embracing theory of creativity might ultimately reduce to how we define the latter. If we broaden it to mean simply 'cleverness' then obviously there can be several other explanations, mostly elucidated by an understanding of general intelligence and the way in which, even in the absence of 'psychotic' modes of thought, that facilitates high achievement. Eminence as a criterion introduces the additional feature of relying on social judgement, perhaps diluting in various ways our evaluation of what constitutes 'true' creativity. In this respect it is interesting to note a comment made by Andreasen on what she interprets as the relative failure of the Ellis survey to demonstrate very significant evidence of psychosis (or the tendency to it) among the eminent persons he surveyed. She suggests that the people studied by Ellis were mainly those who were merely powerful or influential enough to get their names in the *Dictionary of National Biography*, rather than necessarily being intellectually creative.[3] However, it is unlikely that this is an entirely sound basis for making a sharp distinction between 'psychotic' and 'non-psychotic' forms of creativity, if such a difference exists. A certain kind of great achievement, as revealed in power or influence over others, might itself spring from traits of a psychotic nature. We have already mentioned the suggestion that the manic's energy might be an important connecting link between creativity and psychosis. Although personally we believe this to be of only secondary importance, its probable role in motivating innovative acts cannot be ignored. Winston Churchill, an evident manic-depressive who rarely slept, is a notable example. Are we to conclude therefore that eminence cannot be allowed as a yardstick of creativity?

Even if we confine ourselves to the more usual outlets for creative expression – in the arts and sciences – there is similar ambiguity. Here we are reminded of studies carried out some years ago in Germany on the personality characteristics of a large group of professional painters and sculptors.[16, 17] It was found that, as predicted, the artists were more deviant on certain personality traits. However, further analysis of the data indicated that the relationship had nothing to do with the individuals' talent, as judged by expert rating of their contributions to contemporary art. Instead, it reflected how successful they had been in aggressively promoting their rather indifferent work. The authors cynically conclude:

> This outcome does not surprise us because it confirms our experience in this field, namely, that success in the arts is not synonymous with artistic significance or originality.[17]

The most reliable and valid yardstick of creativeness, of course, is retrospective, the capacity for the products of originality to survive the fleeting whims of taste, fashion, or claims as to their truth or value. Fortunately, most of the figures who appear in this book meet that criterion or, if not, they were certainly notable enough for them to have been remembered. That they were also all subject to periods of psychotic breakdown makes them of additional interest and in the next chapter we shall examine precisely what that means and how it might help us to understand their particular form of creativity.

2

Wings in the Head

That it has been possible to reach this point in the book without describing the signs of insanity in detail is a measure of their universality and of the fact that most of us have an intuitive understanding of their general quality. There are few who have not on occasion felt the press of irrational thought, been tempted into unwarranted belief, or experienced the highs and lows of inexplicable mood. However, it is when these pass beyond some threshold of acceptability, both for the person and for others, that the individual is recognised as suffering in a state of psychotic disorder. It is our judgement that all of the authors considered in this book were victims of such disorder and that the accounts of their lives in subsequent chapters can stand alone as evidence of that. On the other hand, we realise that professional clinicians coming to the book might remain unconvinced about some of our chosen examples, as indeed might those readers who only feel comfortable with terms like 'schizophrenia' when they are used in a sense that has been given medical approval. For that reason it is our intention to present, for all of our authors, explicit evidence that they did indeed meet the formal diagnostic criteria for psychotic illness, as used by psychiatrists. This will be done by giving for each subject a brief clinical case description, based on the application of a standard diagnostic schedule, to be described at the end of the chapter.

We hasten to add that we adopt the above procedure without any deep reverence for psychiatric classification as such or for the psychiatric form of describing the person. We are aware of the limited value of both as guides to comprehending the true nature of insanity, especially the more positive aspects we see reflected in the creative mind, and we fully agree with Lyndall Gordon who, when writing about Virginia Woolf, comments 'Our language has, as yet, no term for madness which is not demeaning.'[15]

Even when used, with effort to avoid evaluative overtones and as a purely descriptive device, psychiatric classification leaves much to be desired; for example in its inability to distinguish clearly between different varieties of psychosis or draw sharp boundaries between the manifestly and the marginally insane, points we shall have cause to enlarge upon later. Set against these deficiencies is the fact that psychiatry – if only by dint of the accumulated experience that comes from having to observe the more unusual among us – has developed a 'language of symptoms' that can prove useful in throwing the features of that deviance into high relief. It is in that spirit that we shall use conventional psychiatric terminology here.

Although precise categories of mental illness are difficult to arrive at, there is at least reasonable consensus about the meaning of the more inclusive terms, 'psychosis' and 'psychotic'. Admittedly, in some popular usage the latter is occasionally employed as a synonym for 'psychopathic', particularly to describe individuals who commit grossly antisocial, and often bizarrely motivated, crimes. As it happens, this use is not entirely wrong, since in many cases the person *is* insane and the psychopathic behaviour is itself a reflection of underlying psychosis. However, in a less evaluative sense, and in the majority of cases, the description 'psychotic' refers to an abnormality of experience and behaviour in which the individual loses control of his or her feelings, perceptions, and ideas, may develop delusional beliefs that have no basis in reality and intermittently lacks insight into the fact that anything is wrong. Experienced subjectively the state may range, depending on the degree of insight retained, from great perplexity and distress to arrogant certainty; observed objectively the behaviour seems grotesque and incomprehensible.

For most of this century it is those disorders gathered together under the heading of 'schizophrenia' that have been used as the paradigm for trying to describe and understand psychosis. Yet even in this form, or forms – for many would prefer to talk of 'the schizophrenias' – there is still no universally accepted set of criteria for diagnosis. To illustrate the point, one of the present authors was recently asked to review a paper submitted to a prominent psychiatric journal, proposing a new set of rules for diagnosing schizophrenia. In the course of their analysis the authors determined the extent to which their proposed criteria agreed with those contained in other existing diagnostic schemes – some ten or twelve of them. Correlations varied over a very wide range. Remarkably, one might think, one of the lowest – indicating almost total lack of agreement – was with a diagnosis arrived at using the criteria introduced by Eugen Bleuler, the man who coined the term 'schizophrenia' in the first place!

Given such disagreement, in trying to convey some sense of what psychiatrists mean when they talk of 'schizophrenia' it is probably more informative to consider the *range* of symptoms that might be found across a group of individuals who have received that diagnosis. The following list, close to that used in this book, summarises the most prominent symptoms:

Delusions that the mind is being controlled by an external force or that thoughts are being inserted or removed or can be heard by others.
Persecutory delusions, such as being the victim of a world-wide plot.
Other bizarre delusions, for instance about the body; e.g. that it is being transformed into that of a werewolf.
Hearing voices that keep up a running commentary in the head.
Hallucinations in other modalities, such as vision, taste or smell.
Incoherent speech, marked loosening of ideas, derailed thought, blunted or inappropriate emotion, and grossly disorganised behaviour.

Any one of the above features *could* result in a person being labelled schizophrenic, providing some other criteria are met, such as the symptoms having lasted for a certain length of time. Yet none, by itself, is vital to the diagnosis being made.

Some other general qualities of schizophrenia can be appreciated by examining attempts that have been made to identify various subtypes. One old classification recognised four such varieties: hebephrenic, paranoid, catatonic, and simple. Although now virtually abandoned, being almost entirely useless in both research and clinical practice, this scheme does draw out some of the ways in which the symptoms of schizophrenia can sometimes cluster together. Hebephrenia was once used to describe a form, typically beginning in adolescence, in which the person complains of auditory hallucinations, talks in an incomprehensible way, and shows totally inappropriate emotional reactions to other people. Such individuals are often of low tested IQ even before they fall ill, certainly afterwards their intellectual performance is poor. This is also true of so-called 'simple' schizophrenia, where poverty of speech and thought, apathy, and flat emotional response are the predominant features. In contrast, paranoid schizophrenics are often of high, sometimes very high, intelligence: their difficulty, as the name implies, is the development of unshakeable persecutory delusions, though in other respects their personality and intellectual functioning are usually well-preserved. Finally, catatonia, in which the person enters a state of total physical immobility, is rarely seen nowadays. However, it is interesting because of its paradoxical nature; the apparent lack of behavioural responsiveness actually conceals very much heightened psychological and physiological sensitivity, with which the sufferer copes by withdrawing into the inactivity of catatonic stupor.

One reason why these categories have proved of little practical value is that particular individuals may shift from one to another over the course of time, a fact which also illustrates an additional distinction that has to be made in describing schizophrenia. While some features, like disturbances in thinking or perception, form its central core, others – social withdrawal, for example – are secondary reactions to the mental distress that these cause. There is, therefore, a longitudinal dimension to the condition that makes it difficult to arrive at hard and fast diagnostic rules. Furthermore – and this probably gives us the best clue as to the intrinsic nature of schizophrenia – there is fluctuation in mental state over a much shorter time-scale. Thus, the person may rapidly and unpredictably veer from one extreme of a symptom to the other. For example, he or she may complain now of thoughts racing through the head, now of having no thoughts at all, or, on one occasion, of being bombarded by external stimulation, making concentration difficult, and, on another, of being fixated on some trivial detail in the outside world.

Although in trying to arrive at a definition of schizophrenia much emphasis has been placed on the disturbances that are found in *cognitive* functioning (perception, thinking, and attention), abnormal emotional response is almost universal. This may cover the whole gamut of emotions, including elation, despair, anger, irritability, anxiety, and inexplicable fear. These may occur either as a primary feature or secondarily, as a reaction to the disrupted mental functioning. However, it is where the emotional component predominates that psychiatrists have traditionally labelled the illness 'affective', rather than 'schizophrenic'.

Two points should be noted here about psychiatric usage of the term 'affective' in defining types of psychological disorder. First, it focuses on those aspects of emotion that have to do with prevailing *mood*, especially changes associated with feelings of depression and elation, though also including other emotional reactions, such as general irritability. Secondly, by no means all abnormal changes in mood signify a *psychotic* disturbance. Indeed in many – perhaps the majority of – cases of, say, depression the altered affect is perfectly understandable as a reaction to external stress, such as loss, bereavement, failure, or social circumstances. Psychotic depression, on the other hand, is more severe, seems to come 'out of the blue', and to the observer appears to have a more biological 'feel' about it. It would be diagnosed if the person complains of or shows such things as: poor appetite and weight loss; disturbed sleep pattern; loss of energy and an inability to experience pleasure; feelings of guilt and self-reproach; difficulty in concentrating; suicidal thoughts; and behaviour that is very greatly slowed down or, alternatively, agitated and restless. Some of these symptoms may be so extreme that the psychotic quality of the condition is clearly evident. For example, expressed guilt may be so deep as to become delusional, generalised to the point where the individual believes that he or she is personally responsible for some major catastrophe or for all of the evil that exists in the world.

A depressive reaction of psychotic proportion frequently occurs alone but in other cases it may be replaced by a state of mania which may also, though more rarely, be found without swings into depression. In mania – technically referred to, unless extremely severe, as 'hypomania' – the individual is more than usually active, is distractible and talkative to the point where meaningful conversation is impossible, is expansive and grandiose in attitude with an inflated sense of self-importance, and may embark on reckless activities, such as unrealistic spending, gambling, or sexual indiscretions. It is perhaps worth noting in passing that, although this manic-depressive form of psychosis is frequently interpreted as an alternation between two *opposite* mood states (representing abnormal extremes of sadness and happiness), that is almost certainly wrong. Thus, many manic-depressives, even in their 'up' phases, describe feelings of depression and it is probably more correct to think of their psychotic state as a whole as a rather peculiar co-existence of irritable moods.

Although it is the mood disturbance that stands out in affective psychosis, individuals who meet the criteria for either the 'unipolar' or the 'bipolar' form (as they are sometimes called) sometimes also show features reminiscent of schizophrenia, as we shall see for several of the subjects evaluated in this book. Such mixture of affective psychosis and schizophrenia may be revealed in changes in the symptom profile that are observed when the person is studied over a period of time, or it may be evident within a single episode of illness. In these cases some psychiatrists resort to the description 'schizoaffective' which, although itself an old term, is now often used in recognition of the fact that the traditional categories of schizophrenia and affective psychosis really only represent varieties of insanity as they occur in their pure forms.

In addition to these informal clinical observations, there are several other, more scientific, reasons for believing that schizophrenia and affective psychosis are not as distinct from each other as was once thought. Thus, recent statistical analyses – applied with the aim of trying to demonstrate that the symptoms of manic-depression and schizophrenia form two separate groups – have shown that there is actually no obvious dividing-line between them.[6] Nor, looked at from a genetics point of view are they clearly distinguishable: cases of manic-depression, for example, can often occur against a family background of schizophrenia, and vice versa.[20] Finally, the treatments for these two 'types' of psychosis are by no means specific, drug therapies found useful in one frequently also proving effective in the other.[14]

Of course psychologists, unlike their medical colleagues in psychiatry, have never really been convinced of the reality of such categorisations of psychosis. We can appreciate one reason for this if we examine the question, not from the viewpoint of *symptoms* used to try to distinguish schizophrenia from affective psychosis, but by looking at the underlying psychological processes that are responsible for the two states. Here, far from finding differences, we find crucial similarities. A good example, relevant to this book, surfaced in the previous chapter where we discussed 'overinclusive thinking' as an extreme, clinical, manifestation of divergent thinking. The notion of overinclusive thinking actually arose originally from studies of *schizophrenia*; yet, as already mentioned, it is found as, if not more, commonly in people diagnosed as suffering from mania, helping to account for the wild 'flight of ideas' typically observed in that condition.

Another, quite separate, reason why the idea of watertight categories of psychosis has never seemed very plausible to psychologists stems from the difficulty of defining the outer boundaries of insanity and the existence of so-called 'borderline' disorders that carry the overall flavour of schizophrenia or manic-depression, but which are not severe enough to meet the diagnostic criteria for either.[24] These halfway conditions have long been of interest, though until recently mainly among psychoanalysts or other writers outside mainstream psychiatry. Now, however, they are being formally recognised as mild, but genuine, variations of full-blown psychosis. One example, which is certainly related to schizophrenia and which we shall come across again, is 'schizotypal personality disorder'. Here the individual shows mild or transient psychotic-like symptoms, such as strong 'magical' or superstitious thinking, including illusions of the presence of another person; paranoid suspiciousness and hypersensitivity to criticism; aloofness in interaction with others; and odd, vague, digressive speech. Another borderline manifestation of psychosis is 'cyclothymia' in which the mood swings of manic-depression are evident, but less marked.

If terms like 'affective psychosis', 'schizophrenia' and 'schizoaffective disorder' have a use, therefore, it is merely as labels of convenience, as shorthand descriptors of the flavour of a given individual's form of insanity – and even then often only at a certain point in time and subject to qualifications as to the severity of disability. For many other purposes it is more informative to regard different 'types' and degrees of psychosis as variations on a single underlying theme of psychopathology; with particular forms of psychotic reaction being dependent on the co-existence of other, essentially unrelated, intellectual and personality traits that colour the individual's behaviour. In this respect it is very illuminating to consider what happens when people are given so-called 'psychedelic' drugs, such as LSD. In our experience the latter – which mimics 'natural' psychosis rather well – produces a range of reactions that closely parallels those found in schizophrenia and affective disorder, subjects' reactions being highly predictable from a knowledge of their underlying personality. In other words, the cyclothymic become hypomanic, the schizoid more withdrawn, and the hypersensitive somewhat paranoid.

In the light of the foregoing, psychiatry itself is increasingly being forced to admit that the firm categories of psychosis with which it has tried to work for many years are of limited value. It may be asked why psychiatry has made such heavy weather of coming round to that view. The main reason has been its long-standing commitment (still evident in some quarters) to the idea that each of the different forms of functional psychosis is really a distinct type of brain disease, equivalent to those studied in neurology. In other words, psychiatrists have used as their analogy disorders such as Huntington's chorea or Alzheimer's disease, which are known (or can be assumed) to have a discrete organic cause in the nervous system and which are like other infective or degenerative physical diseases, except that they happen to affect the brain.

Yet the above comparison has never worked, nor could it have been expected to. Quite apart from nearly a hundred years of intensive research having failed to demonstrate such a cause of functional psychosis, there is another important reason why it is totally inappropriate to draw on analogy with the neurological diseases proper. A characteristic of the latter is their solely *deteriorating* impact, the fact that when even their mild signs are present they bring about only incapacity and inefficiency of function. Furthermore, such deficit is a primary, intrinsic feature of those diseases, usually having a progressive course. Functional psychosis, on the other hand, is radically different. It is true that during bouts of acute psychotic illness – or as an accumulating effect of several episodes – there may be impaired social and intellectual functioning, but this has more the appearance of a secondary consequence and, in any case, is by no means seen in all individuals. More significantly, as is already clear from our discussion so far, functional psychosis also contains within itself a potential for the very opposite of deficit, the occasional capacity for superlative functioning and high achievement; this is the paradox of which we wrote in the previous chapter. Such conjunction of the excellent and the awful is never found in any genuine neurological disease.

If the functional psychoses are not ordinary brain diseases, then what are they? Elsewhere one of us has offered an opinion on that question, together with appropriate supporting evidence.[8] Here we shall merely try to summarise the main points that are immediately relevant to the topic of this book.

A crucial first step in our account takes up again a theme, introduced in the previous chapter, about the continuity between the normal and the psychotic. The argument here is that the psychological tendencies responsible for the symptoms of psychosis are not the prerogative of the clinically psychotic. On the contrary they are a natural feature of the human condition, present in everyone to a greater or lesser degree. In other words, just as people differ in extraversion, intelligence, and proneness to anxiety so, too, do they differ in the extent to which they show *psychotic* characteristics. Such traits are widely distributed in the general population and, as considerable research over the past decade has shown, are easily measurable with self-rating questionnaires, of which there are now very many.[9] One example is a questionnaire devised some years ago by one of the present authors for detecting 'schizotypal' traits in normal people.[10] The items in this inventory were modelled on the list of symptoms used by psychiatrists to diagnose the borderline condition of 'schizotypal personality disorder' referred to earlier, but toned down for use with non-clinical populations. Research with this questionnaire (and others like it) has demonstrated that schizotypal personality traits are frequently found in psychologically healthy individuals. In other words, when asked systematically about it, many perfectly normal people freely admit to having had mild 'symptoms' reminiscent of schizophrenia, such as hallucinatory experiences and other sensory illusions, inexplicable mood change, feelings of unreality, strong 'telepathic' thoughts bordering on the sense of being influenced from a distance, and distorted thinking of almost delusional quality. At the level of reported experience, therefore, there seems to be a genuine continuum running from the obviously psychotic, through a borderline (though still clinically diagnosable) form of disorder, to the normal, but schizotypal, personality.

Although schizophrenia and the associated traits of 'schizotypy' have been the main focus of interest, research has also shown similar continuity with affective psychosis. Indeed, the results of very recent work reveal two interesting parallels with the conclusions reached about the psychotic illnesses themselves.[4] First, when we examine a very wide range of psychotic traits in normal people, using questionnaires that contain different kinds of item, we find that they tend to group into clusters closely corresponding to the different ways in which clinical psychosis manifests itself: in emotion, in perception and thinking, and in socially deviant behaviour. Secondly, however, these clusters also show a certain degree of relatedness or overlap. As in the clinical domain, there seems to be a common theme of 'psychoticism' which nevertheless, in a given individual, will be revealed as a unique blend of several different constituent elements, each of which is continuous with some recognisable symptom pattern found in psychotic illness itself.

Study of these various components of psychoticism as found in normal people has not been confined to the superficial level of observable traits, measured by questionnaires. On the contrary, the development of such instruments has only been a first step, preparatory to examining the reasons people differ on such traits. The guiding principle of that research has been the idea that the personality differences partly reflect underlying *physiological* differences in the brain, each person having a characteristic temperamental make-up that is represented at the biological level as a 'type of nervous system'. This principle is a quite general one that has been applied to several 'dimensions' of personality. The simplest and most obvious example concerns individual differences in the susceptibility to anxiety. There it is well-established that part of the reason people differ, even as adults, is because certain regions of the brain responsible for triggering fearful behaviour are simply more reactive in some individuals than in others.[16]

Examining psychotic traits from a comparable point of view is more tricky because it is still unclear precisely what properties of brain activity are likely to prove crucial to a description of the schizotypal nervous system. The best clues are almost certainly to be found by studying those aspects of brain function which, if they become deranged, could account for the symptoms of psychotic illness, and currently a considerable amount of research is in progress testing out various possibilities.[9] Details of the experiments themselves do not concern us here, but some of the ideas that have emerged from them are of interest because they add further to our understanding of how, looked at from a biological perspective, creativity can be connected to psychosis. We shall return to this point later in the chapter. However it is first necessary to consider another important consequence of the view of psychosis being presented here.

Although many people possess the psychotic traits we have been discussing, only a few will show the signs of even a borderline disorder and still fewer will develop a full-blown psychotic illness. What can we learn from this about psychosis? Actually two questions are being posed here. First, what determines whether the outcome for the person is a morbid one, leading to disordered behaviour and experience? Second, if psychotic traits are so widely distributed – and apparently perfectly compatible with mental health – how can they also be associated with such disintegrative states as schizophrenia?

The answer to the second question requires that we look at psychosis from a slightly different point of view from that adopted in most medical literature. There, as we have seen, psychotic reactions are always referred to as *diseases* – which they are, to the extent that they involve serious disruption of the nervous system's behaviour. However, the term 'disease' is slightly unfortunate in this context because it conjures up notions of a 'cause' that has little or nothing to do with the natural state of the organism but which is imposed on it, having a discontinuous effect; as, for example, in infectious diseases. However, this is almost certainly not true of disorders like schizophrenia, which are better visualised as *aberrations* of otherwise normal physiological and psychological processes which for some reason pass beyond their usual adaptive limits; here the term 'dysfunction', rather than disease seems more appropriate.

It should be emphasised that nothing unusual is being stated here. There are many comparable examples in the psychological sphere, as well as in the domain of physical disorder. Again, take anxiety as an example. As a personality trait, this is a universal characteristic, necessary not just for survival but also, at moderate levels, for motivating optimum performance on many everyday tasks. Yet exactly the same trait, if too high, can disrupt and disable, in some cases bringing about the symptoms of anxiety neurosis. Some physical illnesses, known as systemic disorders, also have a similar quality. Thus, very high blood pressure can become established as a pathological state – 'essential hypertension' – which can help to precipitate strokes or heart attacks. However, performing its adaptive function blood pressure is merely a natural physiological trait, though one that can vary over a wide range even in healthy individuals. In all of these cases – anxiety, blood pressure, or psychotic temperament – the underlying trait, as well as describing differences between people, also acts as a *disposition* to the appropriate dysfunction to which it contributes. So-called psychotic 'disease' can therefore best be seen as a normal, healthy characteristic gone wrong.

The other question posed above – Why do some people become ill and others not? – is less easy to answer, except in the most general terms. Certainly, it seems reasonable to assume that individuals whose temperamental make-up is more 'psychotic', and who therefore have a greater predisposition to psychosis, will be in greatest danger of passing over the threshold into overt illness, just as those of anxious temperament are more likely to develop an anxiety neurosis, and persons whose blood pressure is more labile will carry an enhanced risk of heart attack or stroke. But since in all of these examples the relevant traits act only as dispositions, the actual outcome in any given individual will depend on the interaction between vulnerability and other factors that trigger illness, leading to symptoms. Unfortunately, in the case of psychosis it is still unclear precisely what these additional factors are; unlike, say, cardiovascular disease where it is possible to point to very particular things, such as smoking and diet.

Nevertheless, we can say something further about the vulnerability itself; namely that the psychotic temperament does seem to be under strong genetic control. It has been shown, for example, that identical twins resemble each other quite closely on schizotypal traits.[11] In addition, immediate relatives of diagnosed psychotics show schizotypal characteristics more frequently than would be expected by chance.[21] These results are not too surprising given the research findings discussed in the previous chapter and suggest that what is inherited as vulnerability to psychosis forms a broad set of dispositions that include both temperamental and cognitive features.

Taken against the background of considerable other evidence about the genetics of psychosis (especially schizophrenia) we can therefore certainly conclude that inheritance plays a major role in determining susceptibility. Usually this has been emphasised as an attempt to make a statement about which people in the population are most likely, given other interacting events, to develop psychotic illness; in fact that is how we initially phrased the question here. However, from our present perspective it is actually more pertinent to turn the question round the other way and ask: why is it that some people, despite having a strong genetic disposition for psychotic illness do *not* actually break down – or, even if they do, are partly protected from its more devastating effects?

Concern for this issue has recently surfaced in studies that were indeed set up originally to try to isolate the factors that determine which among a selected sample of children are likely later in life to have a schizophrenic breakdown.[26] Typically, these are long-term, follow-up investigations of the children of known schizophrenics – and therefore chosen because, on purely genetic grounds, they should be at greater risk. Predictably, a greater than average proportion of such children do develop symptoms of schizophrenia – or of some related 'borderline' condition, such as schizotypal personality disorder. However, what has often gone unnoticed is that in most cases this does *not* happen and, even more interesting, in some the outcome is what has been called 'outstanding'; that is to say, the individual turns out to be a highly competent and sometimes very creative adult. Such observations have given rise to the notion of the 'invulnerable child' and are now leading to a radical re-appraisal of the results of risk research, with a shift of emphasis towards trying to understand the factors that enable some individuals to survive, or even profit from, their disposition to insanity.

A clinician who has written extensively on this topic is Anthony, who has also discussed the implied association between psychosis and creativity.[1] One important point which Anthony makes is that the essential quality of the psychotic temperament is emotional hypersensitivity or 'skinlessness', with which the child copes by developing a degree of resilience to painful thoughts and events. Invulnerability may be achieved and expressed in several ways, of which one is the flight into creativity. According to Anthony, this may vary in the extent to which it is effective in keeping actual psychosis at bay. In some cases it will be entirely successful, resulting in a 'healthy' form of constructive competence and creativeness in which, though outer-directed, the individual is not afraid to explore his or her inner world. In others, however, the coping is always uncertain and psychotic breakdown a constant threat. Of these Anthony writes:

> With this group, vulnerability is deep-seated and long-lived. From the very beginning, they seem to lack the 'protective shield' and the constitutional buffering between themselves and the world around. The hypersensitivity that permits such free exchange between outer experience and the psychic interior may conduce to two outcomes: 'breakdown' when the primitive content takes over and allows the milieu of irrationality and unrealism to prevail without constraint, and an upsurge of creative productivity delicately controlled by the ego. . . . Thus, many creative artists and writers manifest cycles of vulnerability and resilience determined by the ebb and flow of the creative urge.

By way of illustration Anthony quotes several famous writers including one (Virginia Woolf) considered in this book as well as Kafka and Hans Christian Andersen who, Anthony recalls, had both a psychotic grandfather and a father who became deluded. Commenting on Andersen he notes:

> His main interest was in his little puppet theatre, and this is where he began to create his stories. . . . His 'skinlessness' was only too obvious. . . . His own reason he gave for his survival was that he was supremely capable of withdrawing into fantasy away from actual reality, thus transforming an unkind and often belligerent world into a fairy story. . . . During the act of creation, he achieved a few glorious moments of relief, but once the writing was over, he relapsed in a constant sense of aching depression and deprivation.

Although writing here with a different purpose from our own – and exclusively from a psychodynamic perspective – Anthony nevertheless articulates for us the final theme that remains to be developed in this chapter, which concerns the formal similarities between the mechanisms of mad and creative thought. We have already, in the previous chapter, examined this question rather superficially, by noting the modes of thinking they have in common, described as overinclusive thinking in the clinical, and as divergent thinking in the creativity, literature. However, much more recent ideas developed in academic psychology, and applied to the clinical phenomena of psychosis, allow us to take the account rather further than that. We are referring to theories, based on detailed laboratory studies of both normal schizotypal and diagnosed schizophrenic subjects, about how the 'psychotic' brain processes information. The theories in question arose originally out of a joining together of empirical research and clinical observation, some of which go right back to the very earliest descriptions of schizophrenia and it is therefore instructive to consider, first, what Bleuler himself believed to be the essential features of the 'disease' that he had named.

Bleuler proposed that most fundamental in schizophrenia is the loosening that occurs in associative thought, later to be studied as overinclusive thinking. He further suggested that an immediate secondary consequence of this is a 'splitting' of mental life, leading to autism. Here 'autism' refers to the domination of consciousness by fantasy, by internally generated thoughts which the psychotic individual finds increasingly difficult to distinguish from ideas that originate in perceptions of external reality. Even Bleuler himself considered what most of us would now recognise as a truism: that 'autism' is a feature of normal mental life, accounting for the emergence, or in some cases deliberate exploration, of ideas that arise without logic from unconscious layers of the mind. The difference between the normal and the schizophrenic is, then, solely a matter of degree, depending upon the extent to which the products of autism become fixed in place or, alternatively, remain under rational control. Strömgren draws the comparison as follows:

In non-schizophrenic persons . . . this thinking becomes subject to an incessant critical correction process which has the purpose of adapting the verbal expressions of thought to communication with other human beings. . . . The normal feedback from the surroundings does, however, not function in autistic schizophrenics, and their language thus becomes more and more private and incomprehensible. The precursors of delusions and hallucinations are constituted by fantasies and illusions, wishful thinking and fallacies which formally are identical with those experienced by normal persons. But here again schizophrenic autism makes a distinction between fantasy and reality decreasingly interesting with the result that delusions and hallucinations become equals of, or even superior to, the real experiences. The foundation for the superiority of autism in schizophrenia consists in its indispensability as a protection against unbearable emotional stresses which threaten the catathymically oversensitive schizophrenic. In the non-schizophrenic personality the autistic mechanisms are flexible, in the schizophrenic they are fixed.[25]

If it is indeed the loosening of control over associative thought – Woolf's 'Wings in the Head' – that is the basic mechanism responsible for autism then the question arises: what is it about the mind that modulates this process, allowing it some free rein, though being capable on occasions of going badly awry, leading to psychosis? The answer to that question, in essence at least, was provided nearly thirty years ago, by a perceptive schizophrenic introspecting about her own psychotic experience.[18] In a now well-quoted passage from her account, in which she was trying to capture the feeling – commonly reported by schizophrenics – of being flooded by stimulation, she wrote:

> So the mind must have a filter ... sorting out stimuli and allowing only those which are relevant to the situation into consciousness. ... What happened to me was a breakdown in the filter.

Simultaneously with clinical observations such as these, academic psychologists were also beginning to incorporate a similar idea into their models of normal cognitive functioning and most contemporary theories of human information processing contain the notion of a mechanism that screens and selects the products of consciousness; necessarily so, since organised thought would be impossible without some device that allows the mind to choose from among the many stimuli – both internal and external – with which it is constantly bombarded. Early versions of these theories were quickly taken up by clinical researchers looking for a formal way of examining what their patients – like the one above – were telling them and many experimental studies were carried out, guided by the hypothesis that schizophrenic features like overinclusive thinking are due to very weak filtration of the contents of thought, resulting in the psychotic individual finding it difficult to pursue a logically connected train of ideas. The same theories were also used to explain the normal variants of overinclusion – divergent or allusive thinking.

On the clinical side the view still prevails that schizophrenics have difficulty, as one author has put it, 'limiting the contents of consciousness'.[12] The theories in academic psychology that might explain this have also become more sophisticated, making it possible to identify more precisely the stage of information processing at which the crucial filtering effect occurs. Processing of stimuli goes through a sequence of phases. The first is automatic, occurring below the level of awareness, and involves rapid, parallel scanning of a large array of potentially significant events. Only a proportion of these are passed on to the next stage of conscious analysis. Selection almost certainly involves a process of active inhibition which screens out, among other things, unwanted or inappropriate associations between thoughts. Using specially arranged cognitive tasks it has been possible to show that this inhibition is weaker than average in psychotic individuals, otherwise ignored information being relatively more available for conscious processing.

Applied to clinical psychosis, information processing theories naturally highlight the *disruption* of intellectual functioning that can occur when the mind is overwhelmed by ideas pouring indiscriminately into awareness. However, there is now evidence that the mechanism responsible for this can act in a similar fashion in some normal individuals; as one would expect these are people high in schizotypal traits.[3] The only difference between them and the psychotically ill seems to be the greater intellectual control they retain in managing the freely associated ideas which an equally weak filtering system allows into consciousness. The same cognitive mechanism responsible for the deleterious effects of psychotic disorder can therefore also be seen as a gateway through which the raw material of creativity, originating below immediate awareness, is passed for elaboration by the conscious mind.

The theories that have guided these insights into the mechanisms of psychotic and creative thought do not, of course, specify what it is about the *brain* that might account for the differences observed in schizophrenic and schizotypal individuals. Information processing models are essentially of the 'black box' type; that is to say, although assuming that processes like filtering do have physiological correlates, the models themselves are formulated in purely psychological terms. For our purposes here that may not seem to matter very much. However, it is important for two related reasons. First, it is clear that psychotic illness involves, if nothing else, a serious disruption of brain activity. And, secondly, as discussed earlier, a continuity view of psychosis rests very heavily on the idea that it is the type of *nervous system* they have in common that connects the normal to the abnormal. Any biological data that are available must therefore further enhance our understanding.

Biological research into psychosis has taken, and continues in, many directions. Currently one of the most viable theories is that psychosis has something to do with peculiarities in the functioning of the two brain hemispheres.[5, 22] Although going back well into the nineteenth century, in the past two decades this idea has generated a vast amount of research by psychologists, physiologists, neuroanatomists and other scientists. The work has demonstrated that psychotic individuals do indeed show some imbalance in hemisphere organisation that could account for their bizarre psychological experiences. Interpretations of the source of this imbalance have varied, but most persuasive is the theory that it reflects an unusual form of communication between the two halves of the brain, involving the anatomical structure (the *corpus callosum*) that joins them together.[13, 27] Indeed, it has been suggested that it is here that the 'site' of psychosis lies; not in a strictly anatomical sense but as a functional property, determining the way the *corpus callosum* modulates the flow of information between the hemispheres.

To appreciate the significance of this idea it is necessary to look briefly at some general features of the lateral arrangement of the brain as it relates to psychological function.[2] This can be best understood as the two hemispheres being engaged in a co-operative exercise, to which each contributes according to the task it is specialised to perform. Here two features should be noted. One is the left hemisphere's predominant role in speech and language. The other is the different modes of information processing adopted by the two halves of the brain. The left, consistent with its primary language capacity, is sequential and analytic in its style and has often been regarded as the rational half, responsible for the organisation and expression of conscious thought. The right hemisphere has a more global, less focused, free-ranging style and, being 'silent', can only influence conscious awareness indirectly.

Interestingly, there is also a close correspondence between these two processing modes and the two stages of information analysis referred to in the psychological theories described earlier. Thus the right hemisphere is well-placed to undertake the early parallel, preconscious scanning of large amounts of information, the left taking on the later function of conscious elaboration of selected items. The delicate balance of cooperation between them – occurring across the *corpus callosum* and involving some kind of filtering process – is therefore of crucial importance in allowing the left hemisphere to remain responsive to the right hemisphere's influence, yet sufficiently in control to avoid overloading of conscious, directed thought.

The conclusion from *psychological* research that information processing is unusual in psychotic individuals thus finds an exact parallel in theories emphasising the functioning of the corpus callosum as the *physiological* vehicle for psychosis. The studies on which these theories are based, incidentally, have involved the use of test procedures that make it possible to assess the relative contribution of the two hemispheres to psychological performance, usually on tasks that demand the processing of linguistic information. Differences in the patterns of performance observed on such tests – including reduction of the usual left hemisphere dominance in language, as well as intruding effects emanating from the right hemisphere – have led to the conclusion that in psychosis there may be enhanced communication between the two sides of the brain.[5] However, the same has again been found to be true of some normal schizotypal individuals and, notably, the genetically related children of schizophrenics.[7, 17] This suggests that the quality of interhemispheric control merely represents a particular style of cerebral organisation which can certainly become a potential biological vehicle for psychotic disorder but which, in favourable circumstances, constitutes a brain mechanism responsible for the flexibility of thought found in some creative people.

The experimental research just described has given substance, in several respects, to some older or less empirically based ideas about psychosis and creativity. The schizophrenic's and schizotypal individual's hypersensitivity, which many clinicians have emphasised, can be traced to weak modulation of stimuli that impinge upon the mind, leading to an undue awareness of events – both internal and external – less available to others. This can have disastrous consequences, in some cases sending the person into an insane state. In others of similar nervous system and temperamental make-up it can, through the relaxing of controls over rational thought, facilitate the entry into the autism of which Bleuler wrote and from which much healthy creativity springs. At a neurological level this interplay between conscious and unconscious influences on thought almost certainly depends upon the lateral organisation of the brain, and on a particular involvement of the right hemisphere. Although physiologically naive to suggest, as some have, that the *seat* of creativity lies in the right hemisphere, the latter's contribution must be considered of unique importance, given what is known about its style of cognitive processing.[19]

All of the approaches to psychosis and creativity considered here – clinical or experimental, psychological or physiological – have laid stress on, and indeed provided evidence for, a common theme: the continuity between the healthy and the pathological, the constructive and the destructive. This slant on the topic has been deliberate, in order to draw out connections that are often ignored or, if they are recognised, swept aside as too uncomfortable to contemplate. However, we feel it is also important, in concluding our account, to re-emphasise some earlier points. Psychotic illness itself is frequently a *discontinuous* event and mostly inimical to organised thought. Furthermore, true creativity is relatively uncommon even in those individuals who never overtly break down but whose mode of thinking resembles that of the diagnosably psychotic: it is rarer still in those who do pass beyond the threshold into clinical disorder.

The authors discussed in the remainder of this book are therefore of unique interest. As individuals who used language as the medium for their art they probably take us closer than any other kind of creative person to the heart of our topic; given, that is, the nature of psychosis as a disorder, essentially, of linguistic expression. Furthermore, all of them, despite on occasions entering states of manifest psychosis, remained sufficiently fluent to articulate their experiences, either in their fiction or in records of their lives, or both. They have therefore left us with an unusually rich source of material through which to examine several questions about psychosis and creativity already raised, but as yet unanswered, in this and the previous chapter. Why, for example, were they unique? And were they so as individuals? Are there any common themes running through their lives and writings that can elucidate our understanding both of creativity and psychosis? In the final chapter we shall return to consider those questions.

However, one question which has to be settled in advance of that is: were our chosen authors truly psychotic, as judged by current clinical criteria? As we shall see, in some individual cases this has been disputed. In others there is little or no disagreement. In yet others an answer has never, as far as we know, previously been sought. Our own solution has been to subject the material about each author to a formal analysis, applying a psychiatric assessment procedure that is widely used in research and clinical practice. The procedure in question is the *Schedule for Affective Disorders and Schizophrenia*, or SADS.[23] This comes in two forms, that used here being the SADS-L, or Lifetime Version, which enables the assessment to be based, not on a single episode of illness, but on accumulated information about the person, covering the longer time periods over which our subjects could be studied.

The SADS-L provides precise criteria for diagnosing a spectrum of psychological disorders but, as the name implies, its main focus is major psychotic illness: schizophrenia, affective disorder (depression, hypomania, and manic-depression) and the mixed condition of schizoaffective disorder. Our aim was to determine whether our authors met the criteria for any of these forms of psychosis and, if so, to ascertain in each case which 'diagnosis' provided the best description. Our method of proceeding was as follows.

First, one of us (GSC) developed a simplified version of the SADS-L, extracting all of the items relevant to the diagnosis of psychotic illness. Since the SADS-L is normally used in a face-to-face interview situation these items are mostly in the form of questions and here the original wording was retained. Our modified schedule was then applied to each of the subjects by one or other of two of the present authors (either GW or RP). She was asked to draw on her knowledge of the subject's life material and reply to each question, supplying evidence, as nearly as possible using the subject's own words, that was sufficiently detailed for the answer to be evaluated properly against the original SADS-L criteria.

Completed in this form the schedule for each subject was then scored (by GSC), using the rules contained in the SADS-L. The procedure adopted was to err as far as possible on the side of conservatism, scoring each reply as 'psychotic' only where this seemed reasonably certain. Where replies were ambiguous or lacking in detail further information was requested before reaching a decision: in some cases this was supplemented by material obtained from elsewhere.

Use of the above method clearly has some weaknesses, the most obvious being that ours were not 'blind' assessments and could clearly have been influenced by our preconceptions about the subjects. Against this can be set the fact that the following chapters present very full accounts of their lives and works which should at least allow readers to make their own judgments, especially as we have included (in an appendix to the book) details of our 'SADS-L' procedure.

Another difficulty is that of assessing the mental state of individuals who are no longer alive. Although less of a problem with twentieth- or late nineteenth-century figures, this becomes more serious with individuals from an earlier age, for three reasons. The first is sheer lack of information. The second is the shifting nature of society's concepts of insanity, which requires some disentangling of the significance of whatever information is available. Thirdly, there is the possibility that abnormalities judged by us to be psychotic in a *functional* sense were actually due to organic brain diseases unrecognised at the time; for reasons discussed previously this would rule them out of court for our purposes. Unfortunately, there is no real solution to these difficulties and again we can only leave it to the reader to arrive at his or her own conclusion on the basis of the material presented.

Finally, although not a criticism of our method – indeed, if anything, quite the contrary – it should be noted that for several of our chosen authors it was possible to arrive at more than one 'diagnosis' that fell within the general category of psychosis. Where this was so it will be discussed, together with other comments, in the brief 'case descriptions' attached at the end of each of the chapters that follow.

3

Mediaeval Madness

The spectrum of human behaviour remains fairly constant throughout the ages. Human beliefs and activities change, feelings and responses change hardly at all. The attitudes of Job's comforters are unsurprisingly the attitudes of many people today when faced with mental illness, just as Job's symptoms are recognisable as those of a severe reactive depression. The symptoms of psychosis as we know them today appear in all literatures from the earliest times. Egyptian papyri, Greek myth and medicine, Roman history, the Old and the New Testaments all contain examples of what we now recognise as psychotic episodes; some of them, like the legend of Orpheus, associate creativity and psychosis.

Although God specifically warned Job's comforters not to postulate his sins as the cause of his sufferings, the Middle Ages preferred, like most ages, to ignore what God said. To the mediaeval mind, madness was a direct result of, and punishment for, unacknowledged or unrepented sin. In the widely-read Saints' Lives of the period, sinners are frequently struck with madness, to be restored to sanity when they have repented and been absolved. It was admitted that occasionally the good were afflicted too, and that in these cases God was probably testing their faith, or even possibly allowing them their purgatory on earth, but on the whole the Church found it more satisfactory to believe that madness was punitive and well-deserved. The loss of reason was a just punishment for an evil life, which was the result of the misuse of reason. The folk in Hell, said Vergil to Dante, were *'le genti dolorose/c'hanno perduto il ben dell'intelletto'* – the miserable race who had lost the good of intelligence.

While literature and religion stressed the moral causes of insanity, there were some commentators who, working from pure observation, suggested other causes, physiological or emotional. Bartholomaeus Anglicus, a professor of theology at Paris, discussed in his encyclopaedia *De Proprietatibus Rerum* the three major types of insanity; frenzy, amentia and stupor, which he associated with excesses of choler, melancholy and phlegm. It was known

49

that fasting could cause hallucinations, and extreme weather conditions were thought to affect the mind. Frenzy was used as a description of rapid mood changes and raving, amentia could refer to violence or terror, stupor to apathy and poverty of response. He enumerates also many symptoms easily recognisable as those of psychosis. The depressive patient is 'feynt, ferdful in herte without cause . . . Some wene that they sholde deye anone unresonably . . . some love and desyre deth'. Of schizoid and deluded patients he says, 'Soche holden theyr peas whan they sholde speke to-moche whan they shold be styll . . . And some wene they close and conteyne the worlde in theyr hondes . . . and therefore they put not theyr hondes to take mete . . .' Paranoid patients 'fall in to full euyll suspiccions without recouer and therfore they hate and blame theyr frendes, and sometyme smite and slee theim'. The night-mares and perception of strange smells that we shall see in our more modern writers were as prevalent in mediaeval times: 'He dremyth dredful dremes of derknesse and ferdfull to se, and of stynkynge sauoure and smelle.'

Froissart in his *Chronicles* describes the probably schizophrenic Charles VI, who set out on a punitive expedition to Brittany, in spite of being ordered to rest by his doctors, who had evidently recognised the signs of an approaching attack. He had had severe headaches and depression, and was made nervous by a warning of treachery from a madman who ran out of the woods. Startled by a lance accidentally falling on a helmet, he attacked his own men, killing four, and could not be disarmed until he was exhausted. The doctor who attended him, Guillaume de Harselly, was evidently experienced in cases of mental illness, and warned the royal counsellors that other attacks of the same kind were to be expected. The king's next relapse resulted in permanent disability; this was regarded as a divine punishment for his early excesses.

Canon law prescribed that every physician, before attempting a cure, must persuade the mentally ill to apply to the physicians of the soul, their confessors. No physical remedy could succeed unless the spiritual remedy had first been applied. After that, the possibilities for the disturbed were very much what they were to remain until the introduction of the major tranquillisers – and indeed what they had been from Roman times. The violent against themselves and others were shut up, sometimes in darkness, they might be bound to prevent harm, they might be flogged or starved. The less disturbed needed to be freed 'from cause of matere of besy thoughtes ... and somdele be ocupyd'. In other words, they needed release from stress, and occupational therapy. Celsus suggested that they should be gently argued with rather than opposed, and that music and light reading might help to turn their thoughts into a more rational channel. Medical literature, though bound to note and discuss the physiological causes, in no way contradicted the strong belief promoted by all other literature of the time, that madness was punishment for sin.

Mediaeval literature has frequent references to insanity, in sermons and saints' lives, where holy men struggle with the insane and usually cure them, by the power of God, or where the violent against Christians ultimately become mad; in homiletic literature, where the figures of Nebuchadnezzar and Herod present fearful lessons; and in Arthurian romances, where Tristram and Lancelot are interesting figures to the modern psychologist. Both of them have psychotic interludes, occurring after particularly stress-loaded incidents, both are in guilt-producing situations (Lancelot doubly so, since he has inadvertently betrayed the woman he adulterously loves) and both, in losing their reason, lose their humanity. They run wild into the woods, filthy, skeletal and naked. Lancelot, although befriended by a hermit, cannot be brought back to a normal state of mind because the hermit is too poor to feed him properly, and 'for defaute of sustenance he waxed more wooder than he was aforetyme', and became violent, breaking the legs and arms of those who tried to help him. Both knights have to be bathed, shaved and properly clothed, and well looked after before they come to themselves, and Lancelot is 'sore ashamed' of his madness, and asks that it be kept from common knowledge. It has been suggested that the wild man, or wood-wose, who appears so often in medieval literature, is a conventional figure typifying madness and deriving from the mad king Nebuchadnezzar, who was 'driven away from among men, and did eat grass like an ox, and his body was wet with the dew of heaven; till his hairs grew like the feathers of eagles, and his nails like birds claws.' But all literary conventions have their origin in life; is it not possible that the wild men were psychotics driven out of towns and settlements by a society unable to cope with them? They either died there from hunger or exposure, or were taken back into their community when they had recovered sufficiently to present no menace.

Margery Kempe (c. 1373–??)

In an age when sin and madness were so strongly associated, the only reason for confessing to having been insane would be that complete recovery showed divine forgiveness of whatever sin had caused the madness in the first place; and this is the reason advanced by the two mediaeval authors who admit to having been mad, Margery Kempe and Thomas Hoccleve. Hoccleve was a scribe by profession, and was therefore able to write his own confession, but the difficulty in considering the case of Margery Kempe is that she was illiterate, and dictated her account of her life to two different scribes, one a poor writer and the other a priest. We are therefore presented with a book which was not 'written in order . . . but like as the matter came to the creature in mind . . . for it was so long ere it was written that she had forgotten the time and the order when things befell'. It is likely too that the priest tidied up and eliminated any traces there may have been of disordered thinking or language, as he almost certainly corrected any theological mistakes, for his own safety. Ruskin (who will be discussed in a later chapter) also wrote his autobiography in old age, and without our knowledge of his life from other sources we should have a distorted picture of his childhood, and should know nothing at all about his marriage. Yet he had letters and journals, as well as his own books, to help in his compilation; Margery had nothing but her own memory. What is valuable about her book, therefore, is not its accuracy, but its testimony to her thoughts and feelings.

She was the daughter of a respected and well-to-do burgess of Lynne (as King's Lynn was then called) who had been five times Mayor, and Alderman of the High Guild of the Trinity. Doubtless he gave her a good dowry when she married another burgess, John Kempe. Though she told her husband 'shrewdly and shortly' that she thought she had married beneath her, he proved on the whole a sympathetic and supportive husband in what cannot by any standards have been a normal or comfortable married life. Margery became pregnant soon after her wedding, was continually sick during the pregnancy, and had a difficult childbirth. She sent for her confessor because she was in mortal sin; she had withheld from him in confession a sin of which she was ashamed, but because he spoke sharply to her, she did not confess it at all this time either. Fearful of damnation, and angry at the priest's reproof, she went out of her mind, and was 'wondrously vexed and laboured with spirits for half a year, eight weeks and odd days'. Her breakdown cannot be better described than in her own words: 'She saw, as she thought, devils opening their mouths all inflamed with burning waves of fire, as if they would have swallowed her in, sometimes ramping at her, sometimes threatening her . . . night and day, during the aforesaid time'. They told her she must give up Christianity and deny, not only God and all the saints, but her father, her mother, and all her friends. 'And so', says Margery with a touch of complacency, 'she did. She slandered her husband, her friends, and her own self. She said many a wicked word, and many a cruel word; she knew no virtue or goodness, she desired all wickedness; like as the spirits tempted her to say and do, so she said and did'. The devils urged that she should kill herself and be damned with them in Hell, and it was evidently to contain her attempts at suicide that she was 'bound and kept with strength day and night'; even then she 'rived the skin on her body against her heart with her nails most spitefully'. Then, after eight months of this, she had, one day when her keepers had left her alone, a vision of Christ, in a purple silk mantle.

Soon after this, Margery 'became calmed in her wits and reason, as well as ever she was before', and was able to cope with her usual occupations, 'wisely and soberly enough'. But in her personal and religious life she was very far from wise or sober, which might lead theologians to think that the apparition of Christ which she saw was a hallucination rather than a pure vision. Traditionally the visionaries of the Church have been either opponents of Christ, like St Paul or St Eustace, who were converted by their visions, or men and women already leading lives of heroic sanctity, like St Teresa or St Francis. Far from leading a more Christian life, Margery after her breakdown thought only of outdoing her neighbours, for 'all her desire was to be worshipped by the people'. To this end she dressed in the most outrageously modern and expensive clothes, 'so that they should be the more staring to men's sight'. This, naturally, caused a good deal of gossip. Then, to increase her income and her reputation, she plunged into business enterprises for which she was ill-equipped and inexperienced; in three or four years she had lost most of her money and people refused to work for her, 'it was advised about the town . . . that neither man nor beast would serve the said creature'. But at least these antics attracted attention; 'then some said she was accursed;

some said God took open vengeance on her; some said one thing and some said another'. It has been the habit of the saints to try to avoid attention; Margery seemed to try to attract it.

One night as she lay in bed with her husband, she heard 'a sound of melody so sweet and delectable, that she thought she had been in Paradise'. After this (but only 'when she was in any company') she could not restrain herself from saying, 'It is full merry in Heaven'. Naturally enough, this called forth the response, 'Why speak ye so of the mirth that is in Heaven? Ye know it not, and ye have not been there any more than we'. She made herself even more unpopular by bursting into tears whenever she heard music, 'with great sobbings and sighings after the bliss of Heaven'. She also wanted to put an end to any sexual intercourse with her husband, though formerly both he and she had had great enjoyment from it. Her husband, who had put up with a great deal, and was to put up with much more, was not yet prepared to lose his marital rights. But Margery had ways of getting what she wanted.

She began to get up at two or three every morning, and was in church most of the day, often sobbing 'boisterously', and making a great outcry for her sins. Not unnaturally, the congregation complained about this. 'Many people thought she could leave off as she liked', and others 'slandered and reproved her' for not looking after her home and children. Many of her former acquaintances refused to speak to her. Two years after her conversion to strictness of life, she was sexually attracted to a man she knew well, although she seems to have had just before this a grandiose sense of her own imperviousness to sin. 'She was so strong . . . that she dreaded no devil in Hell . . . She thought that she loved God more than He did her . . . She many times desired that the crucifix should loosen His hands from the Cross, and embrace her in token of love.' When the man first tempted her and then rejected her, she was 'all shamed and confused in herself', was afflicted with horrible temptations to lechery and despair, and 'the devil put into her mind that God had forsaken her'. She was in depression for about a year.

Then she heard Christ speaking to her, saying that she would have victory over all her enemies, and that she was to give up the hair-cloth that she wore and her continual saying of the Rosary, but must stop eating meat. (Christ was very apt to tell Margery to give up things she had become tired of; he was later to tell her to eat meat again.) She now began to have the strange experience of finding herself taking part in the life of the Holy Family. She was present at the birth of the Blessed Virgin, who was then given over to her care for twelve years, and at the Visitation and the birth of St John the Baptist and even at the birth of the Saviour, when she was allowed to provide bedding for the Virgin and swathing-clothes for the Child. She went with them into Egypt after seeing the three Kings present their gifts. Later, her husband became impotent when he tried to make love to her – by the power of prayer, Margery insists, but the reader may have reservations.

When she had made the rounds of the many churches in Lynne, she was 'urged in her soul to go and visit certain places for ghostly health', and her husband, either from kindness, or afraid that she would get into trouble, accompanied her. On the way back from York, they finally resolved their marital problems; he was to make no sexual demands, she was to give up her Friday fasts and pay his debts before starting on her pilgrimage to the Holy Land. Then they went on to Bridlington, Canterbury and 'divers places of religion', where Margery was often in trouble because of her noisy weeping, which went on nearly all day, 'both forenoon and afternoon also'. Her husband, poor man, often left her 'as if he had not known her, and left her alone amongst them, choose how she might'. Yet, she admitted, he was 'ever a good man, and an easy man to her . . . and had compassion on her, and spoke for her as he durst, for dread of the people'. But there seemed to be no way of keeping her out of trouble; her maid, 'seeing discomfort on every side', first refused to obey her, and then left her. She was often hauled up before sheriffs for what would now be causing a breach of the peace, and before Bishops to see whether she should be burned for heresy, and frequently ended up in prison. Like the prophets of the Old Testament, she was compelled to reprove sinners, especially those in high places, such as the Archbishop of Canterbury; and, like the prophets, she did it with immense tactlessness. Some dignitaries did befriend her, usually to get her away from their own localities.

It must have been a relief to everyone who knew her when, in 1414, she started from Yarmouth on her pilgrimage to the Holy Land. Almost immediately there was trouble with her fellow-travellers on account of her 'great weeping and boisterous sobbing', and her continual exhortations to the good life, which she would not cease from even at meals. Some of them evidently knew her, for they said 'they would not put up with her as her husband

did when she was at home and in England'. They would not let her
speak at table and made her wear a white canvas apron and a short
gown 'so that she should be held a fool'; but, said Margery with
unholy self-satisfaction, 'she was held in more worship than they
were, wherever they went'. They turned her away from their
company, but she reached Bologna before they did.

In Jerusalem, her 'crying and roaring' took on a new form. When
she came to Calvary, 'she fell down because she could not stand or
kneel, and rolled and wrested with her body, spreading her arms
abroad', because she had a vision, or hallucination, of the Crucifixion. For the first time she gave vent to loud screams, which
became her usual method of attracting attention from that time:
'this manner of crying endured many years after this time, for
aught any man might do, and therefore, suffered she much despite
and much reproof'. She had these cryings often, she says com-
placently, while she was in Jerusalem and Rome, but when she
returned to England, they were much less frequent; then they
occurred once a month, once a week, daily, seven or fourteen times
a day, and at last 'whenever God would send them', in church or in
the street – never, apparently, in the privacy of her own home.
'The crying was so loud and so wonderful that it made the people
astounded unless they had heard it before'; she 'made wondrous
faces and expressions' too. Her hearers found it difficult to believe
that this screaming was involuntary; some thought she was drunk,
or ill, or possessed by an evil spirit, but most of them just wanted
her out of the way: 'some wished she was on the sea in a
bottomless boat'. Groups of pilgrims never wanted her company,
but Christ told her to go with them, 'whether they would or not'.
By the time she reached Venice, they had had enough: 'they would
not go with her for a hundred pound', and left her on her own. She
reached Rome via Assisi, and, though she found shelter in a
hospice for pilgrims, she was soon turned out.

When God the Father announced that He wished to marry her,
she would have preferred the Manhood of Christ; nevertheless,
she was married to the Father in the presence of the Son, the Holy
Ghost, the Virgin, the Twelve Apostles, St Katharine, St Paul, and
numerous other saints and virgins. After this she began to hear
strange sounds and melodies 'that she could not well hear what a
man said to her at that time, unless he spoke the louder'. Once she
heard the sound of the Holy Ghost, which was like a pair of
bellows in her ear, though it later turned into the sound of a dove,

then of a robin that sang only in her right ear. She smelled strange scents, and saw 'with her bodily eyes' small white things, as thick as specks in a sunbeam, which appeared at night as well as in the daytime. For sixteen years after the heavenly wedding, she felt 'a flame of fire' in her breast, which God told her was the heat of the Holy Ghost. She might have found it confusing that, in spite of having been married to the Father, it was God the Son who told her to treat Him as her wedded husband and kiss Him as much as she liked in bed, but Margery took things like that in her stride.

Having given away all her money in Rome, she begged her food, or existed on charitable donations. It was the year when the canonisation of St Bridget was confirmed, and Rome was full of pilgrims. Margery had a particular devotion to this saint, whose *Revelations* she had heard read aloud in an English translation. In fact many of her visions seem to be a sort of sacred one-upmanship on St Bride, who also had visions of the Holy Family, but was not allowed to play nearly so intimate a role in its life as Margery. Then again, Margery saw the Blessed Sacrament flicker like a dove's wings, and was told by Jesus, 'My daughter Bride saw me never in this wise'. And Margery's visions outdid in splendour anything that was narrated 'in either Hylton's book or Bride's book, or *Stimulus Amoris*, or *Incendium Amoris*, or any other that she ever heard read'.

Although she was penniless, she managed to get back to England: Margery never had much difficulty in finding people who would give her money to go a long, long way away. Her husband took her back to Lynne where, unaccountably to the reader, since she had paid all her debts before she left for Jerusalem, she found herself heavily in debt. She went to church in Lynne, and there gave her first really loud scream. This met with a poor reception. Some thought she had epilepsy because she 'wrested her body . . . and waxed all blue and livid like the colour of lead'. It is not surprising that many citizens 'banned and cursed her', nor is it wholly surprising that there were some among them prepared to give her money to go on a pilgrimage to the shrine of St James of Compostella in Spain. Some of her best friends said rudely to her, 'Why have ye given away your money and other men's also? Where shall ye now get as much money as ye owe?', and when she was given forty pence she bought herself a furred cloak with it rather than paying off any of her debts. Still, she reached Bristol, and waited there for a ship, 'with plenteous tears and boisterous sobbings, with loud cryings and shrill shriekings', and, although her fellow-voyagers threatened to throw her overboard, she got to Spain and back to Bristol in a month. She soon set off for Leicester, where she sobbed 'hideously' and was put in prison with two unlucky fellow-pilgrims. However, there were people there who were 'greatly desiring that she had been out of that country', and she bustled off to York, where the Archbishop paid a man five shillings to lead her out of the town. At Beverley she was arrested; so, unfortunately, was the Archbishop's man, which brought the Archbishop breathing fire to Beverley. Margery, always totally serious herself about her mission, seemed unable to avoid leading others into farcical situations. She was arrested again after crossing the Humber, and again three miles out of Ely.

When at last she reached Lynne, she succumbed, not unnaturally, to 'many great and divers sicknesses'. She may have had another breakdown, since she speaks of 'a great sickness in her head ... so that she feared to have lost her wits therethrough'. Nevertheless, she says that whenever she could persuade her scribe to let her dictate to him, 'she was hale and whole suddenly in a manner'. All this time, her cries and weepings had so increased in volume and in duration (sometimes she cried for five or six hours) that she was forbidden to go to church, and had to be confessed and absolved in a private chapel. Her 'high revelations' ceased, and she had delusions from the devil instead; he sent her 'foul thoughts and foul memories of lechery and all uncleanness'. She saw 'horrible sights and abominable, priests, heathen and Christian', showing her their genitals, and the devil told her she must fornicate with them all. 'She could not say nay; and she must needs do his bidding; and yet she would not have done it for all this world. Yet she thought it should be done, and she thought these horrible sights and cursed memories were delectable to her, against her will'. She was brought almost to despair, until after twelve days the hallucinations ceased.

All this time she kept up her cryings and roarings, indeed, when she was 'barren of tears a day or half a day', she was much depressed. She 'could find no comfort in meat or drink or conversation, but ever was gloomy in face and behaviour till God would send them to her again, and then she was merry enough'. It was natural that her children (those who survived) should be repelled by her bizarre antics. She tells us that when she met with one of her sons 'against his will', they quarrelled, because she, 'some deal moved with sharpness of spirit', insisted on telling him to flee the perils of this world; the young man, doubtless angry at his mother's squandering of his inheritance, 'sharply answering back'. He acquired some unpleasant skin disease, and his mother would not pray for his healing until he begged her forgiveness.

Later he married abroad, and when Margery was about sixty years old brought his German wife and child on a visit to her, but died when he had been in England about a month. His father died shortly afterwards, and Margery was given permission by her confessor to escort her daughter-in-law as far as Ipswich, where the latter was to take ship for home. Here, she was 'commanded in her heart' to go over the sea with her daughter, who was not at all pleased: 'there was no one so much against her as her daughter, who ought most to have been with her'. Margery was rather fearful about disobeying her confessor, but Jesus assured her that he could overrule a priest, and she set off without money or luggage. She stayed in Danzig five or six weeks, to her daughter-in-law's horror and embarrassment, since she had her cryings and roarings 'as well as if she had been at home'. Then a chance encounter with a man going to see the Precious Blood at Wilsnak in the Duchy of Brandenburg determined her to accompany him. It was not a successful pilgrimage: 'the more she wept, the more irked was her man of the company, and the more he tried to go from her and leave her alone'. Ill, insulted, lice-ridden, afraid of rape, she still 'kept on with her fellowship with great anguish and discomfort', till they reached Aachen, where a rich English woman gave Margery leave to accompany her back to England. But after a few days of Margery's company 'the worshipful woman sped herself fast out of Akun with all her retinue'. Somehow Margery got to Calais, where she met 'divers persons who had known her before'; they would not let her know which ship they were sailing on, but Margery 'speered and spied' until she found out, and put her luggage aboard. The persons who had known her before secretly got ready another ship, though 'what the cause was, she never knew', says Margery ingenuously. She had her revenge; she hastily boarded their ship, leaving her belongings on the other ship, and prayed not to be sick. She wasn't, while the persons who knew her before, especially the rich woman, were 'voiding and casting full boisterously and uncleanly'. In spite of trying to help them on the voyage, Margery was left alone at Dover. She travelled via Canterbury to London, where she spoke 'boldly and mightily' against the vicious, did a good deal of sobbing and crying, and was turned out of several churches. When at last she reached Lynne, she found a very angry confessor, and his 'full sharp words' are almost the last we hear of Margery; we do not know what happened to her after her book was finished.

Margery's 'visions' appear not to be typical of those of more orthodox mystics. Some of them happened, she said, when 'her eyes were ever together-ward as if she would have slept', some she saw 'with her ghostly eye'; most of her experiences with the Holy Family she describes just as she does her other, more ordinary experiences. It seems likely that the visions of the devils and of Christ that she saw during her first breakdown were actual hallucinations, as were the later seeing of obscenities, and what she called the 'flickering' of the Sacrament. The white quivering lights which she so frequently saw probably resembled the white 'eels and strings' that Ruskin complained of, and had their origin in the psychotic brain. Her many 'seeings' of Christ and the Holy Family may have been delusions which she actually lived through, as Ruskin lived through his conflicts with the Devil, or they may have been deliberately induced auto-hypnosis deriving from the *Revelations* of St Bridget, to whom Margery had a special devotion. But most of the content of Margery's thinking was derivative. She heard readings from Hilton's *Scale of Perfection*, from which she may have absorbed her preoccupation with virginity. Her desire to kiss lepers probably originated in the story of St Katherine, which she would hear read on the appropriate feast-day in church. Her prodigious roarings and weepings would be licensed in her mind by the examples of St Mary of Oignies (whose book she had heard in an English translation), St Bonaventure, St Elizabeth of Hungary and an unnamed priest she had heard of who wept 'so wonderfully that he wetted his vestment'.

These outcries became her trademark, by which she was known everywhere she went. If they were an attention-seeking device, they were successful; even when she was turned out of the church as she frequently was, the eyes of the whole congregation were on her; sometimes, she reports proudly, people stood on stools to see her better. But this imitation of well-established exemplars is another mark of the psychotic rather than the genuine mystic. Everything that Margery says can be traced to what she would hear in sermons and readings. Her few originalities are so naive as to be laughable (such as her picture of the Persons of the Trinity sitting on different-coloured cushions) or so deranged as to be pitiable.

Margery Kempe has been diagnosed as a case of religious hysteria who never recovered from puerperal fever, a victim of sexual repression, and as a hysterical personality who had psychotic episodes with pathological distortion of the sexual impulse. It is more likely that she was a schizophrenic, for whom the religious beliefs of her day provided a means of escape from the daily life with which her inadequate personality could not cope. Her hyperactivity and restlessness were taken up in the constant roaming, first about the churches in her own neighbourhood, then to religious sites in England, then on pilgrimage in Europe, all of them respectable things to do. This solitary travelling, in an age when travel was dangerous, may seem to show her as an indomitable and independent woman, like Mary Kingsley in the nineteenth century; but in fact, like most psychotics, she was extremely dependent on others. She set up everywhere she went a series of dependency relationships, attaching herself either to the compassionate, the powerful, or the merely expedient, when her lack of judgement often led her to be rejected, robbed or ill-treated, but – again a psychotic trait – she seemed unable to learn by experience. She needed continual reassurance, and although she had been told by God himself that all her sins were forgiven and that she would not need to go to Purgatory, she confessed and had herself absolved four, five or six times a day. Her complete indifference to her fourteen children must also be abnormal. Were they looked after by servants or grandparents while she prayed, sobbed and travelled? She mentions that once, having just given birth to a child, she was ordered by Christ to get up and go to Norwich, though her journey appeared to be without purpose. At another time, He told her that she had conceived again, and when she, fearful that this would interrupt her 'contemplation', asked how she should look after the child, Christ replied casually that he would find it a keeper.

Her roaming about served another purpose: it enabled her to pour out her life-story, her experiences and her 'revelations' to a perpetually new audience. In other times she would have been obsessively at her pen or her typewriter; as it was, she harassed her scribes and possible scribes continually – to death, it would appear in the case of the first one. She had the psychotic's need to discharge the contents of the over-charged brain, and she notes how often she was ill when she was unable to dictate, and how much relieved, and physically improved she felt when she could.

It is significant that, in an age when belief in miracles, extreme saintliness and revelation were of the stuff of daily life, so many of her contemporaries believed Margery to be mentally ill; only, probably, the superstitious, the credulous and the ignorant believed her to be a genuine mystic. But at least her psychosis gave students of English literature and social history a book which can claim to be the first extant long prose narrative in the English language, and the first autobiography by a psychotic personality.

Thomas Hoccleve (1368/9–1426)

Like Margery Kempe, Thomas Hoccleve followed a secular calling, and like Chaucer, his contemporary, he wrote only in his spare time. His working life was spent as a civil servant in the important government Office of the Privy Seal in Westminster, where Chaucer was Clerk of the Works. In spite of his breakdowns, Hoccleve achieved a position of seniority and in due course retired with a pension. His professional work as a scribe meant he could command the means and materials for copying his work, and he was able to supplement his income by writing verses. His access to patronage, too, was gained through Privy Seal connections. He used his poetry as an autobiographical outlet, incorporating detailed personal matter about his illness into the dull routine of conventional composition and translation. The autobiographical passages are the most lively part of his work. Although literary critics have been cautious about assuming that Hoccleve is indeed writing about himself in these passages, rather than adopting a conventional autobiographical stance which is in fact a fiction, there are strong arguments to support the reality of his claims. Much of what he says about his money troubles and his illness is consistent with the evidence of extant records which show his salary was often in arrears, and that at the time he says he was ill his salary was being collected for him, indicating his absence from work. Again, it would have been professional suicide for a civil servant to describe the indignities of derangement and to represent himself as having been mad, unless the facts were as well known to his colleagues and masters as he says they were; while to try, on the other hand, to put his known condition in a better light, as Hoccleve does, is sensible only if the fact of his illness was well known but his recovery less well recognised, which is what he claims. Moreover, it is difficult to believe that anyone who can be as dull as Hoccleve can, when using literary conventions, could suddenly become as lively as he does by merely adopting a new one: the 'autobiographical' convention. There can be little doubt that Hoccleve is describing his own experience.

From an early date – extant records suggest 1407 to 1410 – Hoccleve was obsessed by anxiety about his financial security. His salary should have been adequate, with the perquisites of office, and though salaries were often not paid promptly, he seems never to have been in need. He admits he was extravagant as a young man, and liked to show off by over-tipping the ferryman. One balade, addressed to 'Maister Carpenter', has come down in his own hand, with a marginal list showing that the poem, which is a begging letter, could be recycled, and addressed to a new recipient on each occasion. According to this poem, his dread of foreclosure by his creditors is keeping him awake at night. Another poem of this period, addressed to the Duke of York, complains of his poor eyesight. Clearly this, had it really existed, would have threatened his livelihood, but there is no evidence of its being anything more than imaginary. Insomnia and deteriorating sight are recurring themes in Hoccleve and in the work of other writers studied here.

Hoccleve's longest and most popular work, judging by the number of surviving manuscripts, is the *Regement of Princes*, written 1411–12. This work belongs to the genre of the 'Mirror for Magistrates'; it offers conventional advice to kings and rulers on all relevant themes. The irrelevant parts are those in which Hoccleve's obsessions crop up. The poem is some 5500 lines long, but the first 2000 are Hoccleve's personal introduction, purporting to explain how he came to write the rest. Dialogue is one of Hoccleve's favourite forms. Accordingly, his introduction takes the form of a long conversation between himself and an old man, a Beggar, who approaches him while he is walking in the fields after a sleepless night at Chester's Inn, where the clerks lived. His description of the anxiety he is suffering suggests Cowper's later experience of madness, when the nightmares of waking and sleeping states merge indistinguishably; and his mental state brings on a sensation of alternating extremes of temperature:

The smert of thoght, I by experience [pain]
Knowe as wel as any man doth lyuynge;
His frosty swoot & fyry hote feruence, [sweat]
And troubly dremes, drempt al in wakynge, [anxious]
My mayzed heed sleepless han of konnyge, [muddled;
wisdom]

And wyt dispoylyd, & so me be-iapyd, [cheated]
That after deth ful often haue I gapid.

It is interesting that Hoccleve's old Beggar embodies all that Hoccleve most fears: poverty, old age and helplessness in the face of them.

Confronted by the figure of the Beggar, Hoccleve at first remains withdrawn in his 'seekly distresse'; he refuses to speak to him, then begs him to go away:

talke to me no more
Thy wordes al annoyen me ful sore

Voyde fro me; me list no compaignye;
Encresse noght my grife; I haue I-now.

But the old man insists, and Hoccleve eventually confesses that his great problem is anxiety ('encombrous thoght'), and the Beggar offers to cure him, if he will unburden himself and listen to Reason. The Beggar claims it is by speaking of his troubles that he has himself been cured, after a severe change of fortune which has brought him from wealth to his present condition. The dangerous alternative to the psychiatric help he is offering is Despair. He therefore counsels Hoccleve to have faith and so avoid damnation. Although Hoccleve believes in the sacrament he has no wish to prove dark theological matters (or, probably, to enter on a long psychoanalysis, which, though free, will mean listening as well as talking). The Beggar tells him he has done him good already, and asks him not to spurn but to honour the experience of old age, claiming that poverty has shown him God. Hoccleve now apologises for his earlier attitude and welcomes his help, embarking on a long exposition of his case. He speaks of the trouble he has in getting paid, his fear of old age and its isolation and poverty when he can no longer work; and he describes the privations and pains of his working conditions. He must concentrate all day, not talk or sing like other workmen; the work gives him back, stomach, and worst, eye trouble. After twenty-three years of this his eyesight is nearly spoiled. He again apologises, this time for his long moan, and asks advice. The Beggar's view is, reasonably, that Hoccleve's income should be enough even though he had a wife, and has by marrying her, cut off the possibility of a career in the Church. He must be practical. On the spiritual plane, the Beggar advises him to be reconciled to God's will and his own lot in life. He should avoid sins for which a change of fortune may well be God's punishment. Hoccleve is distressed by the corruptions of the time (which recur in the main work as well as here). He feels his faithful services are not valued, and he longs for death. The Beggar reproves him, then turns to practical advice. Hoccleve should apply to Prince Henry for patronage and protection, using his talents as a scribe and making a translation on the duties of a Prince. They part, but it is arranged that they can meet again any day in White Friars, near Chester's Inn, at seven in the morning. Hoccleve duly begins to translate his sources for the main work next day. It seems that writing and translating is temporarily effective, or at least that the Beggar's use for an introduction to the poem is of no further service, because no further meetings between them are recorded.

However, if there were good effects from the *Regement of Princes* enterprise, they were only temporary. 1421–2 finds him once more using a dialogue convention to describe his woes, and it is now evident that there have been serious developments in the interim. In his new poem, the *Complaint*, it is autumn. He lies awake and thinks how, since his last illness, the will to live has left him. It is his sense of swelling sorrow that is making him burst out into his poem. He recalls how God visited him with sickness, as he does others, and how he suffered a 'wyld infirmytie', as everyone knew, that 'me owt of my selfe cast and threw'. He lost his memory, but it returned, and it will be five years on 1 November since he recovered. The bitter injustice which is afflicting him so deeply now is that in spite of the fact that he has been perfectly all right ever since, no-one will believe it. People who used to seek him out in Westminster Hall and in London now turn away and avoid him. He might as well be dead. He is embarrassed as well as frustrated when he hears people say he may go mad again when the hot weather comes, when he has maintained his sanity for many summers. It is pure conjecture on their part. He remembers how people said he looked like a wild steer, gazing about on all sides, holding his head too high, and how they said his brain was buckish, and totally devoid of sober reasoning power. He says his gait, too, was like that of a roe, starting hither and thither, not staying, not stopping; he was brain-sick. One man said his feet and eyes were in constant motion. Hoccleve knew his opinion wouldn't be valued, and this saddened him. He tried earnestly to look cheerful, but their words made him shake with fear, sweat and turn hot and cold. At home, in the privacy of his room, he went straight to his mirror to see if he looked normal, but he realised he might not be a good judge of that. But all that is in the past. Now he is well, he is being wronged. It might be better to keep out of sight, but then there will be worse gossip. Some people still think him mad, but God has cured him, and in any case they shouldn't judge by appearances, which are deceptive. Although he is unhappy and feels it is time to die, he thanks God he is well again. He is going to translate a work of consolation, in which a mournful man ('Thomas' in the margin of Hoccleve's own manuscript) holds a dialogue with Reason. Reason argues that trouble is the punishment for sin, and should be born patiently, as a means to salvation. Hoccleve has taken Reason's words to heart, and will now put up with the gossip about his illness. He bids farewell to sorrow, hoping henceforth to unpick with patience the lock of his disease, taking his punishment, and seeking to amend his life, giving thanks, and asking for mercy.

He enlivens things further by continuing with a sequel, the *Dialogus cum Amico*. In a clever piece of bridgework between the two, the poet is interrupted by an old friend who comes knocking at the door and calling his name. The visitor wants to know what Hoccleve is doing, and when he finds out, implores him not to publish his *Complaint*, but to let people forget about his illness. Hoccleve knows they still remember; he still hears them talking about him. He insists that God ought to be thanked publicly for his cure, just as any other physician would be in such a case. He (unlike those he holds guilty of some of the corrupt practices that seem to obsess him both here, and in the *Regiment of Princes*, the coin-clippers and counterfeiters), has done nothing wrong. His friend changes the subject and asks what else he means to write, and Hoccleve says he will translate Suso's *Lerne to Dye*. He is fifty-three ageing, losing his sight, and should prepare for death. His friend fears the difficult work may overtax his weak brain. He is afraid too much study has caused him to regress to his former state of madness, and urges him to wait until he has regained stability. The worst may be over, but the illness is still lurking. Hoccleve is distressed at such mistrust. His friend vows steadfastness in friendship, but repeats his warning: his illness came from too much study, and he shouldn't do it again. This Hoccleve rejects outright: his long sickness sent him out of his mind, not too much study. The friend gives way, and a compromise is reached: Hoccleve won't overdo it. In the view of his friend, Hoccleve is unwise to trust his own judgement rather than the friend's, but a programme of translation, with patronage in mind, is drawn up. The friend is to visit him from time to time to make sure he proceeds with discretion. Unlike the Beggar, the friend does return once, looks over Hoccleve's work (a translation from the *Gesta Romanorum*), and goes home to fetch him a better copy, including the moralising of the tale which Hoccleve's copy lacks, and which he immediately begins to translate. The borrowed book may be a fiction taken from Isadore of Seville, one of Hoccleve's sources, but the liveliness, and the determination with which Hoccleve insists on going his own way, whatever his friends advise, is lifelike enough.

Advice not to write, in mediaeval times and later, is of little use to any of the authors considered in this book. When original composition is too demanding, translation, sometimes with original additions, is the next best thing.

Hoccleve, besides being a clerk, was an admirer of Chaucer. The best portrait of Chaucer was one he had made from life for his patron's copy of the *Regement of Princes*, where it accompanied Hoccleve's praise of his master.

Hoccleve's interest for us is accidental: the pressures of his mental illness pushed him into vivid personal confession in an age in which autobiography was almost always purely conventional. In different ways, but for similar reasons, Hoccleve and Margery Kempe began a new kind of writing.

Case Descriptions

Margery Kempe
All psychiatric assessment procedures contain an instruction to set aside as diagnostically insignificant any experience that occurs as

part of a shared religious or subcultural belief system. To follow that rule uncritically for Margery Kempe would make it virtually impossible to reach any conclusion about her from a modern psychiatric viewpoint, given the religious climate of her times. A diagnostic evaluation of her must therefore assume that, even judged against that contemporary background, she showed evidence of genuine psychopathology. In Kempe's case the problem is slightly eased by the fact that even she recognised her state after the birth of her first child as a sickness of mind and we should not regard this as an isolated episode of 'puerperal psychosis' that was unconnected with her continuing aberrant behaviour.

Whatever the spiritual significance of her experiences, Kempe has certainly attracted attention from others as a mediaeval example of psychiatric disorder; for example in Dale Petersens' *A Mad People's History of Madness* and in Porter's more recent *A Social History of Madness*. Porter, although regarding the diagnostic exercise as trivial, quotes Drucker's view that Kempe represented a case of hysteria, overlaid with psychotic episodes. According to our evaluation, judged against the SADS-L criteria we have used, the psychotic element is much more manifest. Thus, we find in Kempe both manic and depressive features to an extreme degree. In manic periods, which seemed the most common, she was grossly overactive and reckless in behaviour, rarely slept, talked incessantly, and showed typical grandiosity in her claims that Christ had singled her out for special revelations. When depressed she was beset with 'sudden sorrow and grief', afraid of eternal damnation, 'mourned and sorrowed as though God had forsaken her', suffering her 'to have as many evil thoughts as before she had good ones'. During her first episode she was also suicidal, reporting that 'she despaired of her life, weening she might not live' and that 'she would have destroyed herself many a time at their [the devils'] stirrings . . .'.

In addition to these signs of affective psychosis Kempe also showed features of schizophrenia, notably hallucinations, occurring in several modalities. She continually saw visions – for example, of Christ and of scenes from the Gospels – and once 'the Sacrament shook and flickered to and fro, as a dove flickereth with her wings'. She also sometimes 'felt sweet smells with her nose . . . They were sweeter', she thought, 'than ever was any sweet earthly thing that she smelt before'. But most typical were her auditory hallucinations:

Sometimes she heard with her bodily ears such sounds and melodies that she could not hear well what a man said to her at that time, unless he spoke the louder.... These sounds and melodies she heard nearly every day for the term of twenty-five years.

Given this mixture of affective and schizophrenic features a modern psychiatric diagnosis for Margery Kempe would most likely be 'schizoaffective psychosis', precipitated in the first instance by childbirth.

Thomas Hoccleve

Assuming, as we do here, that Hoccleve's description of psychological breakdown is genuinely autobiographical we find recognisable signs of the nature of the illness in the author's writings. Mitchell, in his analysis of Hoccleve's works, calls it 'an emotional disorder which bordered on insanity'. Medcalf goes even further, quoting a clinician's opinion that Hoccleve suffered several episodes of a manic form of affective psychosis. While agreeing with this description of Hoccleve's illness as of psychotic severity, our own evaluation is that it had a more depressive quality, many of the symptoms described by Hoccleve meeting the modern criteria for serious depression. In his *Complaint*, for example, Hoccleve refers several times to his feelings of general despair:

> The grefe abowte my harte so [sore] swal
> and bolned evar to and to so sore,

and:

> drowpynge and hevye and all woo bystad;
> small cawse had I me thowght[e], to be glade.

In the prologue to that work he writes, too, of his sleep disturbance:

> ... as I in my bed lay,
> for this and othar thowghts whiche many a day
> before I toke sleape cam none in myne eye,
> so vexyd me the thowghtfull maladye.

His withdrawal from company and his inability to communicate with others are also clearly evident. 'I hadd lost', he says, 'my tonges key'. And through it all there are constant thoughts of death:

> Gretar plesaunce were it me to dye,
> by many folde than for to lyve soo;
> sorrows so many in me multiplye,
> that my lyfe is to me a wery foo;
> comfortyd may I not be of my woo;
> of my distrese se none end I can,
> no force how sone I stinte to be a man.

Two other features reveal the severity of Hoccleve's disturbance, while it lasted. One is the effort he expends, in his long *Dialogue with a Friend*, to convince others that he is now well. The second is the extent to which his friends recognised the change in him. Using the terminology reminiscent of contemporary descriptions of madness (cf. those by the thirteenth-century encyclopaedist Bartholomaeus Anglicus) Hoccleve relates what others said of him: that he was incapable of sober reasoning, that his brain was buckish, that his gait was like a roe's, darting hither and thither, and that his eyes were constantly in motion. This last sign, although not of diagnostic significance here, is nevertheless of some interest and we shall return to it, together with some other features of Hoccleve's mental state, in Chapter 10.

4

The Powers of Night

CHRISTOPHER SMART (1722–71)

Hoccleve's death marked the end of the first quarter of the fifteenth century. In the two hundred years which followed English literature saw the flowering of the Renaissance. Neither the writers of that period nor their audience were unaware of the rewards of madness as a subject. Some seemed fascinated by it, particularly by its dramatic presentation. It was a staple of the revenge tragedy as Kyd, Tourneur or Shakespeare conceived it, and plays by Dekker, Lyly, Webster, Ford and Middleton all made use of madness on stage, and of actors specially trained for the parts of madmen. Kyd's *Spanish Tragedy* and Shakespeare's *Hamlet* show a careful study of the language of madness. In view of the harsh treatment of the victims of mental illness in hospitals like Bedlam, where members of the public or the acting profession could study their behaviour at first hand, it is not surprising that no striking instances of writers proclaiming themselves mad by writing about their own affliction have come to light in this period. Malvolio's treatment, in Shakespeare's *Twelfth Night*, when he was supposed to be mad explains the desirability of keeping such an affliction quiet. Not until after the middle of the seventeenth century do we once more find a government clerk making use of verse as an outlet after he has become psychotic, and then, as he writes from the asylum, he has nothing to lose by revealing himself. James Carkesse worked in the Navy Office of Samuel Pepys. According to Pepys' *Diary*, he was educated at Westminster School, and became a scholar of Christ Church, Oxford, in 1652. Pepys met him in 1665. He was not as good a poet, nor as good a clerk as Hoccleve, and was discharged from his job as unfit for office on 8 March 1667. He appealed, and was reinstated by the Privy Council, but unable to continue his employment for long. In 1678 he was confined in a madhouse in Finsbury. He conceived his mission to be a religious one, 'to reduce Dissenters unto the CHURCH'. His book of verse, *Lucida Intervalla* (1679), does

little for his reputation as a poet. He uses doggerel and lampoon as
weapons against his captors. What he writes is of interest because
it shows his attitude to his illness, and to the importance of
relieving the pressures of his illness. He seems to have been a
difficult patient. In 'The Cross Match' he argues with his doctor,
who fails to appreciate Carkesse's thesis that violence is justified
in a good cause, and he defies anyone who is in any way
concerned with his incarceration. He considers himself the victim
of a plot, regards the asylum as Hades, and refuses to accept that
he is mad. He shifts his ground, arguing first, that he has feigned
madness and that the doctor is a fool to be taken in; and second,
that his doctor has mistaken poetic genius for madness because he
is a fool. The one constant is that the doctor, not the patient, is a
fool, or mad. 'The Riddle' concludes firmly:

> 'Tis Quacks disease, not mine, my Poetry,
> By the blind Moon-Calf, took for Lunacy.

In 'The Mistake' he says he won't survive the harsh treatment and
cold of his prison, and that his erratic behaviour is a response to
this treatment. 'On the Doctors letting him Blood' maintains that
the treatment is useless unless his doctor will use his lance 'to prick
my Poetick Vein', yet he is incensed 'On the Doctors telling him,
that 'till he left off making Verses, he was not fit to be discharg'd'.
Carkesse believed that madmen vent their rage by words on air,
poets by ink on paper. As to doctors:

> Physitian heal thy self, we say; but know it,
> In earnest said to the Self-curing Poet.

While Carkesse thought writing could cure his condition, Smart
looked on much of his output as a vehicle of praise to his Creator
for his cure. In 1756 he suffered a severe bout of fever. It was to
celebrate recovery from this illness that he wrote his *Hymn to the
Supreme Being, on Recovery from a dangerous fit of Illness*. The poem
describes his conversion, and marks the turning-point in his life.
Its theme is the recovery of a man who, in the very moment of
death, is saved, and dedicates the rest of his life to God, a theme
derived from the Biblical account of King Hezekiah. The style and
feeling of the poem is exalted, but it is written with perfect lucidity,
and a firm sense of the tradition of Christian conversion.

It is not clear whether the condition Smart is describing was purely physical, or of a psychotic nature, but two verses suggest he was mentally as well as physically afflicted in 1756:

> But, O immortals! What had I to plead
> When death stood o'er me with his threat'ning lance,
> When reason left me in the time of need,
> And sense was lost in terror or in trance,
> My sick'ning soul was with my blood inflam'd,
> And the celestial image sunk, defac'd and maim'd.
> . . .
> My feeble feet refus'd my body's weight,
> Nor wou'd my eyes admit the glorious light,
> My nerves convuls'd shook fearful of their fate,
> My mind lay open to the powers of night.
> He pitying did a second birth bestow
> A birth of joy – not like the first of tears and woe.

Before his conversion in 1756, Smart's life had been very different from what it was now to become. He was born in Kent, to a Durham family which possessed its own coat of arms. On the death of his father in 1733 he was sent to Durham, to be educated within the sphere of influence of the family. He went up to Cambridge in 1739, to Pembroke College, as a sizar, was awarded a College scholarship in 1740, a degree in 1743, and a College Fellowship in 1745. This last appointment would have procured for him a secure income and a safe environment for life, had he remained in it. He held a Praelectorship in Philosophy (1745) and in Rhetoric (1746); but his Cambridge duties were not too onerous. By 1744 he was already spending some of his time in London, where Dodsley was his publisher. He felt the attraction of the literary life of the metropolis. However, life in Cambridge was not dull. In 1747 he wrote, produced and acted in *The Grateful Fair, or, A Trip to Cambridge*, and had acquired a reputation as a wit. His colleague, the poet Thomas Gray, six years his senior, was becoming concerned for his reputation in other respects by 1747 when he wrote to his friend Thomas Warton about Smart's conduct: 'His debts daily increase (you remember the state they were in when you left us)'. Smart was deaf to advice, however, and in his play, which is bursting with wit and humour, 'He acts five parts himself and is only sorry he cant do all the rest. He has also advertised a collection of Odes; and for his Vanity and Faculty of Lying, they are come to a Jayl, or Bedlam, and that without any help. . . .' His friend Dr Burney, not a Cambridge man, expressed similar concern at Smart's lack of discretion: 'While he was the pride of Cambridge and the chief poetical ornament of that University, he ruined himself by returning the tavern treats of strangers who had invited him as a wit and an extraordinary personage, in order to boast of his acquaintance'.

If Smart's hyperactivity and conviviality were already causing comment – and the mention of Bedlam suggests a degree of exaggeration in these tendencies – at least he had the protection of his College and his friends while he remained in Cambridge. But in 1749 he committed a greater indiscretion when he left Cambridge for London, to live on his wits. Although he was no longer resident, Pembroke kept his name on the College books until a still greater indiscretion made that impossible: he married, and what was worse, married a Catholic, in 1752. The inevitable consequence of his marriage was that he forfeited his fellowship, and the security it had given him. His wife, Anna Maria (Nancy) Carnan, was the stepdaughter of the printer John Newbery. A further consequence of this rash act was the birth of two daughters dependent on him; Marianne (Polly) was born in 1753 and Elizabeth (Bess) in 1754. For the time being, Smart's literary success continued. Between 1750 and 1755 he entered poems five times for the annual Seatonian prize at Cambridge and won every time. In 1752 he published *Poems on Several Occasions* with Newbery. But when the fever struck in 1756 he was obliged to give up the periodical work by which he made a living in London. When he recovered, he had experienced conversion, and from that time on he refused all offers of writing work that was not for the glory of God. What was more, he considered it his duty, not only to pray in public himself, but to induce his friends to join him, often at inconvenient times and in conspicuous places. Mrs Thrale, whose source of information was probably their mutual friend Dr Johnson, puts the state of affairs in a nutshell:

While Kit Smart thought it his duty to pray in Secret, no living creature knew how mad he was; but as soon as the Idea struck him that every time he thought of praying, Resistance against that divine Impulse (as he thought it) was a Crime: he knelt down in the Streets & Assembly Rooms, and wherever he was when the thought crossed his mind – and this indecorous conduct obliged his Friends to place him in a Confinement whence many mad as he remain excluded, only because their Delusion is not known.

Smart had become a nuisance. In March 1757 an application was made on his behalf to St Luke's Hospital for the insane, a private asylum opened in 1751 by a group of London philanthropists. He was admitted on 6 May, and remained in the care of Dr William Battie, a distinguished physician and a Cambridge graduate who had himself held the scholarship which Smart held after him. Although Battie was not a religious man, Smart was fortunate that he was a humane doctor, who believed in treating Smart's kind of illness with sedatives and drugs and not with cruelty. He would have fared less well in Bedlam, or in some of the more notorious private establishments of the time. Smart had always attracted friends, and they served him well now, securing him the necessary recommendation to St Luke's by a bookseller, perhaps a connection of Newbery's, who had become a banker, probably one of the bankers who formed a majority of the Governors of St Luke's. Visitors were not allowed. He probably did not see his wife or children while he remained there. On 12 May 1758 he was discharged as incurable, but his name remained on the books, so that he could be re-admitted, but no longer without charge. Smart's nephew and biographer, Christopher Hunter, records the fact that 'After an interval of little more than two years, Mr Smart appeared to be pretty well restored'. The 'pretty well' sounds a cautionary note. As Hunter says, 'his mind had received a shock from which it never fully recovered'. It seems that after his discharge he remained in Dr Battie's care for some time, probably at the doctor's private residence.

Smart's friends were not all alienated by his misfortune, because on 26 January 1759 David Garrick presented a successful benefit for him, acting a leading part himself, at Drury Lane, and Newbery and Carnan published one of the plays performed, also for Smart's benefit. A letter from Thomas Gray to his friend Mason on 18 January expresses surprise that 'poor Smart is not dead as was said'. Mason fears death might have been the better part, and asks Gray to contribute to the benefit on his behalf. Mason's reservations were well founded. 'But is he returned to his senses? If so, I fear that will be more terrible still', he writes. His fears were real enough. During 1759 Smart was again consigned to a madhouse, this time in Bethnal Green. His younger daughter remembered being taken to visit him there by her mother. In 1759, while Smart was confined, his family moved to Dublin, although his wife returned two years later to Reading, they were never reunited. Smart suffered the isolation which all those afflicted with mental illness suffer, and of which he, in his later poems, Cowper, in his letters and poems, and Clare in his, complain so poignantly.

Few of the friends who had written complimentary tributes to Smart at the time of his release from Dr Battie's asylum expected him ever to be able to write again. They were mistaken. His conversion led to an upsurge of praise the pressure of which could not be denied. He was released from confinement in January 1763, and in that very year published, with other poems, *A Song to David*, his masterpiece. A collection of *Hymns and Spiritual Songs* covering the Church calendar appeared in 1765, together with his translation of the Psalms and a translation of *The Fables of Phaedrus*. In 1767 there followed a verse translation of Horace in four volumes. For children he published *Parables* in verse in 1768 and *Hymns for the Amusement of Children* in 1769. There were also two libretti for oratorios probably dating from 1765, as well as other miscellaneous poems. No doubt some of these productions were the result of friends' efforts to re-establish Smart in a condition of solvency. But the main thrust of them was towards a religious revival. After his conversion, Smart saw himself (as the surviving fragments of *Jubilate Agno* make clear) as obedient to Christ in all his works. On entering the asylum involuntarily, he voluntarily made vows of Poverty, Chastity and Obedience. His marriage to his wife was now a spiritual marriage only. Now, in his 'jeopardy' as he called the imprisonment in the asylum, 'I am the Lord's News-Writer – the scribe evangelist'. '*For by the grace of God I am the Reviver of ADORATION amongst ENGLISH-MEN.*' By his writings he was confident he could modernise and re-vitalise the worship of the Church of England. In *A Song to David*, which must have been written in the asylum, as it was publicised soon after his release, David, who represents the Poet and is thus a symbol for Smart himself, leads the hymn of Adoration in which all Creation joins, every creature making his individual and characteristic contribution. Smart's short prefatory note is elaborate and slightly inaccurate, but emphatic on the subject of David's excellence, his consecration of his genius, and his high worthiness for 'The transcendent virtue of praise and adoration'. Contemporary reaction to this magnificent poem is typified by a critic in *The Monthly Review* in 1763 who thought he knew that Smart was forbidden the use of writing materials in the asylum and that he had written it 'with the end of a key, upon the wainscot'. Smart's nephew Christopher Hunter, in his edition of 1791, thought it belonged to a group of poems which had been 'written after his confinement, and bear . . . melancholy proofs of the recent estrangement of his mind'. It was natural enough that those who knew Smart's recent history should look for evidence of his recent condition. But if the poem is exalted in the Classical and Renaissance tradition of bardic poetry, Smart's understanding of his position is perfectly clear. In *Jubilate Agno* he writes:

> Let David bless with the Bear – The beginning of victory to the Lord – to the Lord the perfection of excellence – Hallelujah from the heart of God, and from the hand of the artist inimitable, and from the echo of the heavenly harp in sweetness magnifical and mighty (A41)

Smart associates the harp not only with praise, but also with creativity, as two of the verses in *Jubilate Agno* show:

> *For God the father Almighty plays upon the Harp of stupendous magnitude and melody* (B246)

and:

> *For innumerable Angels fly out at every touch and his tune is a work of creation.* (B247)

In 1756 he had opened his poem *On the Goodness of the Supreme Being* with an invocation to Orpheus (the Gentiles' David) which beseeches him for inspiration for his great religious theme:

> ORPHEUS, for so the Gentiles call'd thy name,
> Israel's sweet Psalmist, who alone couldst wake
> Th'inanimate to motion; who alone
> The joyfull hillocks, the applauding rocks,
> And floods with musical persuasion drew;
> Thou who to hail and snow gav'st voice and sound,

> And mad'st the mute melodious! – greater yet
> Was thy divinest skill and rul'd o'er more
> Than art and nature; for thy tuneful touch
> Drove trembling Satan from the heart of Saul,
> And quell'd the evil Angel: – in this breast
> Some portion of thy genuine spirit breathe,
> And lift me from myself each thought impure
> Banish; each low idea raise, refine,
> Enlarge, and sanctify; – so shall the muse
> Above the stars aspire, and aim to praise
> Her God on earth, as he is prais'd in heaven.

Even earlier, in 1751, he had had the same theme in mind when he began *On the Immensity of the Supreme Being*:

> Once more I dare to rouse the sounding string
> The Poet of my God – Awake in glory,
> Awake my lute and harp – my self shall wake.

The *Song to David* is Smart's mature sacred and heroic ode on the theme of David. As early as 1746 he had pondered such a work, writing in his preface to the *Ode for Musick on St. Cecilia's Day* of the 'fine subject . . . that is David's playing to King Saul when he was troubled with the evil Spirit'. He had been 'much pleased' with the suggestion, 'but was deterr'd from improving it by the greatness of the subject . . . The chusing too high subjects has been the ruin of many a tolerable Genius'. By the time of his confinement and release, he was deterred no longer.

While Smart's contemporaries failed to appreciate the sublimity of his *Song to David*, later critics have signally failed to agree on its construction and Smart's own note of explanation does not quite match the case. Browning, who revived it in the late nineteenth century, thought it showed Smart rising from sanity to transfiguration, or, as Rossetti put it, from Earth to Heaven. Architectural and musical comparisons have been made to explain its structure, and numerological interpreters have made play with the mystical numbers implicit in its succession of twelve virtues, seven pillars, ten commandments, four seasons, five senses and five degrees. Smart himself says in *Jubilate Agno* '*there is a mystery in numbers*' (C19). The repeated use of the word 'ADORATION' and 'Glorious' have also provided a basis for critical interpretation. All agree that the structure is there. Its exact nature has not emerged to the satisfaction of all readers.

From *A Song to David* to his *Translation of the Psalms of David* was a short step, and perhaps a necessary one for Smart. Structure for the translator is not the problem it is for the composer of an original work of the order of the *Song*. His structure is provided for him by the original. The Psalms translation was first advertised in January 1763 and was published in August 1765. The probability is that a large part, even most, of the work was done in the madhouse, and that Smart finished it after his release. It is exactly the kind of work that might be suited to a poet of Smart's mind recovering from a severe mental illness. Linguistically, the text presented no challenge, as he allowed himself to be guided by the two translations already in use in the Anglican liturgy, those of the Book of Common Prayer Psalter, and the Authorised Version of the Bible. Technically, Smart gave his delight in varied versification free play by making use of twenty-five different stanza forms, generally taking one stanza for each verse of every Psalm, and using neologisms, puns, aphorisms and turns of wit as he found opportunity. Theologically, he used the Psalms translation as one way to promote his intention of revitalising the Church of England, by Christianising his version. 'In the translation', he announced, 'all expressions, that seem contrary to Christ, are omitted, and evangelical matter put in their room'. The Old Testament savagery of a vengeful and jealous God gives way to the teachings of Christ, and David becomes often the Christ he prefigures, and becomes very much Smart. Smart was not the first to try to modernise the Psalms, which had played a central role in Anglican worship since the Reformation. Watts had earlier published *The Psalms of David Imitated in the Language of the New Testament, and Apply'd to the Christian State and Worship* before, others had followed. Smart went further than any of his predecessors in this attempt to provide, according to his prefatory note, a version 'Adapted to the Divine Service'. He wanted it to replace the official versions in the liturgy. His evangelicalism was not extreme; it lay within the limits of Anglican tolerance. But his hopes of superseding the liturgy with any such matter were doomed to failure. He completely misjudged the question, and his translation was ignored by churchmen as well as by the editor of the influential *Monthly Review*, who had been irritated by Smart's angry response to earlier criticism, and dismissed it with short shrift. Smart's claims that he had the support in this enterprise of 'many of the Bishops and other dignified Clergymen' seems to have been completely unrealistic. The work of translation itself, quite apart from his grand conception of his purpose in undertaking it, must have afforded him some solace. He adds many a personal note, for instance in Psalm 31, which he expands to give full measure to the woes of the scorned man imprisoned by his enemies. Among other personal touches, he introduces seafaring imagery on several occasions: Christ is helmsman in Psalm 31, and in Psalm 89 he adds to the raging sea of verse 9 a reference to the navy which is very expressive of his Englishness. As with Cowper, sea imagery struck a chord with Smart, and he chooses to use it in his 'Epistle to John Sherratt' in 1763. In this poem he thanks his benefactor for obtaining his release after 'Well nigh sev'n years' of captivity:

> And all thy motive God alone;
> To run thy keel across the book,
> And save my vessel from her doom,
> And cut her from the pirate's port
> Beneath the cannon of the fort,
> With colours fresh, and sails unfurl'd,
> Was nobly dar'd to beat the world;
> And stands for ever on record,
> IF TRUTH AND LIFE BE GOD AND LORD.

The application of seamanship to Smart's release from Potter's madhouse in Bethnal Green strikes the reader with more force, however, than its addition here and there to the language of the Psalms.

In the *Psalms of David* Smart had his pattern laid out for him, even if he chose to embroider it a little. In the third work of this asylum period, the *Jubilate Agno*, he was much more ambitious. He kept the design, but cut it to his own material, merely using David's poetry as a model for his own original composition. If *A Song to David*, in which he attempted a new and regular form of the ode, was written on an upswing of creativity at the beginning of a psychotic episode, and the Psalms translation made during convalescence afterwards, *Jubilate Agno* is particularly important because its internal dates strongly suggest it was composed during his confinement, and from day to day of his illness, during the period 27 July to 30 January 1763, just before his release. In St

Luke's Hospital he would not have been allowed to engage in demanding intellectual work. Dr Battie believed in avoiding extremes of pleasure or anxiety, and recommended only those occupations which absorbed the patient's attention without creating strain, such as copying lists of names. Smart may well have begun thinking out his remarkable composition while he was in St Luke's. It survives in four separated fragments, was not published in his lifetime and probably remained incomplete. He probably revised it as it went along and his recurring use of various kinds of lists as a basis for the structure of the work may well reflect Dr Battie's influence. The last fragment, D, consists entirely of a list of names. The most dominant structural factor in the work is that much of it is cast in the form of canticles. The paired lines closely follow the parallel verse-form of the Psalms, the first statement in each pair generally beginning with the word 'Let' and the second with the word 'For'. Fragments A and D contain 'Let' verses only, Fragment B contains only 'For' verses after verse 295 (ending in verses 695 to 768 which contain the celebrated passage 'I will consider my Cat Jeoffry', an animal Smart was apparently allowed to keep at Bethnal Green). Skilfully reconstructed by his modern editors, Smart's poem yet remains too much in draft form to reveal its patterns fully, but it shows an elaborate network of complex verbal associations. The overall plan appears to resemble the *Benedicite*, beginning with a call to all nations and all creatures to rejoice:

> Rejoice in God, O ye Tongues; give the glory to the Lord, and the Lamb.
> Nations, and languages, and every Creature, in which is the breath of Life.
> Let man and beast appear before him, and magnify his name together.

The species of creation are then called on to give praise one by one, using a succession of lists: lists of names, Biblical or contemporary, linked with the lists of birds, fishes, plants, trees and gems. D51 may provide a clue to Smart's intentions

> Let Knightly, house of Knightly rejoice with Zoronysios a gem supposed by the ancients to have magical effects.
> Star – word – herb – gem.

The four words 'Star – word – herb – gem' may refer to contemporary occult philosophy, which saw a continuous order of relationship in nature. The 'Let' verses carry this part of the pattern, while the 'For' verses make a continuous sequence of their own; and within the sequence, each 'For' verse supplies a comment on the preceding 'Let' verse. This comment may be of a moral, biographical or prophetic nature. The system is seen working according to this plan in Fragment B, but even there it is not consistently maintained. Perhaps it was not intended as an overall plan. Some fragments are linked by the lists of names, A4 to B295 going from the Biblical book of Genesis to Revelation; fragment C returns to the Old Testament while D is a list of contemporary names. As Smart's editors have shown, the wide range of reference would easily be available within the compass of a few standard books, which he knew and could have obtained in the Bethnal Green asylum. Internal dating in Fragments B to D indicates with all but certainty that they were written on a daily progression; B at the rate of three pairs of verses a day from 27 July to 29 October 1759; one verse a day from 30 October 1759 to 1 June 1760; and three verses a day from 2 June to 26 August 1760; C at the rate of two verses a day from 21 February to 12 May 1761; and D at the rate of one verse a day from 12 June 1762 to 30 January 1763. Although there are some irregularities, Smart seems to have had a fixed task allocated for each day and to have kept to it. Fragment A is more difficult to analyse as the evidence is incomplete and the habit of keeping to a set rate of progress may not have evolved at the A stage of composition; but it could have been completed between June 1758 and April 1759, in a shorter or longer time depending on whether he wrote one verse or three each day. Repetitions in the text, as well as breaks of pattern, suggest the four fragments may represent stages in composition between A and C, with a more complex scheme emerging as it developed and an entirely new beginning in Fragment D.

It is likely that had Smart completed his revisions and published the work he would have included an explanatory preface, as he does in *A Song to David* and the Psalms translation. As it is, he had given enough indication of his intention in the work, quite apart from its Psalmodic basis, to make it clear. The title refers to Psalm 100, the *Jubilate Agno*, and to Christ as *Agnus Dei*. The opening lines of Fragment A are a call to worship and a declaration of praise. B43 refers to the work as 'my MAGNIFICAT', and B332 explains his motive:

For by the grace of God I am the Reviver of ADORATION amongst ENGLISH-MEN

As in the Psalms translation, he is much preoccupied with the Christian outcome of Old Testament doctrine, and his particular concentration of effort is on his own countrymen, and his own Church. He insists on this: (A433) '*For the ENGLISH are the seed of Abraham*'; (B225) 'St. Paul is the Agent for England'. That Smart identified himself with other disciples as a missionary is apparent from a long passage in Fragment B, beginning at line 123:

LET PETER rejoice with the MOON FISH who keeps up the life in the waters by night.
For I pray the Lord JESUS that cured the LUNATICK to be merciful to all my brethren and sisters in these houses.
Let Andrew rejoice with the Whale, who is array'd in beauteous blue and is a combination of bulk and activity.
For they work me with their harping-irons, which is a barbarous instrument, because I am more unguarded than others.
Let James rejoice with the Skuttle-Fish, who foils his foe by the effusion of his ink.
For the blessing of God hath been on my epistles, which I have written for the benefit of others.

He blesses God 'that the CHURCH of ENGLAND is one of the SEVEN ev'n the candlestick of the Lord' (B225). His own role is emphatically stated: 'I am the Lord's News-Writer – the scribe-evangelist' (B327). Smart assumes a prophetic as well as an evangelical mission. He identifies himself with the prophets of the Old Testament in addressing contemporary life, and echoes St Paul when he sees himself keeping the streams of doctrine pure: '*For I am inquisitive in the Lord, and defend the philosophy of the scripture against vain deceit*' (A130). His genealogical lists suggest a need to search for and establish his own identity. In assuming the mantle of David and writing his own psalms, he may even be expressing in this work a sense of identification with David as a type of Christ. At the very least he sees himself as descended from Agricola, steward of England, and as Christ's deputy, when he says in B137:

> Let Agrippa, which is Agricola, rejoice with Elops, who is a
> choice fish.
> *For I am descended from the steward of the island – blessed be the name*
> *of the Lord Jesus king of England.*

In B151 he compares himself to Christ even in the matter of his
lunacy:

> *For I am under the same accusation with my Saviour – for they said, he*
> *is besides himself*

That Smart should have been stigmatised as a madman in all his
publications after his confinement is not surprising, if any of this
fragmentary, unpublished work in progress was known to his
contemporaries. Apart from the grandiosity of the plan, and the
exaltation of the mood of *Jubilate Agno*, the work reveals the man in
all his undefended innocence: 'For I blessed God in St. James's Park till
I routed all the company'. The intricacies of association which link
Creation and the Millennium to his personal hopes, griefs and
anxieties have proved a minefield for scholars. He received visits in
the asylum, and Boswell reports that on one occasion, probably in
1760, Dr Johnson thought Smart ought to be locked up; his opinion
varied, as no doubt did Smart's condition, from time to time. He is
reported to have said to Dr Burney:

> I did not think he ought to be shut up. His infirmities were not
> noxious to society. He insisted on people praying with him; and
> I'd as lief pray with Kit Smart as anyone else. Another charge
> was that he did not love clean linen; and I have no passion for it
> myself.

It was through one of several friends who had remained loyal to
him through the seven years of his 'jeopardy', in two asylums, that
his release was obtained: apparently Sherratt walked in and
removed him from custody. The note of triumph which concludes
the Epistle of 1763 in which Smart 'hail'd the restoration day' 'with
the lyre', the instrument of David, indicates the extreme difficulty
those once detained had in securing their release. Sherratt seems to
have been an eccentric himself. But Smart may have owed his

freedom in some measure to a House of Commons Committee of Enquiry into the problem that year.

The subscription list for the translation of the Psalms, launched in 1763, attracted a brilliant list of his friends and supporters, including William Cowper. Unhappily, many of the 700 subscribers must have failed to deliver the second cash instalment and take up their copies when the book was published in 1765. Granville Sharp wrote to one of these, John Sharp, Archdeacon of Northumberland, relaying Smart's appeal to take delivery of his ten copies. He records Smart's statement that he '"must have finished an unfortunate life in jail had it not been for the good nature of a Friend, who could not bear to see his tears".' Whatever his friends did, Smart was unable to live within his income. They must have felt they had secured his future when a Treasury pension of £50 per annum was obtained for him in April 1766, but his letters continue to reveal his financial anxiety. In 1768 Fanny Burney wrote in her Diary:

> ... He [Smart] ... but last year sent a most affecting epistle to papa, to entreat him to lend him half-a-guinea! ... He is extremely grave, and has still great wildness in his manners, looks, and voice; but 'tis impossible to see him and to think of his works, without feeling the utmost pity and concern for him!

In April 1770 he was again arrested for debt, and this time wrote to an unknown friend: 'After being six times arrested: nine times in a spunging house; and three times in the Fleet-Prison, I am at least happily arrived at the King's Bench [Prison]'. He had been imprisoned for want of bail. Here Thomas Carnan obtained some freedom of exercise for him. Here he must have written his final work, *Hymns for the Amusement of Children*. From here he wrote his last letter, again recorded by Fanny Burney, now Madame d'Arblay, and engaged in writing the life of her father. In it he asks her father's help for one of the other prisoners, saying 'that he had helped him "according to his own willing poverty".' Here he died, after a short illness, perhaps, as his nephew's biography says, of a liver disorder, but more probably of gaol-fever, debility and the shock of re-arrest, coming on top of the disappointment of all his worldly hopes.

Before his arrest in December 1765 Smart completed a translation of Horace, not remarkable for its felicity, but indicative of his need to continue his literary activities at this time, and the natural support afforded by translating. It is remarkable for his description there of the way in which his own original composition had been done. He admires in Horace 'the beauty, force and vehemence of Impression: which leads me on to a more rare and entertaining subject, not anywhere (I think) insisted on by others'.

> Impression, then, is a talent or gift of Almighty God, by which a Genius is empowered to throw an emphasis on a word or a sentence in such wise, that it cannot escape any reader of sheer good sense, and true critical sagacity.

He had hit on the same theme in *Jubilate Agno*, B404:

> For my talent is to give an impression upon words by punching, that when the reader casts his eye upon 'em, he takes up the image from the mould which I have made.

This is an illuminating comment on Smart's work, which like that of all three of the poets of this period studied here, breaks clean from the worn-out conventions of eighteenth-century poetic tradition, and brings a new life to poetry. That it is uneven in quality, and incomprehensible in the intricacies of private association, is the inevitable result of his condition. It is tempting to wonder what Smart's genius could have been had he not been tormented by madness; but perhaps without the enhanced perception that came with illness, he would not have written at all.

Case Description

In his collection of essays on genius the distinguished neurologist, the late Sir William Russell Brain, concluded about Smart that 'clearly he suffered from manic-depressive insanity or cyclothymia' and there is much to support that diagnosis. Even before what appears to have been an acute phase of illness in 1756, Smart showed many characteristic signs: impulsiveness, reckless spending, drunkenness and – leading eventually to his confinement – his disinhibited behaviour of praying in public and on inappropriate occasions whenever the spirit moved him. The form of his religious 'conversion' at that time – his belief that he was a person of special importance, having a Messianic mission – is also typical. Less appears to be known about whether his mood swings were severe enough to justify manic-depression as a primary diagnosis; but Smart himself gives us some clue when he writes: *'For I have a greater compass of mirth and melancholy than another.'* (B132.)

Most informative about Smart's general state of psychosis, however, is the *Jubilate Agno*, written during his period of confinement. It is perhaps a technical point whether we regard this work – with its fragmented associations and obscure, perverse and personalised allusions, as an example of schizophrenic language or, as Brain argues, evidence of manic flight of ideas. Certainly, judged from a purely clinical standpoint the *Jubilate* reveals all of the features of psychotic thought disorder, of which, chosen at random from its 1739 lines, we may cite just one example (B590–4):

For the cymbal rhimes are bell well toll soul & the like.
For the flute rhimes are tooth youth suit mute & the like.
For the dulcimer rhimes are grace place beat heat & the like.
For the Clarinet rhimes are clean seen and the like.
For the Bassoon rhimes are pass, class and the like. God be gracious to Baumgarden.

Finally, for the literary reader it should be noted that claims to have penetrated the meaning of the *Jubilate* in no way contradict the conclusion that its form is essentially 'psychotic', since it is well accepted that, with effort, the sense in schizophrenic language can be discerned (see Forrest for a discussion of this point).

5

Buried Above Ground

Cowper's natural genius, and the classical training he received at Westminster School, produced an elegance of style, both in prose and verse, seldom matched even in the neoclassical tradition of his time. It may well be that the charm, wit and polish, as well as the strictness of form in his work, has diverted the attention of his critics, and even of the thirty or so biographers who have written about his life, from the fact that his writing is extensively autobiographical: a characteristic he shares with all the authors studied in this book.

Although Cowper was trained as a barrister, he appears never to have received a brief and to have had very little notion of how to manage money, still less how to earn it. Born a gentleman, he was content to be sustained by his family – albeit minimally – in that station, and by his friends. Writing poetry was the private occupation of a gentleman, and it was not until 1771, when he was forty, that he began to write poems in more than a dilettante manner, publishing, with the collaboration of his friend the Revd John Newton, the *Olney Hymns*. His first solo book of original poems came out in 1782. By the time 'The Task' was published in 1785, he was the best known living poet in England. His chief undertaking after this was the translation of Homer, published after numerous revisions in 1791, to be followed by an abortive attempt at an edition of Milton which had to be abandoned. He continued to write original poems from time to time: 'The Castaway' belongs to 1799, but translation accounted for more and more of his poetic output as time went on and his mental health grew worse.

Fortunately, the social isolation of mental illness meant Cowper was motivated to write many letters, and the distinction of his prose meant his friends valued and kept them. The poems and letters together are an authoritative source of information on his life. The most important source of all is Cowper's spiritual autobiography, *Adelphi (The Brothers)*. The first part, written in 1767, records his experiences as a boy and young man, through two episodes of mental illness. The second part was written in 1770 after the death of his younger brother, John Cowper.

Cowper was born in Berkhamstead. His father, Dr John Cowper D.D., was the son of Judge Spencer Cowper and grandson of the first Earl Cowper. He was Rector, and one of the chaplains to George III. He married Anne, daughter of Roger Donne Esq. of Ludham Hall, Norfolk, who through her grandfather claimed descent from John Donne the poet. On 7 November 1737 John Cowper was born, but within days, on 13 November, Anne died at the age of thirty-four. After six pregnancies, she left two sons, John, an infant, and William, only six years old. William, who had been particularly close to his mother, was then sent to a boarding school in a village seven miles from home, where he was bullied so badly that the chief culprit was eventually expelled. From there he was taken to live with an oculist, to attempt a cure for eye trouble. In 1742, when he was ten, he was entered at Westminster School. Here he enjoyed the friendship of boys soon to become eminent. After an attack of small-pox his eye trouble cleared up, though he was to complain of inflammation of the eye-lids all his life. When he left school at eighteen he spent nine months at Berkhamstead, but his father had re-married on 8 January 1740–41; neither of the brothers found their step-mother congenial. Cowper had already been admitted to the Society of the Middle Temple on 29 April 1748 to study for the Bar, and he left Berkhamstead without regret to live with an attorney, Mr Chapman, to whom he was apprenticed. He was called to the Bar in 1754 as a member of the Inner Temple. Of the Law, Cowper says it was 'a Profession to which I was never much inclined, and in which I engaged rather because I was desirous to gratify a most indulgent Father, than because I had any hope of success in it myself'. He seems to have spent most of his time at his uncle Ashley Cowper's house in Southampton Row, where his young cousins Harriot and Theadora lived, or with his literary associates at the Nonsense Club or the Thursday Society.

In 1753, before he was called to the Bar, and soon after he had settled in the Middle Temple in chambers, the first signs of mental illness appeared. 'I was struck . . . with such a dejection of spirits as none but they who have felt the same can have the least conception of. Day and night I was upon the rack, lying down in horrors and rising in despair.' Cowper does not mention his cousin Theadora in connection with this episode. He had become attached to her before this, and at this time Ashley Cowper, who was himself subject to deep depressions, had discouraged the idea of their marriage. Theodora suffered from melancholy too. Cowper sought distractions, reading and joining Harriot for a holiday in Southampton. But the theme of shipwreck, which was to recur again and again in his writing until it culminated in 'The Castaway', appeared first at this time, in a poem extant in Theodora's handwriting, 'Mortals Around Your Destin'd Heads'. The shipwrecked mariner finds:

> He but escaped the troubled Sea,
> To perish on the Beach.

At Southampton the depression lifted, while he was sitting on a ledge looking at the sea: 'Here it was that on a sudden, as if another sun had been kindled that instant in the heavens on purpose to dispel sorrow and vexation of spirit, I felt the weight of all my misery taken off. My heart became light and joyous in a moment.' In 1756, when Cowper was twenty-five, his father died, apparently without affecting his mental stability.

Cowper undoubtedly fulfilled the requirements of his profession with the minimum of exertion, paying fines where he could avoid keeping terms and attending ceremonies. Still he expected to practise it, declaring in 1758 that though he was not fond of the Law, he was fond of the money to be got by it. 'I . . . have too great a Value for my own Interest to be Remiss in my Application to it.' How little this sensitive, shy, retiring young man could hope to earn at the Bar was soon apparent. The events which brought about his second breakdown were the result of family pressure to undertake at least some lucrative work for which he was qualified. In April 1763 three posts became vacant. Ashley Cowper, Clerk of the Parliaments and patentee, was very anxious to use his influence on Cowper's behalf to obtain one of them, the Clerkship of the Journals of the House of Lords. The incumbent of this office had died. At the same time, two other posts held in the family interest were resigned: those of Reading Clerk and Clerk of the Committees. Ashley first offered Cowper these two posts, because they were more lucrative; perhaps he hoped that Cowper would then, after all, be in a position to marry Theodora, who had been deeply affected by the cancellation of his plans to do so. These two were public offices; the clerk of each was obliged to appear in the

House of Lords, to take minutes and to read acts and papers. It was probably for this reason that Cowper first leaped at the chance of the public clerkships, and then declined them in favour of the backroom tasks of the Clerk of the Journals, whose job was to copy minutes for the House into journals and reproduce them. Ashley consented to this change of mind; the rock on which his plan foundered was that the son of the former incumbent challenged Ashley's gift of the office, and Cowper was asked to present himself at the Bar of the House to justify his claim.

Cowper was a barrister. He was badly in need of the financial security the post offered, yet the threat of a routine public appearance completely demolished his confidence, and his mental stability. Perhaps the prospect of marriage if he succeeded was also a threat. *Adelphi* records his painful efforts to familiarise himself with the work of the Journals office, his daily attendance there and the intense anxiety, with loss of concentration, that he felt. Every time he went there, 'the feelings of a man when he arrives at the place of execution' came upon him. Remembering how relaxation had helped him recover his balance in 1753, he met Ashley and Theadora in Margate in August, but to no avail. Returning to London in October, he said: 'I now began to look on madness as the only chance remaining, I had a strong kind of foreboding that it would so fare with me, and I wished for it earnestly and looked forward to it with impatient expectation'. His only fear was that he would not be ill in time to avoid the examination. His symptoms included sleeplessness and a belief that he was the subject of other people's conversation and even of newspaper reports. He describes his hurried changes of mind, how he thought first of running away to France, then of drowning himself, taking laudanum, stabbing and finally hanging himself, each endeavour proving impractical in the event. An invisible hand 'swayed the bottle down'; the knife blade broke; so did the garter he used, leaving him unconscious, and attracting a servant by the noise of his fall. In despair he asked for Ashley to be fetched, and Ashley recognised that the clerkship, and its attendant examination, must be given up.

To Cowper it had seemed that it was the examination, and that alone, that had rendered him depressed to the point of suicide. The pressure removed, however, the mood did not lighten. On the contrary, his gloom deepened: he felt the sin of despair was unforgiveable and his nightmares intensified. There were physical symptoms: 'A frequent flashing like that of fire before my eyes and an excessive pressure upon my brain made me apprehensive of an apoplexy'. His physician set his mind at rest on that score. As his anxiety deepened he informed his brother of his state. 'In every book I opened I saw something that struck me to the heart.' Generally, the first sentence he read condemned him; and the smell of laudanum, reminding him of his sin, sickened him, so that he could not use it to relieve his insomnia. 'I never went into the street but I thought people stared and laughed at me and held me in contempt, and could hardly persuade myself but the voice of my conscience was loud enough for everybody to hear it. They who knew me seemed to avoid me, and if they spoke to me they seemed to do it in scorn.' He bought a street-ballad because he thought himself the subject of it. 'The eyes of men I could not bear, but to think that the eye of God was upon me ... gave me the most intolerable anguish.' One particular dream expressed his feeling of ostracism from God, soon to become almost continual. 'One morning as I lay between sleeping and awake, I seemed to myself to be walking in Westminster Abbey, walking till prayers should begin; presently I thought I heard the minister's voice and has- tened towards the Choir; just as I was upon the point of entering, the iron gate under the organ was flung in my face with a jar that made the Abbey ring.' He, and he alone, was excluded from the congregation. Now, having wished to kill himself, he wished to live, but only because life saved him from the everlasting fire that awaited him after death. By failing to improve by the mercies granted him in the lifting of his depression in 1753, he had committed the sin against the Holy Ghost, and become a criminal. His brother could not persuade him otherwise. After his arrival he continued to feel isolated, helpless, restless and withdrawn, con- tinually expecting disaster to overwhelm him, but never knowing what, when, or where. When he tried to pray, he seemed unable to remember the Creed. Instead, the phrase that was the creed of Milton's Satan came into his mind: 'Evil be thou my Good'. He repeatedly lost the words of familiar prayers, 'I perceived a sensation of my brain like a tremendous vibration in all the fibres of it.' His knees 'smote against each other' when, he says, 'I felt ... a sense of burning in my heart like that of a real fire, and concluded it an earnest of those eternal flames which should soon receive me.'

Up to this point Cowper's religion had been that of a conven-

tional Anglican. He now came under the influence of Evangelicalism in the person of his cousin, Martin Madan. Madan's background, like Cowper's, was Westminster and the Inner Temple; he
had been called to the Bar in 1748, had experienced conversion
while hearing John Wesley preach and had become an itinerant
preacher; he was eventually ordained in the Church of England. It
was to Madan that John Cowper now turned. His brother felt
himself damned, and Martin Madan offered salvation. Although
Cowper was soothed at first, depression soon overwhelmed him.
In 1763 he left London for St Albans, to become, on 7 December, an
inmate of Dr Nathaniel Cotton's *Collegium Insanorum*.

Dr Cotton's asylum was small, limited to ten patients and with
usually only three or four in residence at a time. He had been
trained at Leyden, and had the reputation of a kind and pious man.
Cowper says he himself at first rejected the idea that he was mad,
but then eagerly agreed to go where he would get help, but was in
a state of delusion when he arrived and was violent, so that several
men were required to move him in and out of the coach in which
his journey was completed. From 7 December 1763 to July 1764 the
conviction of sin and expectation of instant judgment and damnation never left him. His dreams accused him of forgotten sins, until
'At length I thought every motion of my body a sin, and could not
find out the posture in which I could sit or stand without
offending'. Suicide now seemed a duty, but he was closely
watched. He managed to find and hide a stocking-needle, trying
repeatedly to plunge it into his heart in the night, but he broke the
point on a rib and was obliged to give up. Again he had dreams, or
perhaps visions, of intense vividness, once finding himself in a
cathedral-like, light-filled edifice, glimpsed only to be lost forever –
a device of Satan's to increase his sense of loss. He saw a black
cloud in a storm, with a fiery hand coming out of it clutching a bolt
of lightning, which he watched steadily as it was lifted up and then
fell as though 'transfixing an enemy'. Gradually, Dr Cotton persuaded him to converse. This he tried to do cheerfully, though still
'carrying a sentence of irreconcileable doom' in his heart. By May
1764 there was some improvement. His brother raised his hopes by
telling him, on a visit on 25 July 1764, that his despair was a
delusion. 'If it be a delusion then am I the happiest of beings', he
replied. He was still prey to periods of intense anxiety. By chance
he found a Bible which opened at the raising of Lazarus and again
at a passage in Romans stating the doctrine of atonement, and at

about the same time had a dream in which a young child appeared to him and encouraged him. At breakfast one day he felt the cloud of depression gradually lifting; even though he could not as yet see the way to salvation, he began to entertain hope of a God who sought his redemption. For weeks he wept when the Gospel or the name of Jesus was mentioned.

Dr Cotton was not himself an Evangelical, but he was a man who could share Cowper's sense of devotion. Not surprisingly, he wished to test Cowper's new-found joy a little longer before he let him leave his care. Cowper's friends and relations were by no means pleased by his new determination to trust in God's providence and abandon his career, withdrawing from the empty world which they inhabited. It was therefore not until 17 June 1765 that Cowper left the asylum to take up residence at a lodging found for him by his brother in Huntingdon, at a suitable, though not too great remove from Cambridge, where John Cowper was a Fellow of Bene't College. He took with him Sam Roberts, who had been his servant at Dr Cotton's, and a boy, Dick Coleman, whom he hoped to rescue from moral danger and deprivation. For the collection and management of his own funds when he had them, and for the advancement of funds when he did not, Cowper from now on relied on his good friend Joseph Hill, who practised law in London to some effect.

Huntingdon answered Cowper's needs, giving him a place away from London – scene of disaster to which he felt unable to return – and among those who loved Jesus. His illness meant he had to resign the post inherited from his father, as a Commissioner of Bankrupts, and its £60 per annum stipend; so there was no reason for him to go to London on that account. God, through his friends, now provided 'all the comforts and conveniences of life', and he was assured of a living. But after three months he had exhausted his allowance for the year, and although he needed quiet and freedom from responsibility, he began to suffer from too much solitude. One welcome visitor was William Unwin, whose family he had met at church. Cowper was invited to dine with his parents, and with the suddenness of movement which Cowper sometimes showed towards people he liked, he became their boarder on 11 November 1765. At this point *Adelphi* abruptly ends, with the printing of two hymns, 'The Happy Change' and 'Retirement', composed at St Albans during his recovery and published later in *Olney Hymns*.

To end the first part of *Adelphi* with his conversion was appropriate. But once converted, it was Cowper's overwhelming desire to convert others. The second part of *Adelphi*, which ends with John Cowper's death, is a record of his conversion of his brother. Allowing for the conventions of this kind of narrative, Cowper is very frank, and openly admits that after at first talking readily to him, John became rather silent. By the end of two years' discussion of the Gospel, he would not answer at all. It is clear that John was determined to look after William and to keep the peace. They visited each other weekly during Cowper's residence at Huntingdon, and when Cowper moved to Olney John visited him there annually. John's first illness was in September 1769. Cowper went to him, but made little impression as John felt no concern about life or death. In February 1770 John was ill again and Cowper accomplished his mission, John now telling him that he felt born again. He died on 20 March 1770.

Cowper's immediate missionary sphere, however, was in the home of his new friends the Unwins. In *Adelphi* Cowper is open about his obsession – 'from the moment the thought struck me' – about moving in with them. He blamed himself for his feverish anxiety to bring about this desired end: 'But still the language of my mutinous and disobedient heart was, give me this blessing or I die.' His arrival in the household of the Revd Morley Unwin, and subsequent lifelong friendship with Morley's wife Mary Unwin, was indeed a blessing, but *Adelphi* does not mention her by name, nor describe her conversion to the joys of Evangelicalism, only that 'I found we had one Faith, one Lord, and had been baptized with one baptism of the Spirit'. Mary Unwin was seven years his senior. *Adelphi* begins with the loss of his mother and ends with the finding of Mary Unwin. Many years later, in 1790, Cowper wrote of her in a letter to a family connection that she had 'supplied to me the place of my own mother, my own invaluable mother, these six and twenty years'. In the Unwin household Cowper's practical, physical and spiritual needs were met. He remained on good terms with Morley Unwin, who was not, however, one of Cowper's converts, preferring to distance himself from the religious fervour shared by Cowper and his wife and children. Cowper himself seems to have remained blissfully unaware of the revolutionary impact his arrival must have had on the household. In a letter of 20 October 1766 he described the new order of their days, which began with Scriptural or devotional readings from 8 to 9 am, and continued with divine service at 11 am, religious conversation between Mary and himself between 3 pm and tea-time, then a walk with Mary, further readings and conversation at night, and finally finished with hymns or a sermon and Family Prayers. Except for a respite between 12 noon and 3 pm, Cowper and Mrs Unwin were inseparable. Only to Mary Unwin did Cowper speak unreservedly. With visitors and other friends he remained shy and spoke little.

When Morley Unwin died in 1767 Cowper and Mrs Unwin sought an environment more sympathetic to their Evangelical beliefs, and were introduced to John Newton, Calvinist curate of Olney, who, in middle age, after a life of dissipation, had been converted from atheism during a violent storm at sea. They first met Newton in July 1767, and on 10 August went to Olney to inspect their future home. In September they moved into the Vicarage until their own home, Orchard Side, was ready on 15 February 1768. This move was almost as sudden as Cowper's earlier removal to the Unwins' home in Huntingdon. Newton was their only connection with Olney.

Life at Olney was not quite as retired as at Huntingdon. In a letter of 1 March 1768, only two weeks after they had settled into Orchard Side, Cowper complained that Newton had called on him to lead the Prayers at meetings, 'A formidable Undertaking you may imagine to a Temper & Spirit like mine. I trembled at the apprehension of it, and was so dreadfully harass'd in the Conflict I sustain'd ... that my Health was not a little affected by it'. Cowper's sensitivity was ill matched with the harshness and uncompromising certainties of Newton's nature. He protected himself by a degree of withdrawal, in which he was supported by Mary Unwin. In 1771–2 he began to write his contribution to their joint venture, the *Olney Hymns*, which were to bring a new impetus to the Evangelical cause when they were published in 1779. Cowper's 67 hymns make a marked contrast to Newton's. Already they indicate an ambivalence in Cowper's attitude to God and constitute, at least in some measure, a second spiritual autobiography. In hymn 9, 'The Contrite Heart', he speaks openly:

> The saints are comforted I know
> And love thy house of pray'r;
> I therefore go where others go,
> But find no comfort there.

This verse, based on Isaiah 57:15, adds to its text a note of doubt which is Cowper's own. In hymn 38, 'Temptation', Cowper shows the impact of a Calvinist God who both raises and rules the storm:

> Let neither winds nor stormy rain
> Force back my shatter'd bark again.

The threat of punishment, to keep the erring child from becoming a castaway, lies heavily across hymn 36, 'Welcome Cross':

> Did I meet no trials here,
> No chastisement by the way,
> Might I not, with reason, fear
> I should prove a cast-away?

The work, and the responsibility, put a severe strain on Cowper. His cousin Harriot Hesketh told William Hayley, his younger friend and first biographer, he was day and night in a 'constant fever' about his hymns. From the fever of composition, or preoccupation with composition, he was delivered over to the prayer meetings. But the *Olney Hymns* had reached seven editions by 1836.

If, here and there, the Olney Hymns reveal the weight of the Christian beliefs under which Cowper laboured, and sometimes faltered, Newton himself noticed that the tide of religious fervour which had sustained Cowper at first was slackening. Now another event in his personal life precipitated an emotional crisis. Hayley records that some of the Olney community felt Cowper and Mrs Unwin should be married, particularly as her daughter Susannah would be leaving them to marry in 1774. An engagement was entered upon. But as Harriot Hesketh was later to say, it was as a mother that Cowper considered Mrs Unwin. In January 1773 he was overtaken by a depression not unlike those of 1753 and 1763, when marriage to Theodora had been mooted. He was again suicidal and paranoid. He had to be closely watched, and he thought his guardians hated him and wanted to poison him, and that Mrs Unwin despised him. The most terrible experience was a dream in which he heard the words: '*Actum est de te, periisti*' ('It is all over with thee, thou hast perished'). The engagement was broken at once. The noise of Fair-day in Olney Market Place, which Orchard Side fronted, troubled him. He moved to the Vicarage in

April 1773, and did not return home until 23 May 1774. Even then, he still endured nightmares so terrifying that Mrs Unwin stayed in the room with him at night to comfort him. A letter from Cowper to Harriot Hesketh shows that in 1786 she was still doing this, and he reproached himself for the necessity of it. In fact, the *'Actum est'* nightmare seems to have been a turning-point in his life. After 2 January 1773 he never again went to public worship, remaining convinced that the sin of despair made him a castaway. After 1774 he would not go to the Vicarage. He felt himself banished from both. Before he had feared to be an outcast; now he knew himself uniquely one. In 1763 he had written the poem published with *Adelphi* in 1816, and in the *Poems* of 1782, in which he declares himself so far an outcast as to be debarred from Hell itself. It begins 'Hatred and vengeance, my eternal portion', and goes on:

> Man disavows, and Deity disowns me,
> Hell might afford my miseries a shelter,
> Therefore hell keeps her everhanging mouths all
> Bolted against me.

The poem concludes:

> I, fed with judgment, in a fleshly tomb, am
> Buried above ground.

These words represent his underlying conviction from 1773 on.

In 1770, when he wrote the first part of *Adelphi*, Cowper was prepared to admit that in thinking himself damned during the 1763 breakdown he might have been deluded. After 1773 his personal and unique damnation was always a reality and no delusion. He knew, of course, that his nervous condition was a malady from which he might recover, but that was a separate issue. His changed perception of his own spiritual condition made it impossible for him to occupy himself with the religious affairs Newton had pressed upon him. Although Hayley, and to some extent Cowper himself, believed these might have contributed to his nervous collapse, they had kept him occupied. He now turned to other occupations: his gardening, his carpentering and his pet animals. In the Temple he had kept a pet mouse. In 1774 some children brought him three hares, Puss, Tiny and Bess, well-known from his poetry. To these were added three dogs, Beau and Marquis the spaniels, and Mungo a bulldog, a cat and kittens and various birds, some the property of friends who left them in his care. In his love of the countryside and his keen sympathy for the creatures of it he identified himself with both 'the stricken deer' and 'the hunted hare'. His garden was both a refuge and a source of renewal. His poetry speaks of the 'kind offices' of the gardener and of the 'reward' for his toil. The symbolism of the garden, with its restoration of a lost Paradise, was apparent in everything he wrote about it. In this he is in a strong tradition of English poets from Milton on.

Cowper became more concerned with his poetry after the publication of *Olney Hymns* in 1779, following this with *Poems* in 1782. In a letter to William Unwin dated 7 February 1779 he compared his talent in verse to 'a Child's rattle', useful only as it serves to rid him of some 'melancholy Moments'. Newton would have liked him to continue with religious subjects but clearly he could not, and fortunately Newton left Olney in 1780 for a London parish. In 'Retirement', Cowper expresses his ambivalence about the solitude of his moral retreat. He writes of a 'sanctuary' which becomes a 'grave', and of the desirability of 'a friend in my retreat'; he seems to be repeating the Huntingdon experience. The title-page of his book alludes to his status as a Londoner: *Poems by William Cowper of the Inner Temple, Esq.* He had told Joseph Hill, who had invited him, that he would not visit him because London affected his health adversely. But at every stage of his life, until the last years of all, he enjoyed the correspondence and the visits of his friends. As he wrote to Mrs Newton on 4 March 1780, he could not leave Olney: 'It is no Attachment to the Place that binds me here, but an Unfitness for every other. I lived in it once, but now I am buried in it, and have no Business with the World on the Outside of my sepulchre; my Appearance would Startle them, and theirs would be shocking to me'. To Newton himself he is more particular, writing on 4 July 1780: 'The Meshes of that fine Network the Brain, are composed of such mere Spinner's Threads in me, that when a long Thought once finds its way into them, it Buzzes and Twangs and Bustles about at such a rate, as seems to threaten the whole Contexture'. Again to Newton, on 23 June 1780, he compares his mind as he is writing 'to a board that is under the carpenter's plane . . . ; the shavings are my uppermost thoughts; after a few strokes of the tool, it requires a new surface, this again upon a repetition of his task, he takes off, and a new surface succeeds – whether the shavings of the present day, will be worth your acceptance, I know not, I am unfortunately made neither of cedar, nor of mahogany, but *Truncus ficulnus, inutile lignum* (Horace *Satires* viii 1): 'a fig-wood stem, a useless log' – consequently, though I should be planed till I am as thin as a wafer, it will be but rubbish to the last'. Cowper felt worthless, and it was his illness that made him feel so. He wrote to Joseph Hill about his uncle Ashley Cowper's recovery from a depression on 12 November 1776 'Having suffer'd so much by Nervous Fevers myself, I know how to congratulate Ashley upon his Recovery. Other Distempers only Batter the Walls, but They creep silently into the Citadel & put the Garrison to the Sword'. It was to Hill that he confided, in a letter of 25 September 1770, his sense of the external as well as the internal damage done by his earlier breakdowns: 'The storm of 63 made a Wreck of all the Friendships I had contracted in the Course of many Years, Yours excepted. . . .'

After 1773 clerical friends like Newton who wished to speak to him of his spiritual condition had to be distanced to enable him to maintain any mental and emotional stability. He wrote to Newton on 24 September 1780: 'I am out of the reach of consolation, & am indeed a fit Companion for Nobody'. Only Mrs Unwin could encourage him to endure his life, partly because he was accustomed to her and partly because 'it is impossible for any thing she speaks to give me pain'. Otherwise, he was condemned to trifle away his life in 'Amusements which I despise too much to be entertained with'.

In spite of his fears, Cowper not only resumed old friendships in his remaining years, he attached new friends. Lady Ann Austen was another of Cowper's 'sudden' friends. They met in Olney in the summer of 1781 while Lady Austen, recently widowed, was looking for a house near her sister's. She was attracted to Cowper and to Mrs Unwin, and wrote to them from London. In October 1782 she moved into the Vicarage, from then until May 1784 spending a large part of every day except Sunday with the occupants of Orchard Side. Lady Austen inspired 'John Gilpin', and indirectly, 'The Task', through her suggestion of 'The Sofa' as a subject. Writing to John Newton on 24 February 1783 Cowper says 'I am well in body but with a mind that would wear out a frame of adamant, yet upon my frame which is not very robust, its effects are not discernible.' One of its effects was to wear through the close association – almost too close for Cowper to work – with

Lady Austen. After she left Olney the letters continued for only a short time. Lady Austen informed Hayley that she had offered her devotion to Cowper. Inevitably, he withdrew.

By this time William Unwin had taken Newton's place as Cowper's principal correspondent. After a brief respite following *Poems*, 1782, 'The Task' was published in 1785, and Unwin saw it through the press. It was not only autobiographical, but personal in style and subject matter. The growth of 'The Task' out of 'The Sofa' was apt. It was a long work, and at first it continually changes direction, gaining its final unity from the theme of the virtue of country life as opposed to the modern enthusiasm for London.

'The Task' was completed in 1784, and the translation of Homer begun. But this new work, which was to occupy and often exhaust him, with the intense application he demanded of himself, for the rest of his working life, in itself represented a change of direction. Translation, as his friends were to remind him from time to time, was not composition. What it was was a demanding task which he could put down and take up at will. The structure was provided, making no demands on his attention, yet it allowed an outlet for infinite minutiae of technique in the revision. Although the work was published in 1791, Cowper never gave up revising it. It was work in which he could be completely absorbed without the emotional drain of original composition. For many years it was his main occupation.

Soon after the completion of 'The Task' Cowper entered into a correspondence with his cousin Lady Harriot Hesketh, now a widow, which was to produce the best vintage of his letters during the years 1775–91. Their friendship of the London years had lapsed, partly because of religious differences. It now revived with fresh vitality and she visited Olney in 1786, the first of six visits to Cowper and Mrs Unwin, for periods ranging from three or four weeks to twenty-one months over the years to 1795. Cowper had told Unwin, during the Lady Austen period, that the presence of another was 'not altogether compatible with our favourite plan, with that silent Retirement in which we have spent so many years and in which we wish to spend what are yet before us'. The renewed intimacy with his cousin changed this, at least for a time. This new interest was not allowed to deter him from literary pursuits because, as he told her in a letter of 12 October 1785, these were necessary to him. 'My cousin, Dejection of Spirits, which I suppose may have prevented many a man from becoming an

Author, made me one. I find constant employment necessary, and therefore take care to be constantly employed. Manual occupations do not engage the mind sufficiently, as I know by experience, having tried many. But Composition, especially of verse, absorbs it wholly.' His day is spent in writing, reading and exercising. This letter begins with a tribute to Mrs Unwin and her help for the last twenty years. At this time she was still sleeping in her clothes in his room because of his nightmares. Yet he is so obsessed with his cousin that he admits in one letter (7–8 December 1785) that had their correspondence begun a year ago, he might not have thought of translating Homer.

In November 1786 Cowper and Mrs Unwin moved, at the invitation of the Throckmortons, to nearby Weston Underwood, a quieter and more commodious house in beautiful grounds. To Walter Bagot, Cowper wrote on 17 November a sort of lament. Moving is one of those things that 'do not actually shorten the life of man, yet seem to do so'. He had lived longer at Olney than anywhere until 'mouldering walls and a tottering house' – it actually had to be propped up for the next tenant – 'warned me to depart'. It seems likely that the move upset his balance. He regarded his 'old prison, and its precincts' with regret, admitting to Newton on 17 November he 'cannot easily account for it, having been miserable there so many years'. On 29 November William Unwin died suddenly and Cowper told Newton on 16 December that this was 'peculiarly distressing' to him, and that he wouldn't dwell on it. On revisiting his former house he found it 'the image of desolation' and felt like 'a soul that God has forsaken'. He may also have missed his cousin, who had just finished a visit. At the beginning of 1787 Cowper began to lose weight and suffered another breakdown. It was reported in 1890 that he attempted suicide, and Mrs Unwin cut the rope.

After this fourth episode of psychotic illness, Cowper found the Herculean task of translating Homer his best anchor, and spoke clearly to Newton about his preference for this work over original composition. He felt he was directed to it Providentially, after a year of laying his pen aside for want of a subject. 'It has served at least to direct my attention ... from such terrible tempests as I believe have seldom been permitted to beat upon a human mind. Let my friends therefore who wish me some little measure of tranquility in the performance of the most turbulent voyage that ever Christian mariner made, be contented that having Homer's mountains and forests to windward, I escape under their shelter from the force of many a gust that would almost overset me; especially when they consider that not by choice but by necessity I make them my refuge.' He would cheerfully waive the benefits of fame and sit in a dungeon for the rest of his days, if Hope were at his side. 'For the little fame that I have already earned, has never saved me from one terrible night or from one despairing day since I first acquired it!'

One of the first to hear from Cowper when he emerged from the breakdown of 1787 was Samuel Rose, to whom he wrote on 27 July. He complained of continuing pain in the head, and giddiness – 'maladies very unfavourable to poetical employment'; he took medicines and tried to read, but had to avoid anything that 'requires much closeness of application'. On 22 September he complained to Bagot that he would be better if he could resume Homer, but he still could not do it. At least, he said, he could now write a letter, though when Bagot came to see him he was unable to speak to him. To his cousin (29 September) he wrote: 'I have a perpetual Din in my head, and though not deaf, hear nothing aright, neither my own voice, nor that of others, I am under a Tub.' To Newton (20 October) he said 'This last tempest has left my nerves in a worse condition than it found them, my head especially...', and he apologised for having turned him away unseen. 'The sight of any face except Mrs Unwin's was to me an insupportable grievance; and when it has happened that by forcing himself into my hiding-place, some friend has found me out, he has had no great cause to exult in his success ... From this dreadful condition of mind, I emerged suddenly. So suddenly, that Mrs Unwin, having no notice of such a change, could give none to anybody; and when it obtained, how long it might last, or how far it was to be depended on, was a matter of the greatest uncertainty.'

Cowper soon returned to Homer, telling Lady Hesketh on 27 October 1787 that his health and strength were as good as before and employment 'essential' to him. To Joseph Hill in November he admitted he was 'not a little the worse for wear' but could find nothing to do that would not exhaust him more, since ' those play thing avocations which one may execute almost without any attention, fatigue me and wear me away, while such as engage me much and attach me closely, are rather serviceable to me than otherwise'. He told his cousin that Hill advised him to abstain from Homer: 'I might as well advise him to abstain from parchment.'

(Hill was an attorney and one of the Clerks in Chancery.)

Cowper knew he was not cured. In December he wrote to Robert Smith: 'Nature rather patches than mends, and seems by her best efforts to promise nothing more than a respite, and that a short one'. The onset of winter, with bad weather, restrictions on outdoor exercise and reminders of previous illness always made him anxious. His anxiety was heightened by ordinary things, for instance his cousin's silence, though she had warned him she might not be able to write to him in early 1788. He asked her to fix the intervals of her letters in advance; when she did not, 'I heard, saw and felt a thousand things which had no real existence, and was haunted by them night and day' until she reassured him. Yet his health was better than for thirty years, and he talked five times as much as at other times when dining out at the Hall.

In January 1790 a new friendship came into being when his young cousin John Johnson arrived from Norfolk to see him. As a result of this visit – which at first frightened, then pleased Cowper, as often happened when a stranger was introduced – his aunt, Mrs Anne Bodham, sent him a miniature of his mother. The letter in which he thanked her is eloquent: 'She died when I had completed my sixth year, yet I remember her well and am an ocular witness of the great fidelity of the Copy. I remember too a multitude of the maternal tendernesses which I received from her and which have endeared her memory to me beyond expression.' Writing again in March, he says the poem he has written on the picture has given him more pleasure in writing than any except 'The Winter Nosegay', written to Mrs Unwin, 'who has supplied to me the place of my own mother, my own invaluable mother, these six and twenty years'. The poem 'On the Receipt of My Mother's Picture out of Norfolk' reveals again an intensely vivid memory of an experience undergone in childhood. He recalls not only the face and nature of the subject portrayed, not only his grief, but salient details of the aftermath of her death, including the fact that in a misguided attempt to comfort him the servants lied to him:

> Thy maidens griev'd themselves at my concern,
> Oft gave me promise of a quick return.
> What ardently I wish'd, I long believ'd;
> By disappointment every day beguil'd,
> Dupe of to-morrow even from a child.

These lines seem to foreshadow the character of Cowper's later experience: his quick trust of friends who hold out promise, and his deep distrust of the God who mocks him with false promises. He sees his mother on the farther shore of life, in eternal peace:

> But me, scarce hoping to attain that rest,
> Always from port withheld, always distress'd –
> Me howling winds drive devious, tempest toss'd,
> Sails ript, seams opening wide, and compass lost,
> And day by day some current's thwarting force
> Sets me more distant from a prosp'rous course.

This poem is in itself a miniature autobiography.

By the autumn of 1790 Cowper's thoughts had turned, because of the death of a neighbour, to anxious considerations of his own situation. He was conscious of the shortness of life as he saw the leaves falling from the trees, shortly to disappear. He explained to Newton that 'The consideration of my short continuance here, which was once grateful to me, now fills me with regret.' He knew God could cure him and that he ought to believe He would, but he had experienced the transition from hope to despair so often that 'to me is Hope itself become like a wither'd flower that has lost both its hue and its fragrance'. That winter (1790–91) he suffered from his 'nervous fever', which he dreaded because 'it comes attended by a melancholy perfectly insupportable'.

Homer published, Cowper again found difficulty in composing anything, and he wrote to Lady Hesketh in June 1791: 'My chief distress at present is that I cannot write, or at least can write nothing that will satisfy myself'. To keep the melancholy at bay, something had to be found to fill the vacuum left by the completion of Homer and his inability to compose original work. An edition of Milton was mooted and he was retained as Editor by Joseph Johnson. Cowper regarded this as a new profession, following on those of Author and Translator. His friend, the poet James Hurdis, thought he might be better employed in original composition, and Cowper agreed, but in December 1791 Mrs Unwin had her first stroke, and from that time until her death after a second in 1796, her care became Cowper's first priority. 'She has been my faithful and affectionate nurse for many years, and consequently has a claim on my attentions. She has them, and will have them as long as she wants them . . .', he wrote to Samuel Rose on 21 December. The effect on Cowper himself was one of severe shock: 'Another such stroke upon her would, I think, overset me completely.'

By spring she was able to begin walking up and down the garden with him. His attentions were unremitting. However much the burden affected him, his usual preoccupation remained the same and he expressed it to Samuel Teedon on 10 February 1792 in the following terms: 'My days are spent without one symptom of spiritual life, my nights not seldom under a constant impression of God's contempt and abhorrence. Such was the last night. You will say – it was an Enemy that did this. I answer – true; but you and I differ about the person. You suppose him to be Satan, and I suppose him to be Satan's Master. Who shall decide between us?' Teedon had settled at Olney at Newton's suggestion in 1775, and was the Olney schoolmaster. Although not a friend of Cowper's, his reputation for divination caught Cowper at his most vulnerable, and from 1791 onwards there are many letters, despite the fact that at an earlier stage he had found the man obsequious and pedantic. Teedon professed himself favoured by divine dreams and voices, which he described as 'notices', and Cowper received them, keeping Teedon informed of his own condition. Cowper continued to receive some company, telling Newton on 18 March 1792 that he passed the time 'As comfortably as Mrs Unwin's frequent troubles of mind will permit. When I am much distress'd, any company but hers distresses me more and makes me doubly sensible of my sufferings, though Sometimes I confess it falls otherwise, and by the help of more general conversation I recover that elasticity of mind which is able to resist the pressure.' In March 1792 he had heard from William Hayley, Milton's biographer, who had written to ensure that their work on Milton did not overlap. As had happened before, his friendship with Hayley developed quickly, and Hayley was staying with him when Mrs Unwin, on 24 May, suffered a second and much worse stroke. Although she recovered both speech and movement gradually, Cowper's letter to Teedon on 2 June shows his deep anxiety about her. He found Teedon's cheerful 'notices' of her recovery ambiguous. His own dreams suggested a very different outcome. 'I am continually threaten'd with the loss of her . . . Death, Church yards and carcases, or else thunder storms and lightnings, God angry, and myself wishing I had never been . . . Who can hope for peace amid such trouble? I cannot. I live a life of terrour. My prospects respecting this life as well as another seem to be all intercepted; I am incapable of proceeding in the work I have begun, and unless it pleases God to give me a quieter mind shall be obliged to free myself from my engagement, while Johnson has yet time enough before him to employ another.'

Indeed, work on the Milton edition, which began with notes on *Paradise Lost* Books I and II, concerning God's punishment of the Fallen Angels in Hell, was not calculated to soothe Cowper's nervous state, and did not; while his anxiety and sense of obligation to his publisher at the delay only exacerbated matters. Writing to his 'dear friend and Crony-bard' Hayley in June, Cowper told him he missed him so much after his return home that 'I seem'd to feel my Mary's illness a concern too heavy for me without your presence and assistance, and was terrified at the thought of your absence.' His terrors about Mrs Unwin continued and he took laudanum nightly, but hoped to resume work on Milton after a visit at Hayley's invitation to Eartham, to be undertaken, he told Joseph Hill on 21 August 1792, for the benefit of both Mrs Unwin and himself. 'We have had together thirty years and are now become so necessary to each other, that our respective indispositions affect us both equally, and if she is too ill to use her knitting-needles, my pen of course is idle.'

The six-week visit to Hayley duly took place, and Cowper wrote to Lady Hesketh of its benefits. 'As to the gloominess of mind which I have had these 20 years, it cleaves to me even here . . . It is my companion for life and nothing will ever divorce us.' Although he saw much improvement in Mrs Unwin, his thoughts of the future oppressed him. 'God knows what he designs for me, but when I see those who are dearer to me than myself, distemper'd and enfeebled, and myself as strong as in the days of my youth, I am shock'd to my very heart and tremble for the solitude in which a few years may place me. I wish her and you to die before me indeed, but not till I am more likely to follow you immediately.'

They left Eartham for Weston on 17 September. Even before this departure, Cowper had been writing to Teedon of his state of mind, trying to write only when he could do so without being too depressed and therefore depressing. 'I always wake more or less in terrour' taking an hour or two to reach 'any degree of cheerfulness', after which, with the help of various employments and incidents, he could be much as other people: 'Except indeed that I never can forget for a moment my exclusion from the Church of

God and from all communion with him.' He seldom rose without wishing he had never been born. He had seen the face of God twice since 1763, only to have his 'fetters clapt on again'. Now, as to his freedom to approach God, 'I tremble lest I should lose it a third time and recover it never more.' He was untroubled by an adverse review of his Homer, but was inhibited from resuming his work on Milton, as he told Hayley, by the fear of exposing himself 'to the danger of a fresh mortification'. His daily fear of Mrs Unwin's approaching death meant 'My spirits are not good enough nor my mind collected enough for composition of any kind.' In October he told Lady Hesketh he had been unusually depressed since Eartham, and while there, and could not make use of his time before Mrs Unwin came down in the mornings because he was 'palsy-stricken': 'I am bound in magic chains of sloth, and God alone can break them.' While he made no progress on Milton, he was unable to write poetry, still his favourite occupation, since his bad conscience inhibited him. In November he described to Teedon a terrible dream. In this dream, he was looking through a window, alone in a strange room, on the preparations for his own execution four days hence. Beyond execution lay the prospect of everlasting fire, without bodily dissolution. He was trapped in a vicious circle: terror, wrath, guilt, unadvised speech, guilt, terror. In December he reported another dream. He was sitting by the fire in great distress and heard the words 'I hope the Lord will carry me through it', and his imagination was 'left free to create an endless train of horrible phantoms . . . some of them perhaps, more to be dreaded than the reality'. 1783 began with a distressing night, from which he woke to the words 'I shall perish', and 'a whole glass', accompanied by the vision of a wine glass: a combined auditory and visual hallucination. On 2 February 'My despair is perfect': he had lain awake from 4 to 7 am, his fingers' ends tingling, as often happened. Then he fell asleep, dreaming of the impossibility of his salvation; he could not be saved because this would undermine the scriptural statement of Man's insufficiency to save himself, which must be fulfilled. This dream was succeeded by one in which he found himself on the streets of London, when the fore-horse of a dray-team came at him, and Cowper damned the drayman. A day of fever followed, in which he saw the hand of God.

During all this time Cowper found Teedon's 'notices' of little or no avail, and his physical symptoms worsened, fevers and eye inflammation adding to his difficulties in working. On 1 March he wrote to Teedon of a renewed dream of execution. The evening before the day fixed on, he was taking leave of his former home and all its familiar objects. He looked for a memorial to take away with him and found the hasp of the garden door, but rejected it because of the added torment it would bring when clasped red-hot in the fires of Hell. Hayley's invitation to collaborate on a work in June was rejected: 'My poor Mary's condition makes it impossible . . .' His shyness, too, prevented it; he must work 'in a corner, and alone . . .' Mrs Unwin, he told Teedon, was weaker, while Cowper woke to words of divine derision, and increasingly distrusted Teedon's 'notices'. In July, Samuel Greatheed and his wife offered Cowper and Mrs Unwin a home, but Cowper demurred. By the autumn he felt the laudanum and Dr James's powder he had been taking were losing their effect. His efforts with Milton were like those of 'A deaf man treating of Music'. After a violent cold and perhaps fever in late October, he told Hurdis of his relief that the Milton deadline was not till spring. Eventually the project was given up and he finished his revision of Homer instead. Again the new year of 1794 began badly when he woke to the words 'I will never begin to deliver you.' God considered him a 'traytur'; 'I can hope nothing – believe nothing'; he was tormented by the memory of an offence twenty years old, and expected Teedon to give him up, as he had given himself up.

Only twenty-two letters survive from the period 1794 to 1800 and the chief source of information about the last years of Cowper's life is found in those between Lady Hesketh and John Johnson, and Lady Hesketh and William Hayley. In November 1793, when she was sixty, nine years younger than Mrs Unwin, Lady Hesketh came and stayed at Olney for twenty-one months. Hayley visited Cowper twice after the Eartham visit, in 1793 and 1794, the last time they met. In 1793 Hayley had experienced some hostility from both Mrs Unwin and Cowper, and believed she had misrepresented him to his friend. He told Lady Hesketh, who was also finding Mrs Unwin difficult, and had called her the 'Enchantress', that the Magic lay less in Mrs Unwin than 'in the very tender Heart & ardent Fancy of the Enchanted'. In 1794, although Cowper was still willing to receive some visitors, he was not anxious for a visit from his Norfolk cousin John Johnson. His melancholy was deepening: he expected at any moment to be carried away and torn to pieces. He no longer sought the company of Hayley or even Lady Hesketh, and she, because of her own failing health, felt by

July 1795 that she must leave Weston. The possibility of Cowper's
going to Norfolk to live with John Johnson had been discussed in
March 1794; he had been happy there in boyhood, and it was his
mother's early home. It had seemed that the moment to make such
a change would be after the death – which Cowper also expected at
any moment – of Mrs Unwin. Cowper was wasting away before
her eyes, and in May 1794 Lady Hesketh consulted Dr Francis
Willis, famous for his services to George III during his first attack of
psychotic illness in 1788. According to Lady Hesketh, Willis
advocated Cowper's separation from Mrs Unwin. When he visited
Cowper, he wanted him to move near his asylum in Lincolnshire,
but he found Cowper and Mrs Unwin immoveable. When Johnny
Johnson arrived at Weston in July 1795, Lady Hesketh persuaded
him to take them both to Norfolk. She recognised that they were
inseparable. Johnson was persuaded (though Cowper remained
silent) that Cowper wished to go. His real feelings on the subject
were expressed in '*Lines Written on a Window-Shutter at Weston*' just
before they left, and they reflect much the same mood as his letters
to Teedon:

> Farewell, dear scenes, for ever clos'd to me
> Oh, for what sorrows must I now exchange ye!
> Me miserable! How could I escape
> Infinite wrath and infinite despair!
> Whom Death, Earth, Heaven, and Hell consigned to ruin
> Whose friend was God, but God swore not to aid me!

John Johnson found '*Cowper's Spiritual Diary June–July 1795*' in the
boards of a copy of his Odyssey left lying in a closet at Weston. It
records his sense of being 'the hunted hare'. He now saw his
unforgiveable sin as the failure to commit suicide, a thing 'naturally impossible'; he had tried to kill himself – in the absence of other
opportunities since 1793 – by not eating: but it availed nothing. He
felt that he would not reach Norfolk.

Reach Norfolk he did, leaving Weston on 28 July 1795 without
reluctance, and in the certainty, John Johnson's 'Diary' records,
that he would be dragged from the carriage at Olney by his
Tormentors, and torn to pieces. They stayed first at Mundesley,
where he wrote to Lady Hesketh, telling her that he viewed every
vessel at sea as likely to seize him. He deliberately walked to the
edge of the cliff, to a height terrible to look down from, by

moonlight, and saw two miles off a crumbling pillar of rock at high water-mark. It was an emblem of himself, torn from all natural connections, solitary, 'expecting the storm that shall displace' it. On long walks with Johnny he tried to keep his eyelids sheltered from salt winds that had always inflamed them by going in the lanes, under the hedgerows. On one occasion when Cowper was tired, to save him from the crowded inn, Johnny hired a private lodging for him to rest before the return journey of seven miles. On 26 September Cowper told her that Johnny had suddenly departed – he didn't know where. 'Like every thing else that constitutes my wretched lot, this departure of his was sudden, and shocked me accordingly'; and he added, 'I shall see Weston no more. I have been tossed like a ball into a far country, from which there is no rebound for me.' Lady Hesketh and Cowper were never to meet again.

Cowper told Lady Hesketh that he was becoming daily worse, and found death and life equally impossible. His mind wandered when Johnny was reading to him and also when he was writing (although these lapses in concentration do not show in the letters). Johnny persuaded him to write; Cowper expected every letter to be lost. While Cowper was sunk in despair, Johnson, with extraordinary sanguinity, told Kate Johnson, who looked after the household in his absence, that Cowper was 'as well, pretty nearly, as when I first knew him'. It comes as no surprise to learn that Cowper reverted to calling him 'Mr Johnson', and renounced the familiar 'Johnny' he had used before.

Cowper was unwell in the winter of 1796 and Dr Donne, a cousin from Norwich, attended him. His prescriptions of opiates seem to have helped. By Spring of 1797 he was physically better, but Mrs Unwin's health had begun to give way. In the summer he resumed work on Homer. Johnny found his attempts to reassure Cowper were hopeless: 'I might as well talk to the sea'. The death of Cowper's favourite dog, Beau, on 17 November was followed by Mary Unwin's on 16 December. Cowper was taken to see her for the last time on the day of her death, and exclaimed, 'Oh God – was it for this?' Johnny records that he never mentioned her again. The same thing had happened before when he had ceased to speak of Theadora. To spare him pain, the burial took place without his being made aware of it, by candlelight on the evening of 23 December 1796.

Cowper told Hayley that summer that his state of mind was now one of 'Perfect Despair, the most perfect that ever possess'd any Mind. . . .' To Lady Hesketh he wrote: 'My mind has long ceased to be subject to my will, and I despair that it will ever obey it more.' Ever since he came to Norfolk, every day and every hour had seemed his last. By the autumn, he wrote that scenes that once 'he could not contemplate without rapture' were now 'an insipid wilderness' to him. 'The reason is obvious. My state of mind is a medium through which the beauties of paradise itself could not be communicated with any effect but a painful one.'

The voices that tormented Cowper from 1791 to 1795 often occurred in dreams, or at waking. From 1796 until his death in 1800 he continued to suffer the dreams, but the voices pursued him in his waking hours as well. John Johnson recorded both dreams and voices from 15 November 1797 to 23 April 1799, and from 1795 to 1800 kept a journal devoted entirely to Cowper. He hoped, by inducing him to share his experiences, to relieve them. It is an interesting comment on the desperate measures which concerned relatives of the mentally ill will take that Johnson tried to influence the content of Cowper's thoughts: 'I procured a workman to cut a groove in the wall behind our poor friend's bed, for the insertion of a tin tube, through which I hoped to be able to convey to him some comfortable sounds, to counteract those deplorable ones perpetually injected into his Mind's ear, by the unseen enemies of his Peace'. Foreseeably Cowper interpreted Johnson's well-meant messages of cheer in sombre fashion. For Johnson's benefit, he classified his dreams into 'dreams of contempt and horror – some of shame – and some worse dreams of ignominy and torture'. Margaret Perowne, the gentlewoman in charge of Johnson's household, was forty-four when she met Cowper, a few years older than Mrs Unwin had been on first meeting him in 1765. Like Mrs Unwin, she slept in his room to help combat the dreams. He became convinced that both she and Johnson would abandon him, or turn him out, and that they despised him. A voice would tell him: 'You shall be left.' He received warnings that his drink was poison, that the food he ate would turn into a monster inside him, or that he would be attacked while attempting to eat, Johnson described the effect of these ideas in a letter to Hayley in August 1796: 'Poor Mr Cowper says He is Prometheus – and so it will be done to him!' He was 'taken up in his bed by strange women', and when he saw a tree torn up by the roots knew it for an image of himself – 'disjointed by the Rack'. While Johnson laboured to interpret these things cheerfully, Hayley responded to his 'Perfect Despair' letter with a vision of his own, in which he saw the Throne of God and two kneeling angelic forms, one that of Cowper's mother, the other of his own; when he enquired, Cowper's mother spoke of his gradual restoration and his growing fame and honour, 'for the service he has render'd to the Christian world by his devotional poetry'. Hayley procured famous men and religious leaders to write encouragements to Cowper, but in vain. He would have none of it. After Mrs Unwin's death he turned only to Miss Perowne for comfort, even though he lived in constant dread of her desertion.

Although Cowper's decline was reversed a little in 1797, and he gained some weight, and although he seemed to enjoy the outings Johnny arranged for him, including eight visits to Mundesley in 1798, he was deteriorating. When the Dowager Lady Spencer, friend of his cousin Theadora, visited him in July he answered her questions with a yes or no and afterwards declared she had been interested only in the furniture. He continued to revise Homer; but refused other suggestions of work from Johnny. In 1799 a last great manuscript, containing 'Montes Glaciales' ('On the Ice Mountains') and The Castaway was composed. The 53 Latin lines and 64 lines of English translation deal with a theme long familiar to Cowper, and now recalled to his mind in this form by Johnny's reading him a newspaper piece on icebergs: the intractability of destiny. The theme of 'The Castaway', like that of Olney hymn 36 and the words of St Paul in I Corinthians 9.27, is the fear – now a certainty – of being a castaway, like the sailor of whom he had read long ago in Anson's *Voyage Round the World* (1748). Cowper's fate is worse than the sailor's, reflecting the imagery of his last extant letter, to Newton, on 11 April 1799. His hope had been of an eternity spent in Paradise, but 'a storm was at hand which in one terrible moment would darken, and in another still more terrible, blot out that prospect for ever'.

Cowper struggled on with translations, but became seriously weakened in January 1800 when he suffered from dropsy. He died on 25 April, according to Dr Woods, 'from extreme debility'. His last words were spoken to Margaret Perowne when he refused a cordial she offered him in the night: 'What can it signify?'

Case Description

There can be no doubt about the psychotic quality of William Cowper's recurrent breakdowns. Mostly unrelated to external circumstances, the emotional mood of his illnesses was predominantly depressive, with typical symptoms. These included: loss of all appetites; insomnia (but, when he slept, fearful nightmares with early morning wakening); lack of feeling (anhedonia); inability to do anything (except read, and this 'partly from habit'); and several serious suicide attempts. The other characteristic depressive feature – guilt – also reached psychotic proportions, in Cowper's belief that he alone was singled out for eternal damnation and the mockery of God; a delusion sustained by 'horrible visions' and auditory hallucinations, extending at one point to the conviction that others could hear the voice of his conscience. Some paranoid element was also present in his later breakdowns, when he believed that his food and drink had been poisoned.

In a recent clinical evaluation of Cowper, published in the professional psychiatric literature, Meyer and Meyer decided that, according to the American DSM-III system of classification, he would now be regarded as falling into the category of atypical bipolar (i.e. manic-depressive) disorder. Their reference here to 'atypical' covers the fact that, although mainly depressive in mood, Cowper did on one occasion – during his period of hospitalisation – switch into a more elevated state of 'ecstasy': this was considered sufficiently serious for him to be retained in hospital. Meyer and Meyer conclude that 'Cowper's clinical picture, after 200 years, gives no reason for diagnostic uncertainty' and certainly that would appear to be true insofar as on our own SADS-L evaluation, too, Cowper clearly meets the criteria, at the very least, for affective psychosis. However, he could also be said to have shown some schizophrenic features: hallucinations, occasional paranoid ideas and the 'thought broadcasting', referred to above. (Meyer and Meyer's interpretation of Cowper's auditory hallucinations as 'affective', rather than 'schizophrenic', is based on the view that his heard voices were 'mood congruent'; a judgment that is certainly in line with current diagnostic practice, though in our opinion somewhat arbitrary.)

6

Strange Death in Life

Smart was born a gentleman and became a scholar, until his poetic vision took over his life. It was Clare's destiny to demonstrate that it was possible for a peasant to become a poet in English society. That he succeeded was the more remarkable in view of his mental illness. That he needed to achieve a degree of social mobility to be heard at all cannot have lightened his struggle with that illness, but must have added enormously to the stress which both brought it on, and resulted from it.

He was born in the village of Helpston, then in Northampton-shire, the son of a thresher, Parker Clare, and his wife Ann. Parker Clare was the son of a schoolmaster, a Scot, who had passed that way; he went by his mother's surname, taking his father's name as a forename. Both Clare's parents were virtually illiterate, though Parker Clare could read a little of the Bible and had a good memory for the ballads of the day. He was physically strong, and enjoyed some reputation at village festivals as an amateur wrestler. Ann was eight years his senior and came from the village of Castor nearby; her parents were John and Elizabeth Stimson.

Clare's account of his background is found in a document written in 1821, at his publisher's suggestion, to help in the search for patronage. While this autobiography is written with an eye to his audience, and with some evident acquaintance with the literary tradition of such works, it shows the marks of an original mind. He describes Helpston as 'a gloomy village ... on the brink of the Lincolnshire fens'. He himself was 'of a waukly constitution', the survivor of twins, of whom the girl died after a few weeks in spite of seeming the stronger of the two at birth. He was the eldest of four, the other two dying in infancy. While neither of his parents insisted on putting him to a trade for which he showed no disposition, his father took him, because of their poverty, 'to labour with him' and made him 'a light flail for threshing' after the age of ten, and father and son worked together. Other farm jobs came his

115

way, in winter in the barn, and in summer 'tending sheep or horses in the field or scaring birds from the grain or weeding it'. While thus employed he collected folk tales told by the old women 'to smoothen our labour'. But until he was 11 or 12 at least three months of the year was spared for his education, first with an old woman in the village and later with a master at Glinton. His master, John Seaton, found he improved because he was encouraged in his school-work at home.

The Helpston yokels were less impressed by these endeavours. Clare began 'to wean off from my companions and sholl about the woods and fields on Sunday alone'. Some thought he showed the symptoms of lunacy in this. He developed a passion for reading, always taking a book out with him in his pocket. His peers thought this merely qualifying himself as 'an idiot for a workhouse', but their attitude of condemning a lover of books as lazy only intensified his efforts to find solitude for reading, 'to hide in woods and dingles of thorns in the fields on Sunday to read these things'. He saved scraps of brown or blue paper from his mother's groceries to practise writing. Hired by a neighbour who treated him well, to plough his land, 'I got into a habit of musing and muttering . . . as pastime to divert melancholly, singing over things I called songs and attempting to describe scenes that struck me.' His rhymes exorcised the hobgoblins in lonely places supposed to be haunted. Going into town he would look at the ground and mutter to himself and was 'often embarrasd' when overheard and questioned. At about 13 he came across a fragment of Thomson's *Seasons* and determined to possess a copy; the price was 1s. 6d. He prised the money out of Parker and walked to Stamford – to find the bookseller closed on Sunday; however, he managed to slip away from work the next week and obtained it for only 1s.

His next job, in about 1810, was as an apprentice (unbound) in the kitchen garden at Burghley, the seat of the Marquis of Exeter. The Master of the Kitchen Garden was not congenial. Clare's parents must have despaired when he soon returned home 'were I could look in the wild heath, the wide spreading variety of cultured and fallow fields, green meadows, and crooking brooks, and the dark woods, waving to the murmuring winds these were my delights and here I could mutter to myself as usual, unheard and unnoticed by the sneering clown and conscieted cox comb.' His habit of composition deserted him in 'the continued samness of a garden'. Now he could resume and begin writing down his 'musings', hiding what he was doing from his family, and, when caught, pretending his verses were copied from another book. 'I scribbld on unceasing for 2 or 3 years', reciting them and making use of the criticisms of the family without confessing to his authorship.

Clare began to realise he possessed abilities, both in composing poems and in observing nature, that set him above his companions. He obtained a spelling book, then a stock of pencils to keep in his pocket, to write as chance arose. The jeers of his contemporaries when they found he was a poet were 'present death' to his ambitions. He was motivated to reveal his talents by two things: his father's increasingly crippling rheumatism, which forced him out of his regular work, and his own weak constitution: he was unable to work for a year. Clare describes this 'indisposition' – 'for I cannot call it illness' – as originating in fainting fits, which he believes were brought on by seeing, when younger, a man fall from a load of hay and break his neck. 'The gastly palness of death struck such a terror on me that I could not forget it for years'. He was tormented by dreams of grave-digging and charnel houses. He would swoon, and when he recovered felt as though he had been in a dreamless sleep. He knew when such a fit was coming 'by a chillness and dithering that seemd to creep from ones toe ends till it got up to ones head, when I turnd sensless and fell; sparks as of fire often flashed from my eyes or seemd to do so when I dropt'. A Stamford doctor stopped these fits, after which he had only one or two recurrences, yet 'every spring and autumn since the accident happend my fears are agitated to an extreme degree and the dread of death involves me in a stupor of chilling indisposition as usual'.

Spurred on by necessity, Clare found a book-loving friend nearby to whom he revealed himself as a poet. In 1814 he purchased a blank book from Henson, a bookseller at Market Deeping, and again revealed the use he had for it, and Henson asked to see some his poems, warning him of the expense involved in printing a specimen to get subscribers. Clare found work burning lime and raised enough money for this, but with little hope of success until, through Henson, Clare was approached by Edward Bell Drury. Drury's cousin was John Taylor of the London firm of Taylor and Hessey, who became, with Drury, Clare's publishers. *Poems Descriptive of Rural Life and Scenery* came out on 16 January 1820.

Clare records that Drury found him at the Helpston resort for young men, Bachelor's Hall, run by the Billings brothers and a source of Clare's acquaintance with 'John Barleycorn'. But his bachelor days were ending. As he delicately puts it: 'My amorous intrigues and connections with Patty ... now began to disclose dangers which only marriage could remedy.' On 16 March 1820 Clare and Martha (Patty) Turner were married; Anna Maria Clare was born on 2 June, the first of seven children to survive infancy and to join the Clare household. Fortunately for his family, Patty was to prove more practical than her husband, who wrote to Hessey on 4 July 1820 to tell him that Patty 'I think will prove a better bargain then I expected'. By the end of the following January the first book of poems had reached a fourth edition and Clare was a famous poet, but his wife Martha was not his inspiration. That role belonged to a childhood sweetheart for whom Clare entertained 'a platonic affection'. This was Mary Joyce, who is mentioned immediately after the marriage is recorded, and to whom he began writing poems at about the same time. There had been others, less platonic, before Patty. But the Mary of his schooldays at Glinton was to become the wife of his mind now, and at the end, as Patty was the wife of his hearth. In later days he regarded himself as having two wives. The fact that one was Mary and the other Martha is not without significance.

Sketches in the Life of John Clare concludes with a statement of Clare's moderation in matters of religion (Protestant Anglicanism) and politics. In his theology he shared the same ground as Smart, but his fervour was directed towards nature rather than towards religion. He remained an Anglican to the end. In nature he saw Eden. His vision had an immediacy which further undated autobiographical prose fragments confirm. When he was out of work he sought beautiful places and secluded ones, often travelling half a day's journey on foot to find them. His work was not polished, like Cowper's, or wrought in a scholarly tradition, as Cowper's and Smart's could be. 'I always wrote my poems in great haste and generaly finished them at once whether long or short for if I did not they generally were left unfinished what corrections I made I always made them while writing the poem and never could do any thing with them after wards.'

Until his marriage, which seems to have been undertaken more from compassion towards Patty and a sense of family responsibility than from any expectation of happiness, Clare had avoided being pinned down. Even when he enlisted in the militia in 1812, his clearly inadequate services were not required for long. Now he was living in the restricted space of a small cottage, with parents, wife and child. The sudden fame which his first, and as it turned out his only successful, book brought enlarged his prospects in one way. He was invited by the local aristocracy in the persons of Lord Milton and Lord Fitzwilliam, who offered him financial support, and in London Lord Radstock interested himself on his behalf, so that he was provided with an annual income of £40. At that time, £30 would have been the day wages of a labourer, and barely enough to support a single man. Unfortunately it never seems to have been understood by Clare's patrons that it was no easy matter, particularly after the act of enclosure which in 1809 changed the life of the countryman, for a poet to pick up odd jobs to supplement his income. In some ways he discovered this change of fortune added to his burdens. He was painfully shy and could not meet patronage with ease. He was anxious, and promises were made that were not kept. Visitors flocked to Helpston to see the peasant-poet, often actuated by idle curiosity. 'I was often annoyed by such visits and got out of the way when ever I could and my wife and mother was often out of temper about it as they was often caught with a dirty house then which nothing was a greater annoyance.' On the credit side, many friendships and correspondences came from this time, when he was lionised by his public and introduced to London literary society by his publishers. The first of four visits to London came in March 1820. He was accompanied by his friend Gilchrist and the coach passed Cowper's parsonage 'with its melancholy looking garden' at Huntingdon. In London he met writers, artists and poets – though he missed Keats, whom Taylor also published. He met Mr and Mrs Thomas Emmerson on this first visit. Elated by fame and the delight of conversation with like-minded men and women, whose society he could not find in the country, he nevertheless had to return to the country and take a job at harvest-time to make ends meet. He became ill at the end of the year, but went on, 'all madness to write', amid the harassing pressure of visitors and correspondence, with new poems for *The Village Minstrel* in the belief that it was through writing that he would be enabled to support his family. The proofs of the new book were ready by January 1821. By the end of March he was better, but the delay in publishing the new book irked him. Taylor was interested in other ploys besides Clare, and Clare was drinking more than seemed good to Taylor. When the book was published, it missed the success of its predecessor. The fashion which had caught Clare up, was already sweeping by him. Fame beyond his expectations had overstimulated him, and he hoped to make money not only to support himself and his family, but to help his friends, the Billings, with their debts. The disappointment must have been severe, even though Lord Milton came to their rescue when Clare could not. When he was not overactive, Clare fell into idleness and depression.

During a second visit to London in May 1822, Clare met Rippingille, Lamb, Hazlitt, Cary (the translator of Dante), Thomas Hood, Hartley Coleridge and many others at Taylor and Hessey's monthly dinners at Waterloo Place. He visited Hilton, Lamb and Cary, meeting both Charles and Mary Lamb at Colebrooke Cottage. Hood describes Charles Lamb in witty conversation with Clare who is 'a very Cowslip' in the grass-green coat and yellow waistcoat which cause him nearly to be excluded from the dinner by the doorman. B. W. Procter, delighted by Clare's delight in the wonders of London, says he is 'as simple as a daisy': but to Lamb he is 'Clarissimus', or 'princely Clare'. These meetings must have diverted him. But he became ill and depressed again on reaching home. To shake off the 'peasant poet' brand he published under the name of Percy Green in the *London Magazine*, which Taylor had now taken over. Again he addressed poems to Mary; Taylor suggested he should begin work on the next book, *The Shepherd's Calendar*, in August, forestalling Lord Radstock's wish to find a new (and more committed) publisher for Clare. Taylor proposed to bring it out the next winter but in the event it did not appear for four years. The conflicting advice about publishers, as well as the disappointment of delays, took its toll. Then Clare's friend Gilchrist died, and by the end of 1823 he was iller than ever before. The correspondence with Mrs Emmerson helps to illuminate this period. His 'mind was dead'; he suffered from 'loss of memory'; was 'nearly blind'; and he felt 'wandering pains' and 'cold chills'. He suffered for two years, and Dr Darling whom he had met at a dinner in London sent him pills through Hessey, besides other help that was proffered. Believing himself to be dying, he made a will, repented and gave up 'John Barleycorn'. In April he decided, on Taylor's advice, on a third visit to London to see Dr Darling. This took place in May 1824. Although several of his artist friends were in London, the benefits of novelty soon wore off. But he was still able to register new experiences, and one of the most striking was his accidental sight of Lord Byron's funeral cortege passing through Oxford Street. His doctors kept him until 8 August when he went home, fully expecting that this time the illness had him in its final grip. He wrote to Thomas Inskip describing six months' gradual decline and complaining of 'a sort of apoplectic fit' since which he has never had the use of his faculties. He has a 'numbing pain' constantly about his head, 'and an aching void in the pit of my stomach keeps sinking me away weaker and weaker'. If the air of Helpston fails, the next thing to try is 'salt water'. In September he wrote to Cary that he was 'ill able to do anything', but he seems to have been writing feverishly for months after his return in an effort to take his last chance. Some of the poems were not published until after 1835. His prose writings included a journal, further autobiographical writing and part of a *Natural History of Helpston* suggested by Hessey and taking the form of letters to him. The end of 1824 saw him still working despite his ill ease.

The journal Clare kept between his return from the third London visit and the following year, 6 September 1824 to 11 September 1825, records his observations of nature, particularly of birds and flowers, and shows how Clare was able to make an important contribution to the scientific work of other authors. It also shows his anxiety about his work; a dream in which a proof of a poem crumbles to dust in his hand; and his sensitive, even morbid imagination: 'Heard a terrible kick-up with the rats in the ceiling last night and might have made up a tolerable faith to believe them ghosts. . . .' The journal records, too, the difficulties he had with Taylor, who now says he has twice as much material for *The Shepherd's Calendar* as he wants, having given as his reason for delay only a few months earlier that there was not enough. It was at this time that he began publishing in the periodicals poems written in imitation of the old masters. When he confessed this practice to James Montgomery, editor of the *Sheffield Iris*, his letter made it quite clear that he was committing deliberate forgery, and meeting with a degree of success he did not always achieve under his own name. Montgomery had suspected the truth, and asked for proof of authenticity for an anonymous 'old' poem Clare claimed he had copied from the fly-leaves of an old book, but printed 'the glorious offence' anyway. Clare later admitted that the book, as well as the poem, was his own invention. What had begun in admiration of the old poets ended in sending invented finds, sometimes accompanied by a letter to the target editor signed with a false name and written in a disguised hand. This particular poem, 'The Vanity of Human Wishes', appeared in *The Rural Muse* in 1835. This did not prevent Dr J. H. Bell from defending his inclusion of it in a collection of 1846 as genuine, on the grounds that had Clare really written it, it would make him the equal of Burns. He considered that Clare was deluded in claiming it as his own. Clare scored other successes with his imitations of Sir John Harington, Andrew Marvell and Sir Henry Wotton. When Clare asked Cary's opinion as to the 'harm' of compiling a whole book of these imitations, Cary replied in a letter dated 18 January 1829 that he preferred Clare in his authentic identity than in the guise of the Elizabethan or Jacobean poets; the imitations 'want the livelier touches of your pencil'. Clare sensibly accepted this delicate piece of diplomacy.

By the end of 1825 Clare was still receiving advice from Dr Darling, and he was depressed, blaming himself for the illnesses of his children; in 1826 he had added infidelity to his burden of guilt. Difficulty about the publication of *The Shepherd's Calendar*, which Taylor had taken responsibility for and which needed much editorial work which it seems Clare could well have carried out himself more easily, continued to irk him, particularly in view of his financial problems. He worked at the harvest, and felt better. When the book finally appeared in November 1826, after many delays, its expression of Clare's joy in the vision of nature was not reflected in the public's reception of it. Taylor was appointed printer to the University of London in 1827, and had little time for Clare's work. At the end of 1827 Clare was more seriously ill with distress of mind and the physical discomfort of skin eruptions and pains in the head. His mood of despair generated one of his most acclaimed poems, 'Autumn'. In February 1828 he took the advice of Dr Darling and Mr Emmerson and made a fourth visit to London, this time travelling alone, and staying with the Emmersons. He was too ill for much excitement, but saw Taylor and Cary. He suffered sleepless nights, and missed Patty and the children, as usually happened when he was away from them. He left for home after a month and by the end of that year seemed completely recovered, although he was still tormented by feelings of guilt. After harassing struggles with Taylor to sort out his accounts in 1829, Clare found himself, at the end of a decade which had begun with public acclaim, without a publisher, without experience of editing his own work, and with his public lost in the silence caused by Taylor's delays between 1821 and 1827. 'I would advise young authors not to be upon too close friendships with booksellers . . . if a book suits them they write a fine friendly letter to the author if not they neglect to write till the author is impatient and then comes a note of declining to publish mixed with a seasoning of petulance in exchange for his anxiety. . . .' Clare's last book, *The Rural Muse* was published by Whittaker in 1835 and was a failure. Although he continued to write until very nearly the end of his life, there were to be no more books in his lifetime.

In 1830 and 1831 Clare was ill again. In a letter to Taylor dated 7 March 1831 he complains of stomach pains, a burning sensation in the groin, a prickly feeling in the face and temples, sleeplessness, loss of appetite, 'a stupid and stunning apathy & death', and 'dreads'. He suffers a 'sobbing or beating' of the head when he lays it on the pillow; and he has had a dream in which he thought 'the Italian liberators were kicking my head about for a foot ball'. He moved, with the help of his patron, Lord Milton, to a larger cottage with a garden he could cultivate and pasture for a cow, to Northborough, three miles away, in 1832. Although the move meant an improvement which he welcomed for his family – which now included three daughters and two sons, with another son born in January 1833 – it upset him. How much any change in his environment disturbed him may be judged by his reaction to the felling of two elm trees, in a letter to Taylor written in March 1821, and by the poem, 'The Fallen Elm'. Now, once again he expressed his sorrow at change in 'The Flitting'. 1832 saw the publication of his proposals for a book of poems *The Midsummer Cushion* which he edited himself, and hoped to publish by subscription. But he was unable to carry the project through unaided, and it was not published until 1979. In 1833–5 Clare seems to have lost his ability to rebound from illness. His children were ill, and he left Helpston owing £20 with further debts soon added. *The Midsummer Cushion* and *The Rural Muse* show him to have been at the height of his powers in this period, but he was increasingly subject to illness and depression. His letters to Mrs Emmerson became shorter, and he became convinced that he had two wives, Mary Joyce, his first, and Patty, his second. He suffered fits of extreme irritation, but could be calmed by one of his sons who would talk quietly to him to distract him. At the same period he suffered from hallucinations, believing himself bewitched and assailed by evil spirits. An entry in his notebook for 13 October 1832 provides an insight into what was to become Clare's refuge from his torment. He recounts a remarkable dream: 'That Guardian spirit in the shape of a soul-stirring beauty again appeared to me, with the very same countenance in which she appeared many years ago and in which she has since appeared at intervals and moved my ideas into ecstasy. I cannot doubt her existence.' In the first dream, she appears before he had published anything, leading him into the fields and to familiar haunts, among a large crowd. He is shamed by his own insignificance. Then the scene changes, and they are in the shop of a city bookseller, where among the books on a shelf are three lettered with his own name. 'I was very astonished, and turning to look in her face I was awake in a moment; but the impression never left me. I see her still. She is my good genius and I believe in her ideally almost as fresh as reality.' In another dream, used in the poem 'The Night Mare', he is called in a crowd of villagers to judgment. He sees his guardian again, in white garments, and hears his name called. As his guardian smiles in ecstasy, he 'knew all was right, and she led me again into the open air'. As he wakes from the dream the realisation comes:

> 'Twas Mary's voice that hung in her farewell;
> The sound that moment on my memory fell,
> A sound that held the music of the past . . .

The dreams 'gave the sublimest conceptions of beauty to my imagination'; he 'could no longer doubt her existence'; and he writes them down to prolong his happiness 'in believing her my guardian genius'. Nature, the well-known scenery, Mary and poetry are fixed in his imagination when the outward scene changes.

More and greater changes were on their way. In 1835 Clare's mother died. In 1836 he had begun to suffer renewed lapses of memory and in June 1837 he was admitted as a voluntary patient to Dr Matthew Allen's asylum at High Beech, Epping Forest, through the good offices of John Taylor.

Events leading up to this first, voluntary, hospitalisation are described by Clare's first biographer Frederick Martin. His *Life of John Clare* was published the year after Clare's death when people still remembered him; but the book's modern editors point out that Martin's approach is not scholarly and he does not discriminate between fact, hearsay and imaginative reconstruction. Martin says that in the winter of 1835–6 Clare was often violently excited and Patty got one of the children to calm him by leading him out into the fields, which he allowed. He seemed almost recovered, and took to rambling alone all day. Mrs Marsh, the wife of the Bishop of Peterborough, met and recognised him. She knew him as an eccentric poet. She invited him to stay and he said he was expected home that day, but would come later, which he did, staying several days at the Bishop's residence. Mrs Marsh took him to see a production by roving players of *The Merchant of Venice*. During the performance Clare began shouting at Shylock and tried to get on the stage. The performance had to be stopped. Martin describes Clare's singular remarks and habit of swerving from one topic to another. Patty realised he had deteriorated. He kept asking for Mary, and said all his friends had left him. But his condition was not generally known. The Vicar of Helpston, the Revd Mr Mossop, was not aware of it when he invited him to meet someone interested in his poetry. Patty allowed him to go, but in the middle of the conversation he saw figures moving overhead. Mr Skrimshaw, the surgeon from Market Deeping, was called and pronounced him a lunatic. These incidents are plausible, and there must have been many like them.

Dr Allen was well qualified and sympathetic. He encouraged Clare to write, and to walk in the beautiful surroundings of the hospital. In 1840 he reported that he believed he had improved greatly and might have recovered completely and permanently had an adequate pension been made available to him at the beginning of his illness. He thought the state of continual anxiety and the extremes of flattery and neglect he had suffered, as well as over-exertion of body and mind had caused Clare's condition. Physically, he wrote to Taylor, he had improved, but he suffered delusions. He was struck by the way Clare would write fluent, sane and beautiful prose or poetry the moment the materials were to hand, even at times when he could not keep up a sane conversation. In answer to Dr Allen it must be said that Clare's dislike of being exhibited to visitors he did not know may have tended to heighten his delusions. Clare's strongly built father had been a fighter at village fairs, while Clare himself was of weak frame and small stature. When a stranger confronted him, his mind ran on prize-fighting, while the sequence of his thoughts was disconnected. Cyrus Redding, the visitor, sent him Byron's works, and Clare wrote the 'Don Juan' and 'Childe Harold' verses. In his poetry too, the delusions show, despite Dr Allen's view of the matter. His two wives, Mary and Martha, both appear in 'Childe Harold'. Mary Joyce died in 1838. In 1841 he is still writing to her, inscribing a letter to her among the verses in his notebook.

On 18 July 1841 Clare was planning to cast off the apathy of his illness and to escape the walls of his 'prison'. In one of the most extraordinary documents in the language, he relates the results of his sudden determination to endure the asylum no longer, but to act. July 18 was a Sunday. He was feeling 'very melancholly' and met some gypsies during a forest walk, one of whom offered to help him escape on his promise of £50. When they met again 'he did not seem so willing' and later the whole encampment had vanished. Once formulated, Clare's intention remained firm. He was undaunted by setbacks, and after a day's wait, set out for home on 20 July. He slept the first night in a hovel and dreamed of his 'first wife' Mary. He seems to have remained ignorant of her death in 1838. The next day a man on horseback threw him a penny with which he bought half a pint of beer at a public house. He gave up any attempt to beg because two drovers 'were very saucey'. Gravel got into his shoes, one of which had now 'nearly lost the sole'. The second night he found shelter on some stones in a porch, thinking of his 'two wives and both their familys'. On the third day he was reduced to eating grass and chewing some pipe tobacco he had in his pocket, which helped his hunger. Stumbling along 'foot foundered and broken down' he was eventually met near Peterborough by a cart driven by Helpston neighbours who recognised him and threw him some pennies when they heard his plight. He stopped at a public house for 'two half pints of ale and twopenno'th of bread and cheese', and staggered on, 'my feet more crippled than ever', resting on stoneheaps along the highway. Nearer home he was met by a man, woman and boy in a cart:

> when hearing me the woman jumped out and caught fast hold of my hands and wished me to get into the cart but I refused thinking her either drunk or mad but when I was told it was my second wife Patty I got in and was soon at Northbrough but Mary was not there neither could I get any information about her further than the old story of her being dead six years ago . . . but I took no notice of the blarney having seen her myself about a twelvemonth ago alive and well and as young as ever – so here I

am homeless at home and half gratified to feel that I can be hapy any where.

The manuscript concludes with an entry dated 24 July 1841: 'Returned home out of Essex and found no Mary – her and her family are as nothing to me now though she herself was once the dearest of all – "and how can I forget"'. There is a poem with the title 'How can I forget?' On 27 July he wrote a letter 'To Mary Clare – Glinton'. It begins 'My dear wife', and explains that he has written this account of his journey 'or rather escape' from Essex for her amusement; and he declares his expectation that his hopelessness at not being able to see or hear of her will be comforted by the sight of Glinton church, by the feeling that Mary is 'safe if not happy' and by the memory of her. He proclaims himself 'as I ever have been and ever shall be' her 'affectionate Husband'.

At the end of August Clare wrote to Dr Allen explaining that he had 'heard the voice of freedom' and had left without taking leave. He says he could have stayed if only his friends 'had noticed me or come to see me'; he can be 'miserably happy' anywhere, but the keepers 'assumed as much authority over me as if I had been their prisoner', and he wearied of it. Now he is anxious about a pension from the Queen. He wants to be independent and pay his board and lodging at home. He considers himself a widower or a bachelor. Women are faithless; man he never liked. He wishes to be himself for a few years 'and lead the life of a hermit: but even there I should wish for her whom I am always thinking of – and almost every song I write has some sighs and wishes in it about Mary'.

Dr Allen replied. Clare was mistaken about the pension; the Queen had contributed £50 to an annuity fund for him, but no more. He offered Clare a welcome back at Epping, where he could have his board and lodging for nothing and his liberty as long as he did 'nothing to make you unpleasant as a Visitor'. He could lead the life of a hermit all he wished, and Dr Allen would make provision for him. Clare did not avail himself of this offer and in 1845 Dr Allen died a bankrupt after a disastrous business venture with, among others, Alfred Tennyson; so the proffered hermitage would not have lasted long.

Clare's renewed attempt to live at home, where he was now cut off from the hope of finding his Mary, produced poems of despair, mitigated by the consolations of nature. He kept a nature journal, recording observations made on his walks with the old delight and exactness. His notebook records, too, his anxiety about the neglect of those who had praised him in earlier days. He felt he had lost himself. 'Forget not thyself and the world will not forget thee. Forget thyself and the world will willingly forget thee, till thou art nothing but a living-dead man, dwelling among shadows and falsehood.' Near the end of the notebook he writes:

> To live with others is not half so sweet
> As to remember thee.
> Mary.

The last entry is dated 12 December 1841. On 19 December Dr Skrimshire of Peterborough, who had treated Clare before, certified him and he was taken to the General Lunatic Asylum opened at Northampton in August 1838. There he was maintained at the charge of his patron, Lord Fitzwilliam, at the rate for private patients. Dr Skrimshire entered on the certificate the statement that Clare's madness was 'hereditary'; but there is no known evidence of this. Unfortunately the Northampton Asylum records were destroyed during a fire, and only those from the last two years of Clare's stay remain.

When Clare took up his residence the superintendent of the asylum was Dr Thomas Prichard, who, like Dr Allen, believed in and used humane methods with his patients. Clare was free, as a 'harmless' patient, to go into the town, or walk in the neighbourhood. His physical welfare prospered, as it had at Epping, but his mental state seemed to deteriorate. He was deluded, and although he began many poems, few were finished. He retained his early habit of dashing them off, never returning to one in which he had been interrupted for any reason. He complained to one visitor, Spencer T. Hall, that he was tired of waiting to go home. 'They won't let me go, however; for, you see, they're feeding me up for a fight; but they can get nobody able to strip me.' Asked if he felt more proud of his reputation as a poet than as a prize-fighter, Clare replied rather absently, 'Oh, poetry, ah, I know, I once had something to do with poetry, a long while ago: but it was no good. I wish, though, they could get a man with courage enough to fight me . . .' G. J. De Wilde, the editor of the *Northampton Mercury* recorded meetings with Clare in the town. On one occasion Clare quoted Byron and Shakespeare, claiming authorship of both quotations. Challenged on this issue, he replied 'It's all the same. I'm John Clare now. I was Byron and Shakespeare formerly. At different times you know I'm different people – that is the same person with different names.' This statement may throw some light on his earlier literary forgeries. However, Clare's sense of identity with the famous did not stop at poets: it embraced prize fighters and criminals too. De Wilde found him taciturn, and his answers brief. Clare believed in Dr Prichard's power to know whether he was disobeying him, present or absent, and refused to join with some fellow patients in an escape attempt, saying they would only be brought back. They were. 'I told you how it would be, you fools', said he.

At Northborough Clare had suffered from melancholy and from outbursts of anger. At Northampton he was more docile, although he still felt himself a prisoner within 'the English Bastille'. A friend of Miss Mitford's found in 1844 that he believed himself a witness of the execution of Charles I, and recounted the event in graphic detail. Mary Lamb had a similar imaginative power of recollection. He also related the Battle of the Nile and the death of Nelson as one of the sailors present, using nautical terms with great accuracy. Among other delusions, he believed his head had been blown off in the battle and when questioned about this could not explain its evident restoration. On 28 August 1860 Agnes Strickland, a historian, visited him but failed to rouse him from apathy by her praise of his work and her encouragement to write more. '"I can't do it"', he replied gloomily; "they pick my brains out". I enquired his meaning. "Why", he said, "they have cut off my head, and picked out all the letters of the alphabet – all the vowels and consonants – and brought them out through my ears; and then they want me to write poetry! I can't do it."'

Dr Wing succeeded Dr Prichard in 1854. He described Clare's condition as one of 'deep melancholy', with only occasional lifting of the clouds. After Dr Wing's arrival Clare was confined to the grounds of the hospital. Between 1862 and 1864 he suffered 'delusions about his identity', and he was 'haunted by phantoms' and used 'bad language to these chimaeras'. At last he showed 'insensibility to the flowers and sunshine into which he was taken', though he still chose to sit on a window-seat and look into the garden until within three days of the end. He suffered a paralytic stroke on 10 May 1864. On 20 May he became comatose and died.

Clare's earlier poems vary greatly in quality, some of the

ballad-like narrative descending into mere versification; but the immediacy of his response to the sounds and sights of nature never varies. He responded to critics by dropping some of the dialect words, which made the early poems obscure at times. As his illness progressed, so did the emotional depth and maturity of feeling in his poetry. Many poems describe his solitary walks; his awareness of creatures about him and his peculiar sensitivity remind the reader of Cowper and Smart, particularly when he writes of birds, and bring a new contribution to the English Romantic Movement. The many asylum poems are especially moving because they show him contending with his sense of a loss of identity and meaning, and using the formal intensity of the poem to keep control of his life, as he does in the poem 'I Am'. Very few of the poems betray any irrationality in his thinking although the grief they express speaks for itself. His letters, which display the same vivid qualities as his verse, though with less formal control of his ideas, show a clear decline at the end. The last, to John Hipkins, was written on 8 March 1860, at the instance of Dr Wing:

> Dear Sir
> I am in a Madhouse & quite forget your Name or who you are you must excuse me for I have nothing to commu[n]icate or tell of & why I am shut up I don't know I have nothing to say so I conclude
> > yours respectfully
> > John Clare

None of his friends visited him, except for his son John, who seems to have come once to see him. Indeed a letter to his son Charles on 15 June 1847 counsels against it (Charles had died in 1843):

> Frederic & John had better not come unless they wish to do so for its a bad Place & I have fears that they may get trapped as prisoners as I hear some have been & I may not see them nor even hear they have been here.

Yet he continually in letters home enquired about them all, including his father Parker Clare, whose death in March 1846 had been reported to him. In a letter to his wife Patty in 1849–50 he recalls his son Frederick in infancy:

I see him now in his little pink frock – sealskin cap – & gold band – with his little face as round as an apple & as red as a rose – & now a stout Man.

Father and son are strangers because the bad government keeps prisoners like himself in the English Bastille, where 'harmless people are trapped & tortured till they die'. So close in his experience are the joys and despondencies that even as far back as 1831 he had written to Taylor 'I often wish I had never been known beyond 1818'.

The essence of Clare's life as a writer seems to be summed up in what he says to his friend Thomas Pringle in 1832, in a letter of which only a draft has survived:

I became a scribbler for downright pleasure in giving vent to my feelings & long & pleasing painful was my struggles to acquire a sufficient knowledge of the written language of england before I could put down my ideas on paper even so far as to understand them myself – but I mastered it in time sufficiently to be understood by others & then became an author by accident & felt astonished that the critics should notice me at all & that one should imagine I had read the old Poets & that others should imagine I had coined words which were as common around me as the grass under my feet – I shrank from myself with extacy & have never been myself since – as to profit the greatest profits most congenial to my feelings were the friends it brought me . . . – but I wrote because it pleased me – in sorrow & when happy it makes me happier & so I get one & when they please others whose taste is better then mine the pinnacle of my ambition is attained – & I am so astonished that I can hardly believe that I am myself for no body believed that I could do any thing here & I never believed that I could myself – I persued pleasure in many paths & never found her so happily as when I sung imaginery songs to the woodland solitudes of autumn.

Case Description

Like several of our other authors, John Clare has been the subject of past attempts at diagnostic assessment. Although the general psychotic nature of his illness has not been disputed, opinions have been divided on whether, in current terminology, he would be labelled manic-depressive or schizophrenic. Both Kris, a psychoanalyst, and Grigson preferred the latter description. Tibble and Tibble, in their life of Clare, considered him manic-depressive, as did Tennent, former Physician Superintendent of St Andrew's Hospital (previously the Northampton Asylum where Clare was a patient). Unfortunately, the early medical notes relating to the crucial periods of Clare's stay there are missing, and any evaluation has to rely on other material.

Judged as manic-depressive Clare certainly showed severe swings of mood and activity, reflected in his bouts of furious writing alternating with periods of inability to write at all. (In a letter to his publisher, Taylor, he says: 'I fear I shall get nothing ready for you this month at least I fear so now but may have 50 subjects ready tomorrow.') But his more prevailing mood seems to have been one of depression and apathy, which became progressively worse, accompanied by increasing failure of concentration and disturbed sleep. In other letters he writes of these:

> I am very unwell & what ails me I know not but my head is horribly afflicted with a stupid vacancy & numbness that is more than hell itself . . .

and elsewhere:

> I cannot sleep for I am asleep as it were with my eyes open & I feel chills and cold come over me & a sort of nightmare . . . I cannot keep my mind right as it were for I wish to read and cannot . . .

More indicative of schizophrenia are his delusions; for example his belief that he was the poet Byron, and that he was a prizefighter whom nobody dare challenge because of his huge strength. Although these might be judged evidence of 'manic grandiosity', another delusion has a clear schizophrenic quality; i.e. his belief that he was married to his long-dead first sweetheart, Mary. And certainly schizophrenic in form was the comment he made to Agnes Strickland, the historian, when she visited him in the asylum:

> . . . they have cut off my head, and picked out all the letters of the

alphabet – all the vowels and consonants – and brought them out through my ears;

These signs, together with Clare's progressive withdrawal from the world, suggest that a modern diagnostician would label his illness 'schizophrenia with a chronic course'.

7

The Storm-Cloud and the Demon

JOHN RUSKIN (1819–1900)

In 1842 Dickens could write in *American Notes* that the State Hospital for the Insane in Boston was 'admirably conducted on those enlightened principles of conciliation and kindness, which twenty years ago would have been worse than heretical'. It is true that at the time Dickens was writing, there were some humane institutions for the mentally ill – John Clare seems to have been treated with some sensitivity both in High Beech and in Northampton Lunatic Asylum, and Mary Lamb was not badly looked after, at least as long as her brother was alive. As early as 1792 a home for the insane was set up in York by a Quaker, William Tuke, which was run on principles of persuasion and self-restraint. But it is safe to say that in the early years of the century, most institutions for the mentally ill were little better than prisons, and the inmates were neglected and ill-treated.

It was for this reason that, when John Ruskin's grandfather became insane in 1810, he was not taken to a madhouse, but was cared for in his own home. Ten years after his wife's death, he cut his throat, leaving debts of £5,000, an enormous sum for a small tradesman at that time. His son and his niece married four months later, and in 1819 became the parents of a son, John Ruskin, who inherited the severe psychosis of his grandfather.

Margaret Ruskin was some years older than her cousin and husband, and bearing a child at the age of 38 might well seem to her something of a miracle. Her son John was to her a gift of God, and, stern Evangelical that she was, she determined that he should be from birth devoted to the service of God. Her main concern was that he should have a high place in heaven, but she wanted him to be eminent in this world too, and she disciplined and trained him to both ends to the best of her not inconsiderable abilities. His will must be broken to obedience, and he was, according to his own

accounts, whipped from an early age both for deliberate disobedi-
ence and for natural accidents such as falling downstairs or
bursting into tears. But his own memories of childhood, his picture
of the solitary child with no toys but a bunch of keys and a box of
bricks, tracing out for hours the patterns of the wallpaper and the
carpet, must not be too readily accepted. Contemporary letters
show the infant Ruskin as having plenty of toys, but his own
memories in old age, if not veracious, are valuable as an indication
of how impersonal, unemotional, and to some extent deprived and
punitive it seemed to him, and also of what was important to him
in those early years – solitude, and the pleasures of the eye. Other,
more active, pleasures were gradually withdrawn from him; he
saw less and less of his child cousins at Croydon, he was not
allowed to dig in the garden, his mother became so anxious when
he fell off his pony that his riding lessons were discontinued, he
might no longer play with the dogs after one bit him on the lip. He
later came to feel bitterly about his mother's over-protection: 'my
mother had never let me play cricket lest it should quicken my
pulse – step into a boat lest I should fall out, or learn to box lest I
should bleed at the nose'. He had not, he said, 'a single athletic
skill or pleasure'. What was there left for him to do but read and
write, draw and paint and look, look, look at all about him?

He believed that his parents' treatment of him was at the root of
most of his later troubles. At intervals in his later life he was to turn
on them with intense resentment, and to rage at their 'extreme
though selfish affection'. It is likely, and indeed it is affirmed by
several of Ruskin's biographers, that his parents were constantly
on the watch for signs in their son of the family insanity. (If that is
so, it is remarkable that they should have married, since the
nineteenth century had a strong dread of hereditary insanity, and
both parents came of the paternal stock.) There were, in fact, signs
of psychosis in childhood and youth; the over-sensitive response
to visual stimuli and the racing, multi-associative brain. At the age
of ten he wrote to his father, 'After all I shall not get what I have to
say into this letter. Things come pouring in upon me from all sides
and after deafening me with their clamour fall to fighting who shall
get first, kill each other, and do not get in at all.'

Already, too, the child was pouring out words; as in later life, his
difficulty was not finding subjects, nor finding modes of expression, but selecting from the flood of ideas that seethed and rioted in
his over-active mind. He was forced to leave unfinished many of

the projects begun and abandoned before he was ten – the autobiographical encyclopaedia, for instance, intended to run to at least four volumes, or the poem on the Universe, of which hundreds of lines were completed. At eleven, he wrote more than two thousand lines of an *Iteriad*, which described a holiday trip to the Lakes. He kept a journal, he wrote poems and plays, letters and psalms.

His education, by his parents and by tutors at home, added to the pressure on his brain. '. . . What with Livy and Lucian, Homer, French, drawing, Arithmetic, globe work and mineralogical dictionary, I positively am all flurry, never a moment in which there is something that ought to be done.' He was laying the foundation for his lifetime of manic occupation. Already present too was the strange feeling that was to become so strong a part of himself: 'It is odd you always think it would be very pleasant to be where you are not . . . It is singular that almost all pleasure is past, or coming.' He wrote this at 14 years old at his first ecstatic sight of the mountains he had longed for years to see, which were to prove to him 'the seen walls of lost Eden'. Significant too is the fact that although Ruskin was to be a compulsive traveller, he rarely, or with slight variations, diverged from the routes his parents followed in their early journeys with him. When the nomadic impulse took possession of him, it was to take him only over the same ground.

It may not have been a burden at that time for the precocious gifted child to think of himself as destined to greatness, but it did not help him to deal with the world outside his home. When, at the age of 17, he fell in love with Adèle Domecq, the daughter of his father's partner, he could not come to terms either with his own emotions or with her attitude to him; far from admiring him, she found him absurd, even grotesque. He remained for several years obsessed, not with her, for he probably never saw her as a person in her own right, but with her as the object of his passion. Some of his biographers think that this early episode set the pattern for his subsequent sexual orientation towards adolescent or pre-adolescent girls; but it may be that, being himself sexually and emotionally underdeveloped, he was naturally drawn to the physically underdeveloped.

In January 1837 Ruskin entered Christ Church, Oxford, as a gentleman commoner. His mother entered Oxford at the same time, as a lodger in the High Street. Her anxiety about her son's welfare, and her overriding conviction that her first duty was to protect and shield him from the perils of College life forced her to this temporary separation from her husband (though it was greatly mitigated by his weekend visits). But all her care could not save her son from the first of his breakdowns in 1840 – a very minor affair compared with the later ones, but interesting in that it seems to have been misunderstood, or misrepresented, by many of his biographers. There had been warnings of trouble in 1839, when Ruskin was in difficulties with his work, finding it impossible to keep to the strict timetable necessary for an Honours degree. Early in 1840 he heard of Adèle's marriage. Two months later he had a small haemorrhage from the throat, which made his parents anxious to take him abroad for the winter; but it is clear that his illness was not entirely physical in origin, though his father put it about that he had 'injured his health by over Study'.

The family started for Italy in September 1840. John's moods alternated between elation at having left the Oxford grind and despondency at what seemed his failure in every field and his poor health. It was at this time that his lifelong obsession about his eyes first showed itself; he feared he might become blind. On a visit to Vesuvius he recorded that his spirit was lying 'in dark ashes'. 'I wish Vesuvius could love me like a living thing; I would rather make a friend of *him* than any morsel of humanity.' After he arrived back in England at the end of June 1841, he was sufficiently recovered, though still unsettled, to take a Pass degree in April 1842; his papers were good enough for him to be awarded a Double Fourth. He subsequently began work on his first book *Modern Painters*, by 'A Graduate of Oxford'. This had originally been intended as a pamphlet, but, said Ruskin, 'the pamphlet turned into a volume. Before the volume was half-way dealt with, it hydra-ised into three heads, and each head became a volume.'

It was to be the story of Ruskin's life. Every one of his many interests was to 'hydra-ise' until his mind gave way in the attempt to control and order their ever-increasing number. 'I want', he was to say, 'to go everywhere at any time, and be in twenty places at once.'

At the age of twenty-six he travelled abroad for the first time without his parents, much against their wishes, though he was accompanied by his valet and a guide. He wrote every day, sometimes twice a day, to his father, receiving as many letters in return. His moods were still volatile, veering rapidly from despondency to rage or elation, and there were signs of strain in his intense mental activity. He reacted with extraordinary emotion to his first sight of the paintings of Tintoretto and could hardly drag himself away from Venice but for his parents' complaints about his extended absence. His return to England made him feel ill and depressed. 'I fell into a state of despondency till then unknown to me'; he was tormented by 'the perpetual feeling of being in everybody's way', could tolerate neither company nor solitude, and felt that 'the people seem to have put a chill on me, and taken my life out of me'.

In 1847 he became even more unnerved because he fell in love with Euphemia Gray, whom he had first met when she visited his parents' house as a young girl years before, and his parents did not wish him to marry her – or, perhaps, to marry at all. He spoke of 'a strange deadly shadow over everything, such as I hardly could comprehend; I expected to be touched by it, which I was not, but then came a horror of great darkness – not distress, but cold, fear and gloom'. His parents were so anxious about his continued depression that they allowed him to propose to his Effie, but even when she accepted him his gloom did not lift. 'I am so nervous, and weak, and – dreamy – and really ill and broken down', he wrote to her a month before the wedding. 'My father was for many years in the same state, and it ended in his secluding himself from all society but that which he sees in his own house. I inherit his disposition – his infirmities, but not his power – while the morbid part of the feeling has been increased in me by the very solitude necessary to my father ... Excitement of all kinds are [sic] just as direct and certain *poison* to me as so much arsenic or hemlock and ... the *least* thing excites me. From a child if I turned from one side to another as I slept, the pulse was quickened instantly.'

Perhaps such a letter should have warned Effie that her marriage was likely to be difficult. In the event it was disastrous. She seems to have been a good-humoured girl, willing to make compromises, and it was not her fault that the marriage failed. The older Ruskins could not relinquish their emotional hold over their son, nor perhaps did he wish them to do so. The burdens put on the young wife went beyond all that was reasonable, and indeed Ruskin seems never to have regarded her as a person with needs and rights, but as a kind of slave who was to accede to all his and his parents' wishes, and to disappear without complaint when not wanted. Again, this was to be the pattern of his life. He took and gave friendship only on his own terms; he must have his own way and could make no concessions. It is not surprising that he found himself increasingly isolated.

The marriage, which had never been consummated, was annulled in 1854. In his autobiography many years later Ruskin made no mention of his ever having been married. Now he returned to live with his parents as though he had never left, but the old serenity of the family home was gone. Even before the marriage, John James could no longer fully sympathise with his son's sudden intense enthusiasms, nor with his extravagance in buying pictures. Ruskin thought his father to be, if not mean, at least penny-pinching, and was irked by his parents' constant watchfulness and anxiety over his moods and actions. In 1846 he had, while abroad, received a letter from his father, an 'ungoverned expression of extraordinary though selfish affection', and had actually brought himself to throw it on the fire; on which he felt 'a degree of happiness and elation totally different from all my ordinary states of mind'.

His parents had sown the wind, in all good faith, and now they were to reap the whirlwind. They had continually assured him of his unique qualities and destiny, and he had come to believe them. 'I could not write as I do unless I felt myself a reformer, a man who knew what others did not know – and felt what they did not feel,' he wrote to his father. He had, he felt, 'an instinct of impartial and reverent judgement' which fitted him to the work to which he had been 'appointed'. These convictions, however strong, had no foundation; his theories were seldom based on facts, his judgments on social, economic or philosophic matters arose not out of knowledge or reflection, but from mere personal impulse or prejudice. Dante Gabriel Rossetti found many of his opinions about art 'absurd'; he could not justify his criticisms, he could only eulogise or vilify.

With such traits and such convictions of his own absolute rightness, it is not surprising that Ruskin was unsuccessful in social relationships. He could neither collaborate nor compromise, but must dominate or patronise (often with great kindness and generosity, though he took care to conceal his financial donations from his father). He liked teaching where his pupils were deferential and adoring, and would accept his very idiosyncratic methods, but of friends and equals he had few. He wrote to Rossetti: 'I believe that I once had affections as warm as most people but . . . they have got tumbled down and broken to pieces . . . I have no friendships and no loves.'

His dissatisfaction with his personal world led him to try to reform the greater world around him, but again, he had not the patience to found his hastily-formed theories on solid fact, and his prejudices against all modern inventions, such as steam-power or the use of iron in industry, seemed often to be expressed with childish petulance. He crammed enormous amounts of work into every day – drawing, writing, lecturing, teaching, studying mineralogy, navigation and countless other subjects. His mind, he complained, was 'too busy', and it made him physically over-active. His mind darted from subject to subject as his body darted from place to place. From 1840 to 1888 he was never in the same place for long at a time.

His mother's censoriousness ('she combats his opinions and lectures him publicly') and his father's interferences ('my father cannot bear to see me put a letter in my pocket without telling him all that there is in it') made his home life difficult. Their intrusive affection galled him, he said, like hot iron, 'and I am in a state of subdued fury whenever I am at home which dries all the marrow out of every bone in me'. Outside his home there were plenty of critics of his wild ideas: 'genius divorced from common sense', said the *Manchester Examiner*. His parents' unquestioning Christianity no longer supported him and a cloud came over his life and mind during the 1860s. He became unbalanced and rather paranoid, seeing himself as the victim of all sorts of deliberate 'provocations'. 'I live the life of an old lady in a houseful of wicked children', he wrote to the Brownings in 1859, 'they won't leave me to my knitting-needles a moment'.

By 1860 he was beginning to feel a reaction to all the frantic activity of the last fifteen years, in 'the lassitude of surrendered effort and the disappointment of discovered uselessness'. He could not write or think without getting angry. His former achievements appeared to him of no account; he felt 'intense scorn of all I had hitherto done or thought, still intenser scorn of people's doings and thinkings ... and almost unendurable solitude in my own home, only made more painful to me by parental love which did not and never could help me, and which was cruelly hurtful without knowing it.' He was obviously in a depressive state, unusually (for him) languid and exhausted, and unable to make decisions about his life. He could neither be alone, nor get on with any companions. In the summer of 1860, after that enormous autobiographical work *Modern Painters* was finished, he went to Geneva with a single companion. They 'made each other miserable to an amazing extent'. Ruskin was sulky, restless and unable to settle to any work. His depression was not alleviated by the reception given to his articles on Political Economy published in the *Cornhill*. They were, said the critics, 'eruptions of windy hysterics . . . absolute nonsense . . . utter imbecility . . . intolerable twaddle.' The public outcry was such that only four of the projected seven articles finally appeared.

Ruskin's father, apprehensive that his son would be taken for a socialist, was even more apprehensive about his growing predilection for young girls. In 1859 Ruskin had visited a girls' school at Winnington in Cheshire at the request of the headmistress, to teach the girls drawing, mineralogy and Bible studies. Their youthful grace and deference, their uncritical admiration, poured oil and wine into the wounds caused by the hostility and lack of appreciation of the rest of the world. He was also physically attracted, and there was a certain amount of romping and kissing. The elder Ruskin was disturbed by this, but probably more disturbed by his son's growing obsession with the child Rose Latouche, whom he had first met when she was 10 years old. When in March 1861 John James wished his son to leave Winnington and accept an invitation to stay with Lord Palmerston, he received the unreassuring answer, 'You needn't think I'm in love with any of the girls here, and get me out of it therefore – Rosie's my only pet. . . .'

The first signs of real breakdown appeared on 19 April 1861, when Ruskin gave a lecture at the Royal Institution and 'found I had no command of my subject and my brains, and was obliged to give in half-way'. A severe depression continued throughout 1862. 'I don't speak to anybody about anything . . . I sometimes find the days very long, and the nights longer; then I try to think it is at the worst better than being dead.' He even began to think that his fondness for Rose did him harm; she was growing up, no longer the adoring little disciple and playfellow. She was developing ideas of her own, while he would have her remain a child. They had in the summer of 1863 what he called 'a fine quarrel' because she did not help him enough; it did not occur to him that a fourteen-year-old was under no obligation to help a man of forty-three.

His irritation with his father had reached a climax. 'I know my father is ill, but I cannot stay at home just now, or should fall indubitably ill myself . . . I must have a house of my own now somewhere.' In mounting fury and distress he fled to Switzerland, where, he told his father bitterly, he would look for a permanent home. He saw a doctor in Geneva about his disturbed state of mind, saying that he could not work without feeling giddy and losing all power of thought, but it was not of much help. 'The doctors all say rest, rest. I sometimes wish I could see Medusa.' Inert and despondent, he felt that his whole life had been a failure and blamed his parents. 'You thwarted me in all the earnest fire and passion of life', he wrote to them. 'If I had the courage and knowledge enough to insist on having my own way resolutely, you would now have had me in happy health, loving you twice as much . . . Now, my power of *duty* has been exhausted in vain, and I am forced for life's sake to indulge myself in all sorts of selfish ways.' In a highly nervous state, and desperate for a home of his own, he arranged to buy two pieces of mountain property, neither of them suitable for building on; the one on which he finally arranged to put up a house was almost entirely inaccessible. After a time he allowed himself to be persuaded of the impossibility of living on this site, even if the builders could have transported their materials there, and the deal was cancelled; but his unrealistic ideas about money and property were to cause incessant trouble from this time.

For years there had been anxiety on the father's part and resentment on the son's over money matters, but in 1864 Ruskin inherited a large fortune on his father's death. He was unmoved by his bereavement, but he began steadily to give away, spend or lose his inheritance. Perhaps he was unconsciously destroying or diminishing his father, perhaps he was acting in accordance with his beliefs that wealth should be distributed; more probably he was simply acting irrationally. He first invested £5,000 in what he called 'entirely safe' mortgages, but very soon found it 'no less desirable than difficult' to get rid of them, and lost about £20,000 on the deal. He gave away £17,000 to relatives not mentioned in his father's will, but only, he said ingenuously, 'to those I liked best'. He sold some of the pictures and bought others at treble the price. He bought a collection of minerals at the owner's valuation of £3,000, which subsequently proved to be worth less than £500, though he recovered in a costly law-suit about £1,000. Later he was to buy, sight unseen, a house, 'a mere shed of rotten timber and loose stone', which was to cost him enormous sums to rebuild and furnish. He was to pour out money on charitable schemes – a few successful, most wildly and predictably unsuccessful. He would accept no advice and became stubborn and wilful in the extreme. No doubt his mother disapproved, if indeed she was allowed to know what he was doing; but she was in her eighties and half-blind, though she still tyrannised over him to some extent. He was forced to ask her permission to invite his friends home, or indeed to absent himself. But he had his way over some things; he visited Winnington six times in the year after his father's death, much against her will. She almost certainly did not know that he was supporting several needy pupils there. On his visits he played blind man's buff with the girls, and there was kissing and petting: 'the prettiest of them make their lips into little round Os for me whenever I like'.

For some months after his father's death Ruskin could not work, but neither could he be idle. His mind was much on Rose Latouche, whom he had not seen for some years. He met her again in London in 1865, and   .teenth birthday proposed marriage to her. She told him .. ..x her again in three years time. From that moment his emotions were in turmoil.

The story of Ruskin and Rose Latouche has been told many times in detail and it is impossible to do more here than touch on its implications for him. Rose was not a normal girl; she was anorexic and subject to periodic breakdowns, under immense pressures from both parents to live a life (for her) without interest, sympathy or stimulation. She probably understood nothing about sexuality and certainly she was not in any sense in love with Ruskin; but her religious convictions and her sense of his desperate need of her drove her sometimes to try to help him in whatever way she could, which was never the way he wanted. Their relationship was a long affair of separations, misunderstandings, frustrations, occasional rapturous reunions and bitter quarrels. It is extremely unlikely that this diverse pair could ever have married, but had they done so, it would have been as much of a disaster as Ruskin's first marriage, since he was unable to see another person except in relation to himself and ministering to his wants. In his many moments of petulant resentment he saw her as 'an Irish girl of nineteen, who cannot spell – reads nothing but hymn-books and novels – and enjoys nothing so much as playing with her dog', while he was a man 'whom Carlyle and Froude call their friend, and whom many very noble persons call their teacher'. But the stress and pressure of the years until she died were to have a terrible effect on him.

In 1867 his mental condition deteriorated. The Christmas of 1866 was 'the worst Christmas I ever past'. He began to write torrents of letters – many to his mother-substitute Mrs Cowper, later Lady Mount-Temple, but many to journals and newspapers, often about private matters; one, about a confidential conversation with Carlyle, brought him into real trouble. In his diary he recorded many strange dreams, which he regarded as revelatory, and he was constantly looking for – and finding – messages about himself and Rose in the Bible, though not in the least because he had any remnant of his former religious faith. His bizarre and confused ideas at this time led him continually to 'take the Sortes', not only from the Scriptures, but even from Scott and Swinburne, and eventually from Greek mythology. 'Do you see what Proserpina spells? If you take P (for Pet) and R (next the Rose) away from it? Ros-Epine.'

That Christmas, because Rose did not write to him (she 'cursed the day for ever to me into darkness with her broken faith'), he wandered 'giddy and wild' about the Lake District. He began the new year in a fever of restlessness, and wrote floods of letters to Mrs Cowper. Later in the year he had an illness in which he became delirious and saw faces in the wallpaper of his room. When he recovered – if he ever did after this return to any state that could be called normal – he was 'torn by various dispositions to work in fifty ways at once'. *The Queen of the Air*, written in 1869, supposedly about Greek mythology, was in fact investigations into and confessions about his own personal mythology and life. Indeed almost all his work from now on was, embarrassingly to his friends, about his private life and convictions.

His American friend Eliot Norton thought him mad in the summer of 1869. He conceived a vast plan of irrigating the Upper Rhone Valley by trapping melted snow and rainwater, and threatened, if the Alpine Club would not help him, to buy one hillside and get the scheme working himself. In Venice later that summer he experienced a revelation at the sight of Carpaccio's paintings of St Ursula; he was convinced that St Ursula was Rose, or that at least Rose had reincarnated herself, or had some actual connection with the pictured Saint. It was at this time of mental and emotional confusion that Ruskin accepted the Slade Professorship of Fine Art at Oxford and went back to London to prepare for the lectures he was to give in the new year. He recorded a series of very confused dreams, one of a serpent with Medusa eyes and breasts, and could only work by never thinking of anything which might disturb him.

He managed to give his first series of lectures without disaster, although some of his audience were surprised to find him 'acting' his subject, apparently without premeditation, in the liveliest pantomime. His Oxford friend Henry Acland, a doctor, wept with relief at the end of the second lecture, and there were complaints of his inclusion of irrelevant matter. He felt that Rose was unnecessarily cruel, and turned to his young cousin Joan Agnew, who had been living with his mother since his father's death. He came to depend greatly on her, and in their daily letters he developed an extraordinary baby language, in which he was 'di pa' and she 'di ma' and (unfortunately to a modern ear) 'your own wee pussy'.

In 1871 Ruskin began to publish at his own expense a series of letters nominally addressed to the workmen and labourers of Great Britain, but largely in order to pour out the tangled thoughts of his increasingly deranged mind. They appeared under the title *Fors Clavigera*, a title which is in itself a good example of the intricate way in which his tortuous imagination worked: *Fors* has implications not only of chance, hazard or destiny but also of fortitude and strength; *Clavigeris*, the key-, nail-, or club-bearer, epithets used in classical literature of Hercules but also of Janus, the god who looked both ways. This was particularly appropriate for Ruskin, whose readers might one week be surprised to hear that he was 'a Communist of the old school – reddest also of the red', and less surprised three weeks later to hear their wealthy author describe himself as 'a violent Tory of the old school – Walter Scott's school, that is to say, and Homer's'. He had for some time felt much guilt about the sources of his father's wealth, and in the fifth *Fors* letter he proposed a fund to buy land; he was to give a tenth of his property and earnings and asked others to join him in contributing. The legal and practical problems arising out of this scheme, the St George's Guild, proved to be endless and its support minimal. It was in essence founded upon a practical impossibility, an attempt to revert to a feudal past in agriculture and manufacturing. All profits would have been shared, but there were none. These letters showed that there was, as he himself complained, 'terribly mixed work in my head'. This 'mixed work' led him into many charitable enterprises, a few sensible, and many absurd; most of the latter gradually or quickly collapsed, either through lack of supervision or lack of interest on the part of their originator.

In the summer of 1871 Ruskin gave another lecture which roused half Oxford to indignation by an attack on Michelangelo, without any reference to the University's superb collection of his drawings. In December his ninety-year-old mother died; he said that he had never loved her, and he seemed to feel none of the guilt that he had felt after his father's death. While his new home at Coniston was being prepared, he went abroad with a group of companions; but he was irritable and demanding, he complained continually about the destruction of antiquities and the greed and offensive manners of Italians. He hurried his party on against their will, finding Rome 'repulsive', and in Pisa he had to be restrained from violently attacking workmen who were restoring a chapel.

Back in England in the summer of 1872 he again proposed marriage to Rose Latouche, but his vehemence terrified her. He tried to overcome his despair by continual activity, and his behaviour was often bizarre. Joan Agnew married Arthur Severn, the son of Keats' friend, and when she had her first child Ruskin was both anxious and jealous. 'Will oo always ove oos poor Donie just the same?' he wrote to her. 'Me fitened – di ma. Is oo velly much peesed? Pease no be peased too mut.'

His friends thought him too much alone, but he could not tolerate guests. His next series of lectures in Oxford were disorganised and disconnected, and drew very small audiences; his 1874 lectures were cancelled because of 'various anger and distress'. He went back to Italy, his depression deepening and his mind ever more confused: 'one of my chief troubles is the quantity of things I want to say at once'. Everything seemed to him 'so ghastly a confusion and grotesque mistake and misery' that he felt he was on the edge of a breakdown; doubts, despondency and fierce rages shook him continually. Nothing that he had relied on could comfort him; art, landscape, love, had all betrayed him; 'I am left utterly stranded and alone in life and thought'.

Rose was increasingly ill, both mentally and physically. When it became clear that she was dying, Ruskin was allowed to see her again. Her derangement forced him for the first time to see what an enormous strain he had laid on this young thing; he felt guiltily that he should have left her alone. Her death, he said, was 'very bad' for him, and he retreated into a kind of childhood. 'It is so precious to me to be thought of as a child, needing to be taken care of', he wrote to the faithful Mrs Cowper-Temple. He got her cook to make jellies and blancmanges for him, so that he could pretend they were mountains, and make glaciers and 'terrific' crevasses. But he was a child who must be given his own way in everything; Coventry Patmore noticed how irritable he became at the slightest hint of contradiction. He insisted on buying a cottage near Sheffield to be used as a museum for workers – to deter visitors who were not genuinely interested, it was on the top of a steep hill. He poured random exhibits into it, and required the harassed curator to keep his catalogue up to date at all times. The St George's Guild accounts were always troublesome, because of Ruskin's unpredictable sales and purchases and, after their desperate pleas for information were met with a petulant 'I am doing a larch bud, and don't want to leave off', both trustees finally resigned.

Ruskin was continually preoccupied with his past, 'giddy with the lot of things that focus, now, out of past work'; he felt languid and despondent, alienated from the rest of humanity. In August of 1876 he went to Venice for nine months and here he really hovered on the edge of insanity. 'Such a state of hopeless confusion of letters, drawings and work . . . Everything brings a thousand old as well as new thoughts.' He went on to describe a scene too well known to relatives of psychotics: his room in total confusion, letters opened and unopened, manuscripts of four or five different books at different stages, unfinished drawings, unopened parcels, unsent packages, upset inkstands.

Since he had been told by a medium that Rose was always near him, he felt alternately elated at her nearness and depressed by his inability to bring order into his days; sleepless and haunted by 'terrific' dreams when he did doze off, he seems to have wandered incoherently about Venice. His readers could make nothing of his current *Fors* letter, and it began to be whispered that he was insane.

When he returned to Europe he was 'in a dream state . . . not knowing well what I was doing'. 'Messages one after another, crowding in, – so fast, so innumerably', he wrote in his diary on 20 February. On the night of 22 February (when he made the last entry in his diary until April) he was in a state of delusion. He was impelled by the devil to do 'some fearful wrong' (to masturbate), 'which I strove with all my might and main to resist. Every time I did wrong, I heard the voice of the Demon' (a peacock in the grounds outside) 'give a loud croak of triumph.' In order to be ready for an encounter with the devil he stripped naked and marched up and down his room. At dawn a large black cat – real or hallucinatory – jumped out from behind his mirror; he threw it 'with a dull thud' on the floor. In the morning he was found in a state of total derangement.

Doctors were called, chloral and hypophosphite were prescribed, with little effect. Ruskin was abusive to his 'dear Doanie', refused food and had to be forcibly fed, never slept, was restless, continually clapping his hands and raving, wrote his doctor, 'in the same clear voice and exquisite inflection of tone, the most unmeaning words'. He would sometimes attack his doctors, sometimes tenderly clasp their hands. His delusions were mostly paranoid; Joan was the cause of his insanity, had plotted with the Queen to have him murdered, until here he was lying dead in his coffin, and Joan would take over his house and money. He was not only the target of artillery, but himself fired into opera-houses and 'shot whole audiences dead'.

Other delusions were that every thousand years the Devil had to drive in a chariot race for the possession of the earth and that he always won because he knew a special way of overlapping. At another time Ruskin was convinced that a bishop had been sent to the centre of the earth to bring back false reports about the scriptures, but that huge mobs wanted to lynch him, and their screams of 'bishop him' were echoed by the birds outside his window. One 'most tormenting scene' was of a deep funnel, out of which emerged 'with bland assurance' a recently elected bishop, whom Ruskin alone knew to be a hypocrite. By some not-easy-to-follow train of ideas, these scenes led Ruskin to 'a terrible impression of my failure in duty to my father, and of the pain I had caused him and my best friends'. The delusions gradually died away and at the end of the first week in April he was downstairs in his study again.

His doctor, Dr Simon, wrote to Eliot Norton: 'You know . . . all that has brought this dreadful disaster on him, – the utterly spendthrift way in which (with imagination less and less controlled by judgment) he has for these last years been at work with a dozen different irons in the fire – each enough to engage one average man's mind. And his emotions all the while as hardworked as his intellect'. But Ruskin's own idea of the origin of his illness was quite different. 'The doctors said that I went mad from overwork . . . *Mere* overwork and worry might soon have ended me, but it would not have driven me crazy.' 'In every case these illnesses were brought on . . . by acute mental suffering or misfortune . . . It is not the work, but the sorrowful interruptions of it that threw me.' Emotions, he said, 'of indignation, grief, controversial anxiety and vanity . . . are all of them as deadly to the body as poisonous air or polluted water.' In his case, the deadliest emotion was 'too much thinking about my dead Rose'.

Ruskin resigned the Slade Chair in November 1879, through 'ill-health'. In February 1880 he wrote a *Fors* letter about his recent illness and its causes. The physicians, he said, must deal with its medical causes and symptoms, but:

> there were some conditions of it which I knew better than they could; namely, first, the precise and sharp distinction between the state of morbid inflammation of brain which gave rise to false visions (whether in sleep, or trance, or waking, in broad daylight, with perfect knowledge of real things in the room, while yet I saw others that were not there) and the not morbid, however dangerous, state of more or less excited temper and too much quickened thought, which gradually led up to the illness, accelerating in action during the eight or ten days preceding the actual giving way of the brain . . . and yet, up to the transitional moment of first hallucination, entirely healthy, and in the full sense of the word, sane; just as the natural inflammation about a healing wound in flesh is sane, up to the transitional edge where it may pass at a crisis, into morbific, or even mortified substance. And this more or less inflamed, yet still perfectly healthy, condition of mental power may be traced by any watchful reader in *Fors*, . . . that manner of mental ignition or irritation being for the first time a great additional force, enabling me to discern more clearly, and say more vividly. . . .'

His doctors, he added, did not understand that his 'mental wounds' needed to be healed. 'All alike, in whom I had most trusted for help, failed me in this main work: some mocked at it, some pitied, some rebuked – all stopped their ears at the cry; and the solitude at last became too great to be endured. . . .'

In August 1878 Dr Simon was writing to Eliot Norton:

> I suspect that he is more irritable than formerly, and that he is conscious of readier mental fatigue . . . In his financial affairs, he is, I believe, resolute not to change his course; he will . . . entirely

exhaust his few remaining thousand pounds of cash, and will next, from time to time, part with Turners and other chattels while they last; and what *then*, God knows. And the difficulty in dealing with him in these matters does not now consist only in the old wilfulness and the inaccessibility to what you and I would consider 'commonsense' appeals, but ... by our consciousness that we are on very doubtful ground between the sanity and insanity of his mind ... Altogether the position is, I think, sad: and I have little hope of his being secure against very dark sequels.

In spite of Ruskin's own feeling that his breakdown had, at least in some elements, a healing function, the 'very dark sequels' were now to follow in steady succession during the years until his death. In September 1878 he wrote to an enquirer, 'I am far from well ... and I must be LET ALONE.' In 1879 he was not much better; on 17 March his hand was 'trembling with the excitement of the thoughts I have to deal with'. At the end of July he wrote to Mary Gladstone 'In my present state of illness, nearly every word anybody says, if I care for them, either grieves or astonishes me to an extent which puts me off my sleep, and off my work, and off my meat. . . .' In August, in diary entries over which he subsequently wrote the word 'insanity', he began to record 'diabolic' darkness and 'fiendish' weather, which signified to him the triumph of the devil: 'the sky's anger is all against *me*.' A visitor to Brantwood said that 'his distressed look showed that his brain was becoming clouded'.

The beginning of the next year was 'quite the most miserable I ever passed', and throughout 1880 he was discontented, languid and unable to concentrate; his writing was immensely digressive and he found it difficult to organise his thoughts. In 1881, after a month of sleepless nights, finding 'clear guidance' in continual random openings of the Bible, he broke down in the middle of February into a month of 'terrific delirium'. Joan was anxious that news of this fresh episode should not leak out, but Ruskin's behaviour was more erratic and violent than it had been in the earlier breakdown. He gave absurd orders to the servants, swore at them, smashed windows, refused to eat and then insisted on Joan bringing him food. When she did so, limping because she had a sprained ankle, he 'dashed it' all over her, swearing and forcing her out of the room. He was found setting out barefoot to go to

Ireland, or on his knees in the hall in expectation of a visit from Cardinal Manning; he shut the cook in his bedroom and was furious when she was released by the hungry household. It was found impossible to let him roam the house, and a 'trained attendant' was procured. He had hallucinations of dragons and spectres; he tried to get Rose to materialise; he thought he must be crucified in order to 'found a farther phase of Christianity', and that Rose would be 'as the Magdalene'. 'I CAN'T understand', he wrote despairingly to Rose's mother in August, 'how so extremely rational a person as I am can lose their wits, and still more, how they don't know they have lost them at the time. I do think that if I was to go crazy again for the *third* time I should know I was so.'

After this attack, Ruskin remained antagonistic to Joan and her husband, and sent them back to their London home. His secretary, Laurence Hilliard, wrote to Norton in October: 'He seems more and more to find a difficulty in keeping to any settled train of thought or work, and it is sad to see him entering almost daily upon new schemes which one cannot feel will ever be carried out. . . . The influence of those around him is now very small, and has been so ever since the last illness.' He had begun again his lavish expenditure of money on books and *objets d'art*, and his extreme irritability, even in correspondence, had returned. Finding his solitude at Brantwood unendurable, he joined Joan and her family in London, where he became for the third time insane. Joan was pregnant, and professional nurses had to be called in to look after Ruskin.

This third attack 'alarmed and stupefied' him, as did the rapid depletion of his funds. He was forced to send a cherished Meissonier painting to Christie's, in order to pay for extensions at Brantwood and a trip abroad (in which he was greatly disappointed). He was often perverse and irrational, and became increasingly touchy in personal relationships. He had been, at his own suggestion, re-elected to the Slade Professorship again in 1883, but his lectures, though well attended (probably because of rumours of his odd behaviour) were fiercely and vituperatively idiosyncratic. Some of his audience were scandalised and some amused. He was too discursive, improvised freely, was embarrassingly emotional and sometimes could not fill in the allotted hour. The press referred to 'this academic farce', and *The World* appealed for 'some kindly and benevolent veto' to be placed on 'these ignoble antics'.

Ruskin was at least well enough to begin his autobiography, but looking over old diaries and letters made him 'desperately sad'. He began to have nightmares again, and suffered his fourth breakdown, far more severe than the other three; hallucinations, delusions, paranoia, violent abuse, followed by paralysing depressive inertia went on for months. Joan found it imperative to impose some control on his correspondence – he was required to dictate his letters – and on his spending, for his own good and to save his reputation, but he bitterly resented this, and took to calling Joan 'the dragon'. He complained of 'persistent illness – feebleness of thought – and feverish disturbances of the nerves'. In 1886 he had another 'fit of craze' throughout the whole of July, which left him in a state of extreme irritability for months. He had for some time been roaming round the schools near Coniston, and now he began to invite many of the girls to Brantwood for lessons, games and tea on Saturday afternoons. Some parents were anxious, and so was Joan, and after Ruskin proposed to adopt one of the girls, it was decided that his association with the children should stop altogether. This caused fierce quarrels and 'black rages' on Ruskin's part. 'We ought to have always our own way', he wrote furiously, ' – to have no scruples whatever about taking it when we can get it – to be able to kiss anybody whenever we like. . . .' In May 1887 he left Brantwood in one of his rages and went to the Waterhead Hotel in Coniston. There he sent for a local lawyer, Albert Fleming, who was a fervent disciple of his; but his London solicitor, annoyed by Fleming's trying to take over the care of Ruskin, wrote that he had heard 'some very unpleasant rumours' from local magistrates, who 'were resolved that if any complaint came before them, to treat our friend exactly as they would any other person in a similar case'. He warned Fleming that 'prison or a lunatic asylum may be the end of it'. Fleming must ensure that 'no such visitor as could be mixed up with the subject referred to in your letter passes the threshold of his house, and that he has with him a suitable companion whenever he crosses it himself'.

It is evident that for his own safety a complete embargo had to be placed on any association with children. His publisher was willing to lend him money, but stopped doing so when he found it was all being given to 'other people'. It was evidently best for Ruskin to leave Coniston for a while, and in August he travelled south with his valet Baxter. They stayed in Sandgate till May 1888, where Ruskin managed to become infatuated with, and propose marriage to a seventeen-year-old. In spite of not being allowed access to his cheque-book, he bought clothes and model boats, took music lessons, deluged Joan with requests for money and generally behaved as though he still had a wealthy father who would finance all his wishes. But he was ill and confused; an old friend meeting him at an exhibition of water-colours reported that 'there are moments when he does not seem to know what is being said, nor who the speakers are'.

In July 1888 Ruskin set off for Geneva with a courageous young friend, Detmar Blow, whom he liked because Blow obeyed all his orders. But by the time they reached the lake of Thun, Blow realised that he needed help, and they returned at once to Paris, where Ruskin had another episode of psychosis, with delusions and fits of uncontrollable trembling. He was taken back to Brantwood, where he soon collapsed into total breakdown. The mainspring of his mind was now gone, although he was only seventy. He could take little walks, occasionally chat in a confused way with old friends, but his life was effectively over. He died of influenza in 1900.

It is not possible, in a short study of this kind, to assess Ruskin's work for its 'psychotic' content. Certainly most of his immense output has a wild personal exuberance, unusual even in the wild and exuberant Victorian era. His huge proliferation of themes is typically 'psychotic': *Modern Painters*, begun as a pamphlet, swelled into three volumes, and the later *Fors* letters become incoherent in the attempt to trap and enclose the wildly proliferating thoughts: 'Oh me! I had so much to tell you in this *Fors*, if I could but get a minute's peace.' He derived relief, he said, from violent language, and thought that if he veiled it in 'wild inconsequent humour' his readers might not notice his lack of control; so we get such expressions as 'You helpless sots and simpletons! Can't you at least manage to set your wives – what you have got of them – to brew your beer?' 'You fools everywhere!' 'You carnivorous cheats. . . !' Of course there was widespread unease about his uncontrolled ravings; one of his girl readers wrote that people were saying that he was mad, 'really, really mad'. He admitted, 'If I took the Harlequin's mask off for a moment, you would say I was simply mad.' He could not restrain himself in these letters from publishing his most intimate concerns and his most private speculations.

The *Fors* letters were scribbled off at white-hot speed. In his books, which were presumably subjected to some authorial or editorial revision, we do not find such reckless candour or such wild revelations, but there are many signs of abnormal responses, especially after 1869. *The Queen of the Air*, published in that year, shows a complete inability to concentrate on its subject, Greek mythology, and often slides off to Ruskin's obsession with snakes. His conviction that he was always right led him to begin a crusade of social and economic reform 'without reflection or knowledge or judgment', and indeed even his early books of art criticism or history often went directly against the facts. He did not shrink from exposing his most private concerns, the spirit-messages from Rose, personal letters, his delusions about the cosmic struggle of the elements – all went into *Fors*: '. . . conditions of storm and of physical darkness, such as never before in Christian times, are developing themselves, in connection also with forms of loath-some insanity. . . .' His readers were left in no doubt as to the apocalyptic nature of his message: 'I stand . . . alone in conviction, in hope and in resolution, in the wilderness of this modern world . . . I have yet this message again entrusted to me.' But his inner confusion was also shared with them: 'I am miserable because I am always wanting to be something else than I am. I want to be Turner; I want to be Gainsborough; I want to be Samuel Prout; I want to be Doge of Venice; I want to be Pope; I want to be Lord of the Sun and Moon. The other day, when I read that story in the papers about the dog-fight, I wanted to be able to fight a bull-dog.'

The psychotic mind, not so much rambling, as exploding with discursiveness, every thought proliferating hydra-headed into others which in their turn give birth to more, is shown in his work from its earliest beginnings. He refers to 'the eddies of thought which turned the main stream of my discourse into apparent irrelevant and certainly unprogressive inlets', and these 'eddies' may be perceived throughout his work, in continual asides such as, 'Are crocodiles afraid of crocuses?'

Ruskin's diaries record his sleepless nights, his 'quite terrific' nightmares and 'disorderly and discreditable' dreams, often of Medusa-like serpents, of children being used for food, of hands with holes in them, of St Gotthard precipices crumbling under him like sugar, of being a small girl in the power of a sorcerer – sleeplessness and nightmares always occurring in the period before complete breakdown. They also record (as do some of the *Fors* letters) his extreme hypersensitivity at these times to sounds that he normally ignored or found pleasing. The church bells that in the Swiss valleys had been 'a sweet sound' became in Venice 'a reckless discord . . . as if rung by devils to defy and destroy the quiet of God's sky . . . filthy stridulous shrieks and squeals.' The whistle of a boat, the steady calling of a cow for her calf, made him feel, 'Deafness would be a mercy to me.' Once, 'a hideous sound I cannot describe, a prolonged malignant yell, broke from the sky and seemed to fill the earth. I stopped my ears and ran indoors, but the sound followed to the innermost chambers . . . It . . . ended with a kind of spasm and howl that made every nerve shudder.' It was a steam-whistle from a foundry miles away from Coniston.

Diary entries also show his continual anxiety about his eyes in the period before a breakdown. His first complaints about his eyesight occurred at the time of his original breakdown at Oxford; they recurred whenever he was in a similar state of health. 'My eyes hinder me'; 'attack of sight failure after breakfast'; 'eyes weak and quivering'; 'eyes swimming a little in the bad way'; 'my failing sight plagues me; I cannot look at anything as I used to do, and the evening is covered with swimming strings and eels'. That these complaints were nothing to do with any real defect in his sight is shown by his claim in 1883, in one of his stable periods, that 'I see everything far and near . . . as few men my age.'

Ruskin's life and work were influenced by his psychotic episodes. His hyper-activity led to his immense output; it also led, in the later years, to numbers of projects, worthy and absurd, beginning in an access of wild enthusiasm and then being abandoned as some new scheme caught his interest. The proliferation of thought, the 'lateral thinking' and continual cross-referencing of his mind, gave his work a florid discursiveness which at last he himself could not control and which broke down into a frenzied grasping after the multifarious currents which crowded into and struggled to escape from his brain. The speed of his thought, too, made him impatient with all exact scholarship, with any checks on his exuberance and hasty formation of theories which had no basis in fact. His unbalanced dogmatism, his conviction that he could not be wrong, led him to make ludicrous statements in the face of all evidence to the contrary, and caused the break-up of many friendships, so that at last he was driven to say: Pictures are my friends. I have none others. I am never long enough with men to attach myself to them.'

Case Description

At first glance John Ruskin is relatively easy to evaluate from a diagnostic point of view, apparently presenting as a classic case of manic-depressive psychosis of which he showed all the typical features, including the cycling of mood between extremes of elation and despair. In manic phases – which he described as 'happiness and elation totally different from all my ordinary states of mind' – he hardly slept, was irritable, distractable, sexually disinhibited and grossly hyperactive, roaming 'giddy and wild' around the countryside. Thought and speech were corresponding-ly speeded up: 'Messages one after another crowding in so fast – so innumerably.' Grandiosity, another feature typical of the manic, was also evident, in his exaggerated belief that it was his destiny to convert the world from materialism; and, more bizarrely, that during one of his breakdowns he had single-handedly destroyed the Devil (actually the household cat). Phases of depression brought the opposite: a slump into 'utter hopelessness – a real pure despair', with all of the attendant symptoms of lost appetite, inertia, great inability to concentrate, total loss of interest in his usual intense preoccupations and self-criticism (the feeling that his first breakdown was a punishment for his vanity and selfishness).

Despite so definitely meeting the SADS-L criteria for manic-depression, Ruskin also scored on certain items relating to schi-zophrenia. Some of his writings, discussed again in Chapter 10, certainly show the disorganised qualities typical of schizophrenic language. He also suffered both visual and auditory hallucinations, felt himself to be under the influence of an alien force (the Devil), was at times grossly deluded, and was extremely paranoid (on one occasion he even left his own house in fear for his safety). Taken overall, the clinical picture we observe in Ruskin does illustrate the arbitrariness of distinguishing manic-depression (except as a con-venient label) from schizophrenia. The general psychotic nature of Ruskin's illnesses is not, however, in doubt.

8

The Beast Behind the Hedge

A. C. BENSON (1862–1925)

Arthur Benson felt a great affinity with Ruskin, and in 1911, after he had recovered from a major breakdown lasting from 1907 to 1909, he wrote *Ruskin, A Study in Personality*. It may have been partly in an attempt to exorcise the memory of his own trauma that he so conspicuously sweetened and softened his account of Ruskin's psychotic episodes, although of course the sources on which he relied were carefully censored for public consumption. Insanity was still a shameful affliction, and was presented as neurasthenia, the ubiquitous 'brain disease', or nervous trouble. Ruskin, says Benson, lost the balance of his mind through continuous delirium 'arising from some obscure inflammation of the brain', which arose in its turn from overwork. By steadily refusing every kind of work or mental exertion, he was at the end of his life 'rewarded by a tranquillity of life and spirit which he had never before enjoyed'. Benson grasped eagerly at Collingwood's words that Ruskin's friends 'in those trials learnt as they could not otherwise have learnt to know him, and to love him as never before'.

Benson recognised the similarity of Ruskin's illnesses to his own. He might well have been describing his own symptoms when he wrote, 'There had been definite premonitory symptoms. The only thing that might have shown him where he was drifting was rapid alteration of intense excitement, accompanied by vivid dreams and unnatural restlessness, with periods of intense depression'. Yet he was impelled to write, against all the evidence: 'He is often spoken of as having been mad. That is not at all the case. He had no fixed delusion, no insane preoccupation.' It was vital to him to believe that Ruskin's attacks did no damage, and that 'he was in many ways happier and more tranquil in the intervals than he had been before'.

157

Arthur Benson is now known only as the man who wrote the words to *Land of Hope and Glory*, but in his own time he was a prolific and popular author; so popular, indeed, that importunate ladies frequently proposed marriage, and one donated a large fortune to him. Of more than fifty books, only those which deal with his family, friends and relations are of interest for their content; his poems, novels, literary studies, and the volumes of mildly sentimental maunderings which won him his popularity are interesting only because they show one side of his curiously dual personality. 'One side of him', said his brother E. F. Benson, 'was the gentle, musing, meditative man his readers knew'; the other was loud-voiced, aggressive, domineering and wickedly observant. This persona was the writer of a remarkable diary of more than four million words, kept continuously from his thirty-fifth year until the year of his death at the age of sixty-three. Only the four years of his major breakdowns are unrecorded. Using books and diaries it would be possible to construct a biography of Arthur Benson entirely in his own words.

Arthur and his brother Hugh during the course of a holiday in Yorkshire put together a genealogy of the three families from that county from whom their own family (and that of their mother) derived. There had been intermarriages among Bensons, Sidgwicks and Jacksons. Arthur's great-grandfather had married a first cousin; his father and his maternal grandmother were cousins. He remarked on 'the curious decrease of so large a family, consisting of so many long-lived people'. None of his brothers and sisters married, and when the last survivor, E.F., died in 1942, he had no relations nearer than second cousins. There had been a good many histories of insanity, depression, financial irresponsibility and general eccentricity in all three families, and Arthur thought it a good thing that the family was dying out. After visiting his sister Maggie, who was incurably insane, he wrote in his diary: '. . . the knowledge of Maggie's weakness, and how certainly derived it was from papa, and my own tendencies, make it clear to me *why* we are coming, as a stock, to an end – and I don't think it would be *right* to prolong it.'

It may not have been only from 'papa' that Maggie's insanity was inherited. Her mother, Mary Sidgwick, came of a family with psychotic and depressive characteristics. Mrs Sidgwick had severe depressions; two at least of her sons underwent manic or depressive episodes, and Mary herself had breakdowns after the births of her two youngest children. Arthur describes his uncle William Sidgwick as having a serious illness 'brought on by overwork', and as being afterwards prone to 'long fits of silent depression, varied by intervals of almost perilously high spirits', with 'brilliant ideas and sudden impulses, which he seldom had the patience to carry out'.

Edward White Benson, Arthur's father, had fearful moods of depression, of which Arthur wrote: 'I never knew anyone whose moods . . . so affected the spirits of the circle by which he was surrounded.' They were of two kinds: moods in which he was convinced that he was a failure, when he required constant sympathy and reassurance, and moods of fierce and resentful silence, in which no-one could do anything right. If his family tried to be cheerful, they would be devastatingly reproved; if they were silent, they would be asked if their father was not good enough for them to talk to.

His marriage to Mary Sidgwick had not, perhaps, even apart from their fairly close consanguinity, been a very wise one. Edward had, while a master at Rugby, stayed with his widowed cousin, and there had fallen in love with her twelve-year-old daughter. The child was intimidated by her severe and passionate lover, and was married to him when she was 17, without being in love or sexually attracted to him. Six children were born in eleven years. Edward was both wildly anxious about money and given to sudden extravagances, followed by frenzied economies. He would take the whole family on a holiday abroad, 'and then practise an elaborate species of discomfort, in an earnest endeavour to save some minute disbursements'. He would have a tennis-court laid out for the children, and then force them to mark it out with tape and hairpins, and to play with wooden bats. Mary, on the other hand, was carelessly extravagant, and never to the end of her life managed to stay within her more than adequate income. Edward was masterful, domineering, hyperactive and given to fierce rages; Mary was indolent, propitiatory and given to falling in love with younger women. Such a couple was not likely to have a happy marriage, since they were in every way unsuited to each other; and the children of such an ill-assorted pair were subject to all the strains and repercussions of the marriage.

Edward and Mary were not much more satisfactory as parents than as spouses, and had besides contradictory and opposing ideas of discipline. Edward was passionately attached to his children, but they all feared him, and were never at ease with him, said Arthur, 'because he rebuked them constantly, and found frequent fault . . . not from any pleasure in censoriousness, but from a terror, that was almost morbid, of the consequences of the unchecked development of minute tendencies'. 'As a child, the one thing I was afraid of was the possibility of my father's displeasure. . . . This descended upon me as a cloud of darkness. . . . There was an element of injustice in his rebukes, which one merely accepted, as part of his awful and unaccountable greatness.'

Mary Benson, on the other hand, always at odds with her husband, not of much help to him in his exacting task as first Master of Wellington College, absorbed in her infatuations with local young women, was kind to her children when she was with them but left them largely to the care of the old nurse, Elizabeth Cooper, who had been her own nurse. 'I had a devoted admiration for my mother', said Arthur, but it was his nurse whom he loved 'intensely'. The children were in any case probably not much aware of their mother in their first years, since her six pregnancies would have involved a good deal of lying on the sofa, and of being confined to her bedroom for weeks after the birth. Mary never found conjugal relations pleasant ('Oh, the nights! How did I ever live through them!' she wrote long afterwards in her journal). After the birth of E.F. she had a long depressive interlude, when she went to be nursed by friends in Lincoln for several months. After her last child Hugh was born, four years later, she had a prolonged breakdown, and was sent away to her brother-in-law in Germany; even when she was well again, she continually delayed her return, and probably sexual relations with her husband were never resumed. There is evidence that he himself was in a state of breakdown while she was away. Even after she came back to England she did not go home to her children but stayed with her mother for some time.

Arthur's memories of his life at Wellington were not unhappy, but they were all memories of solitary occupations. Although his elder brother Martin was only two years older, they were never companions. Arthur loved to roam about looking at things and finding hiding-places for small collections of treasured objects. (In fact this was a habit of all the Benson brothers, who made 'caches' well into old age.) His early life was, like Ruskin's, mainly spectatorial; it had been, he wrote of himself in a barely-disguised autobiography, 'one more of perception than of anything else;

sights and sounds and scents had filled his mind, to the exclusion of almost all besides'. And indeed he felt that Ruskin was 'the only writer who has described what was precisely my own experience, when he says that as a child he lived almost entirely in the region of *sight*'. His visual perception, like Ruskin's, was unusually vivid; he could, he said, at any time of his life, walk in memory through the gardens at Wellington, recalling 'the minutest details with an astonishing accuracy'. He was timid and unadventurous, middle-aged while still a small child, with an intense dislike of the unknown and unfamiliar, wanting only not to be interfered with, to be left to the daily round of his small affairs. People were only a part of the background of life to him, and it did not occur to him that he would feel any grief if his parents died: 'The strange thing is, that in thinking of it all, I seem always to have been *alone*.'

It is clear to us, though probably it never was to Arthur, that unconsciously he feared and hated the fierce emotions raging round his parents' marriage, and that his chief aim throughout his life was to avoid deep feeling. His love for his old nurse was probably his strongest, and certainly his most constant, feeling; it never changed and it never threatened. Until he went to school at the age of ten, he led two separate lives. While nominally under his mother's care (for Beth would have been occupied with the younger children) he was allowed to roam at will through the huge grounds of Wellington, which contained lawns, flower and vegetable gardens, orchards, lakes and a wilderness, and also through the heath-lands round Sandhurst and Crowthorne. Such freedom, amounting to neglect, was not without its dangers. The heathery scrub was full of vipers and trenches too deep for a child to climb out of unaided, and in one of the lakes Arthur would once have drowned had not a distant gardener heard his cries. But Mary Benson seems to have been unaware of possible hazards to her children. Edward, on the other hand, was only too aware – of moral dangers even more than of physical. When the children were with him every word, every slightest action, came under his unremitting scrutiny, and only too often under his stern reproof. Mary read her children wild romantic books like *Ivanhoe* and *Phantastes*; Edward insisted on their reading improving books such as *Philosophy in Sport*, 'where', said Arthur bitterly, 'the poor boy cannot even throw a stone without having the principles of the parabola explained to him, with odious diagrams'. It was no wonder that the children became in their father's presence wooden dolls, practising 'a sort of diplomacy', careful only to say what would win his approval.

It was probably this continuous and over-riding fear of his father that made Arthur, though large and strong for his age, an unusually timid child. Terror was apt to leap out at him even in his securest haunts. The two towers of the College seemed to follow him 'with hollow melancholy eyes'; there was a particular gravel path which he must avoid because it was 'terrible'; there was a picture of an owl on the nursery wall which he could not look at, and an even more dreadful picture in a *Penny Magazine* of an old saint being menaced by a fiend, which terrified him so much that he could not speak of it, and never afterwards dared to open any of the bound volumes of that periodical for fear of seeing it again. Even at the age of twelve he was still subject to these irrational fears; he saw a ram pumping water, and rushed to his mother screaming that he had seen a man trying to escape from drowning.

Being sent to school was a sickening shock to the child, more because he grieved for his beloved home terrain than because he regretted leaving his family. He had adequate food at school, and was not bullied, but to Arthur it was detestable, 'a place of terrors and solitude', where his only aim was to avoid notice, and be as inoffensive as he could. He made no friends and no enemies, since his father's warnings about 'all sorts of impossible contingencies' made him feel that 'no one could be trusted for an instant, the only safe course was to make no claim, and shield oneself as far as possible against all external influences, all alliances, all relationships'. When the time came to leave, he felt nothing but 'unconquerable relief'.

He won a scholarship to Eton, and by his last two years there was enjoying himself. He was good at football and athletics and made several friends; he even fell timidly in love. But he came to feel that his schooldays had been marred by his parents' obsession with keeping 'all the evil and second-rate and hurtful things' away from him, to such an extent that they succeeded in keeping all the good things away too. 'Much as they would have liked an omelette, they dared not break the eggs'.

While he was at Eton, something happened that was to change his life. His elder brother Martin died at Winchester. Edward Benson was pierced to the heart by this loss of the dearest of his children, and turned to his second son as a substitute for his first. Arthur became an uneasy companion to his father, always aware of his own inability to comfort ('How trivial I was!'), and never able to break away from his childish fear and awe. He could never be the confident friend that Martin had been, able to meet his father on equal terms of scholarship and scholarly pursuits. At last Edward abandoned his attempt to create a replacement for Martin, and turned to his youngest son Hugh, leaving Arthur permanently scarred with a sense of his own utter inadequacy.

He went up to King's College, Cambridge, in 1881, and on 9 November 1882 there occurred what he was ever after to call 'my great anniversary', 'my great misfortune', 'the greatest and most sudden blow that ever befell me'. What happened is shrouded in mystery, though Arthur made opaque references to it in his diary, in the novel which he published pseudonymously in 1886, *The Memoirs of Arthur Hamilton B.A.*, and in some of his other books, particularly in *The House of Quiet*. It seems that a friend whom he had adored at Eton showed himself to be 'utterly corrupted', to Arthur's horror. It is possible that the unnamed friend made homosexual overtures, and that Arthur partly yielded, or at least was tempted. In a late book, *Where No Fear Was*, he wrote of how parents would warn a child going to school about dangers he did not understand, 'And then, long afterwards perhaps, when he has made a mistake and is suffering for it, he sees that it was *that* of which they spoke, and wonders that they could not have explained it better.' Later, in the same book, he wrote of how boys 'go astray, they give up some precious thing – their innocence perhaps – to a deluding temptation ... Neither is it always annulled, even in length of days.'

Whatever the cause, he experienced that night 'a crisis of dereliction' so intense that the very walls of his room seemed afterwards 'soaked with suffering'. In *Beside Still Waters* he described his condition:

Thoughts raced through his mind, scenes and images forming and re-forming with inconceivable rapidity; at last he fell asleep to awake an hour or two later in an intolerable agony of mind. His heart beat thick and fast, and a shapeless horror seemed to envelop him, ... a ghastly and poisonous fear of he knew not what, seemed to clutch at his mind. ... When he rose in the morning, he knew that some mysterious evil had befallen him. ... His suffering appeared to be of so purely mental a character, that he did not realise how much of it was physical.

Later, 'a fierce blackness of depression' settled on him, and 'he became possessed by a strong delusion that it was a punishment sent him by God'. He read the Bible continually, making marks whenever a quotation impressed him as relating to his own case, and soon became convinced that he was beyond recovery. He laboured under 'an agonising dejection of spirit', and the intensity of his suffering 'seemed to shake his very life to its foundations'. Years afterwards he was to write: 'I have often thought I was nearly out of my mind – and have certainly never quite recovered it.'

It is clear from the similarity of these symptoms to those of his later breakdowns that this was the first of his major psychotic episodes. He could not shake off the memory of that November night. 'I have often thought', he wrote in another of his barely fictional autobiographies, 'how strangely and secretly the crucial moment, the most agonising crisis of my life . . . drifted upon me. No day was so fraught for me with fate, no hour so big with doomful issue. The current of my days fell . . . into the weltering gulf of despair.' He felt like 'a wounded creature, who must crawl into solitude', beset by every nervous misery known to man – 'intolerable depression, spectral remorse, nocturnal terrors'. His diary suggests that he may for a short time have been admitted to the mental hospital at Fulbourn. Even when the first horrors had subsided, he fell into a state of 'melancholy quiescence', although even into his purposeless days the 'accursed foe' would leap without warning. Once as he waited with a friend by a level crossing, 'came upon me with a flash an almost irresistible temptation to lay my head beneath the ponderous wheels, and end it all'.

Very gradually the 'aching frost of the soul' thawed, but the long depressive periods remained. In February 1885 Arthur wrote in his diary, 'For more than two years . . . I think it is not an exaggeration to say that I have not had one happy day.' Although he once said that all her children could take to Mary Benson any question or difficulty or speculation 'with complete reliance on her sympathy and understanding', he does not seem to have breathed a word to his family about his condition. His home was now at Lambeth Palace, for his father, after a stint as Chancellor of the diocese of Lincoln, had been appointed first Bishop of Truro and in 1883 had swept on to the See of Canterbury. Lambeth was more a place of Pan-Anglican conferences, meetings of Synod, garden-parties for rural clergy and huge state dinner-parties than a home for the family. Arthur never felt at ease there. At Addington, the Archbishop's country mansion near Croydon, he might have found some remnants of the old family life, but it was inseparably connected for him with his father's low spirits, for the Archbishop on holiday pined for the work he had come to Addington to get away from and required constant amusement and attention to distract him from his bored repinings.

Edward's dearest wish for all his sons was that they should take Holy Orders. Arthur, though he never completed more than Part One of the Tripos (and took three years to do that) went back to King's in the autumn of 1884 to read, as he bitterly put it, 'enough theology to very nearly wreck my religion'. But before the academic year was finished, he was asked to take up a temporary teaching post at Eton, and in order to gain a breathing-space while he looked around to find his real vocation, he accepted. He was to stay at Eton for twenty years, although he never felt that teaching came naturally to him, and he despised many of his colleagues and was at odds with most Etonian policies. If he had any strong wish, it was to write 'feebly imaginative' books. He only partly succeeded in this aim; many of his books were feeble, but very few were imaginative.

For three years he got on reasonably well. He liked some of the younger staff, and parents were keen to have their sons taught by a son of the Archbishop, but Arthur did not consider himself a permanent member of the teaching staff. In 1888 he applied for a Fellowship at King's, with a hastily-thrown-together and unscholarly book on Archbishop Laud. His rejection left him with a lasting grudge against King's. Perhaps this failure contributed to the return of insomnia and deep depression in the summer of that year. 'The curse was on me', he wrote, when he heard in October of the sudden death of his sister Nellie from diphtheria. Nellie had been, he thought, the best of the Bensons, 'gay, adventurous, brave'. She had also been the one person he could talk to about his depression, because she suffered from it to some extent herself, 'that overshadowing of the spirit which is so much harder to bear than physical pain'.

Nellie had been the one who kept the family together, arranging holiday occupations, directing theatricals at Christmas; the only one who was able to ignore the Archbishop's moods and grievances and coax him back to some semblance of normality. Now that she was gone, the Bensons tended rather to retreat into their separate worlds. Sorrow and unavailing regret for her death were added to the cloud of darkness which hung over Arthur. He managed to go on doing his job, and he had one or two holidays in which the cloud seemed to lift a little, but at the end of 1895 he concluded that the years had gone past in acute and deadly depression, '. . . and I record it as my deliberate feeling that I would rather at any time die than live. The whole thing is a heavy enigma. Why should I be born, reared, given a contented temperament with certain definite aptitudes and inclinations, and then pushed, miserable and reluctant, along this stony path?' His parents were urging him to marry – his father especially longed for grandchildren – but Arthur was appalled at the idea. 'It would be *criminal* even to run the risk of handing to another my own miserable disposition – and to admit another into the torture-chamber which I call my life.' Even if his life had not been a torture-chamber, it is unlikely that he would have married. His erotic (or, since he shuddered at the idea of a sexual relationship, his romantic) inclinations were for pretty young men.

The Archbishop had not been well for some time, but his response to the pains in the chest for which he had been ordered to rest and diet was to thump his chest vigorously and work even harder. In October 1896 he died suddenly of a heart-attack. His sons may have feared, even hated, their father, but he had been unquestionably the most dominating figure in their lives (and was, in one sense, to remain so in Arthur's life). Arthur felt 'a sense of ineffectual sorrow such as he had never known before', and thought he might be going to have a breakdown; but in fact his father's death seemed to have a liberating effect on him. He was often 'fretful and wearied', he could be irritable and demanding, he could not bear his daily routine to be altered, but there were no more severe depressions for ten years.

During those years he was a successful Housemaster and got on well with his boys, especially with those to whom he was attracted, but he became increasingly disenchanted with Eton. He found the work soul-destroying, the teaching of classics, which comprised most of the syllabus, dull and useless, and he loathed the increasing glorification of games and athletics. His writing became the outlet for these and other frustrations, and, like many habits that bring relief and relaxation, it grew into a compulsion. He set aside two hours out of every day, no matter how heavy his workload: 'when the sacred hour comes, I sit down to write with an appetite, a keen rapture, such as a hungry man may feel when he sits down to a savoury meal'. From 1886 to 1903, when he left Eton, he had composed or edited twelve books and from then until his major breakdown in 1908 another sixteen. Besides these, he had edited three volumes of the letters of Queen Victoria, and written a two-volume life of his father. (He hated drudgery, so he called on many people to help him with these; his sister Maggie wrote many chapters of the *Life*, and checked and rewrote many others. This may be why it is considered Arthur's masterpiece.) He could fill anything up to twenty-two volumes of his diary in a year. Like Ruskin, he ceased to write only during the depths of a major breakdown.

When he was recommended for the selection and editing of the royal letters, he seized the opportunity to leave Eton, with some regret but more relief, and went to live in Cambridge. Here he found himself rather lonely until he suggested to his former colleague Stuart Donaldson, then Master of Magdalene, that he might become a Fellow without stipend. Magdalene was a rather poor and neglected little College at that time, but even so Arthur had some difficulty in getting elected; many of the Fellows expressed reservations about his having taken only Part One of the Tripos. His Eton colleagues thought his election mere jobbery, and humiliated him by not wanting him on the Governing Body; but still he was enormously gratified by his Fellowship, which exactly suited his needs. He had some undemanding teaching, plenty of attractive young undergraduates to worship, colleagues to bicker with, companions who would allow themselves to be quarrelled with to accompany him on walking and cycling holidays, and (what was very dear to his heart) some academic status. His mother and sister were now living in a beautiful old manor-house called Tremans near the Ashdown Forest, where Arthur could spend weekends and vacations. His life seemed to contain everything he could want or need.

And yet it was during this halcyon period that he published *The House of Quiet*. It appeared anonymously as the autobiography of 'a temperament without robustness and *joie de vivre*', written 'for all whose life seemed dashed into fragments'. In a later foreword, when his flabby and sentimental style made anonymity impossible, he pretended that the apparent writer was an imaginary character, but it is recognisably Arthur himself who describes his own schooldays and his later breakdown and depressions. One chapter, about his depressive moods, was, he said, spoken to the initiated, 'those who have gone down into the dark cave, and seen the fire burn low in the shrine, and watched aghast the formless mouldering things . . . that hang upon the walls'. It describes 'living under the shadow of fear', a boding, misshapen, sullen dread which has no definite cause. These moods are 'preluded by dreams of a singular kind, dreams of rapid and confused action' and 'of a romantic and exaggerated pictorial character – huge mountain ranges, lofty and venerable buildings, landscapes of incredible beauty, gardens of unimaginable luxuriance, which pass with incredible rapidity before the mind'. The dreams themselves are in no way threatening, but as they draw to a close:

> into the dream falls a sudden sense of despair, like an ashen cloud; a feeling of incredible agony, intensified by the beauty of the surrounding scene. . . . Then the vision closes, and for a time the mind battles with dark waves of anguish, emerging at last . . . into the waking consciousness. . . . The first thought is one of unutterable relief, which is struck instantly out of the mind by the pounce of the troubled mood; and then follows a ghastly hour, when every possibility of horror and woe intangible presses in upon the battling mind. . . . It can only be silently endured, like the racking of some fierce physical pain. The day that succeeds to such a waking mood is almost the worst part of the experience . . . the accursed mood leaps again as from an unseen lair, upon the unnerved consciousness, and tears like some strange beast the helpless and palpitating soul.

Although the narrator purports to be recalling his experiences at Cambridge more than twenty years earlier, it is only too evident how very fresh those experiences remain. Arthur here admits, for the only time in his published work, that he contemplated suicide. Perhaps it was dangerous to recall those memories; perhaps he was forced to re-live them, for he had a sense of things going wrong. His house in Cambridge was too noisy, many of the other dons irritated him, his usually pleasant holiday trips had been disappointing, his friends' talk wearied him. At Tremans he quarrelled with his brothers and his moods changed alarmingly and rapidly. He felt that he needed to be alone, and in the summer of 1906 moved into a remote Fenland house called Hinton Hall. He immediately filled it with relays of friends, but after the summer vacation was over he fell into low spirits. 'If I can't be happy here, where can I be? . . . I like solitude, and it does not suit me.' In *The Upton Letters* and *The Thread of Gold*, both published in 1905, there had been references to 'confused and troubled dreams of terror and bewilderment, enacted in blind passages and stifling glooms', and to the 'old enemy's' clutches'. 'I lay in a strange agony of mind, my heart beating thick, and with an insupportable weight on my heart.' In *Beside Still Waters*, straight autobiography disguised as fiction, he dwelt once more, at greater length and in greater detail, on his Cambridge breakdown. He seemed to have some insight into his own nature and its effect on others. The narrator (strangely named Hugh) 'was incapable of pure idling; but he was also incapable of carrying out prolonged and patient labour'. 'He tended to concentrate his thoughts too much on himself; the sudden growth of egotism and introspection began to alarm his friends.' 'Other people were apt to regard the jealous arrangement of his hours as the mere whim of a self-absorbed dilettante.' And then, proleptically, the narrator falls ill for the second time: 'A lingering malaise . . . seemed to bereave him of all spring and energy'.

Arthur now had days of 'vile gloom'; he brooded constantly over his faults and failures, becoming hypochondriac and guilt-ridden. Was he like the rich man in the parable of Dives and Lazarus, awaiting punishment? His incessant writing tired him, but he could not do without it; the exercise he needed for his restlessness bored him; friends irritated him but he could not stand solitude. The 'wild beast', the 'black dog' that he envisaged always stalking him behind the hedge was almost ready to spring. Early in May 1907 he had to rush to Tremans because his sister Maggie had become insane.

Maggie had had rather a hard time since Nellie's death. She had done extraordinarily well at Oxford, and her tutors had forecast a brilliant future for her. But she had gone home to Lambeth, simply to help in the entertainment of eminent clergy and statesmen, which she found difficult because she was shy and had no small talk. She relied a great deal on her sister's spontaneous gaiety and social ability, but when Nellie died Maggie determined to take her place as far as she could. However, Lucy Tait, the daughter of the former Archbishop, came to live at Lambeth, to be a daughter to Edward and much more than a daughter to Mary Benson, with whom she was in love. Maggie found herself unnecessary to either of her parents, and perhaps rather a burden to them. There was a tendency on their part to hurry her abroad for her health and a tendency on her part to hurry home again because she was bored with spas and health resorts. When her father died and the family moved to Winchester, she began to edit and complete some of his work for publication, and became immersed in his letters and papers in order to help Arthur with the *Life*. She began to assume some of her father's characteristics; she became gloomy and domineering, apt to criticise and censure all activities not initiated and managed by herself. She was also only too evidently jealous of her mother's close association with Lucy, and Mary was less than tactful. While continually urging Maggie to have a life of her own, Mary did all she could to keep her daughter dependent and immature, writing to her daily when they were away from each other, requiring to know every detail of her life, especially about such things as her menstrual periods, and refusing to give her any information about sexual matters.

In 1905 Maggie became very discontented, and she and Arthur took to discussing their depressions a good deal. 'I remember', she wrote to him, 'the sickening imprisoned feeling of *desiring* solitude, and knowing that one was absolutely dependent on the people with whom depression had made one nervously at cross-purposes. . . . "All the earth is full of darkness and cruel habitation" is one of the things which used to ring in my head.' As 1906 began, Maggie had rapid mood changes, was irritable and fussy over small details, and worried over her own state of health. Her symptoms resembled Arthur's closely enough for him to be frantic when she collapsed. In February her depression became severe and she had a series of terrifying hallucinations, seeing people with animal faces: 'underlying darknesses and vilenesses, old animal inheritances and evil taints of blood', wrote Arthur shudderingly. She knew there was a figure standing behind her, waiting to strike; the world began to seem phantasmal, 'as if life were a confused cataract pouring into the void'. Then her world collapsed, and she with it.

Arthur was shattered, and did not know what to believe. The local doctor diagnosed cerebro-meningitis, which would probably prove fatal, the nurses called in to look after her said it was hysteria, 'an attempt to convince us she was worse than she thought we believed'. (Poor Maggie! It might well have been that, since her mother and Lucy Tait appeared to ignore her long suffering.) She was taken to a nearby nursing-home for the insane, and Arthur arranged to stay at Tremans for a week, or as long as he could stand it – 'a few bad nights and such pleasant reveries as mine this morning would soon embark me on the same course'. He felt that if he had been offered death at any time that week, he would have gladly accepted it. His waking hour every morning (always the worst hour of the day for him) was like a crucifixion, 'such misery of nerves and mind as I can hardly bear even to record'. He had to sign the papers for Maggie's committal, but felt better when a London specialist diagnosed her condition as 'blood-poisoning due to influenza'.

In August his mother virtually forced him to visit Maggie, when he was already feeling depressed. She herself was taking the carriage to within a few miles of the nursing-home, but claimed that it was impossible for her to call there. 'She doesn't like going', wrote Arthur in his diary, '– no wonder – and yet doesn't like to confess it – And wished to make out that it was my wish or plan that I should go.' He did go, but 'it was very bad, as bad as it could be'. Maggie was at her worst, full of delusions; she said that the nurses poisoned and tortured people, and, as though to bear out her statements, a woman screamed incessantly from the room below, and there were thumps and stamps from overhead. When Arthur bent to kiss Maggie goodbye, she whispered, 'This is a place of torture and living death – and the worst of it is that I am directly or indirectly responsible for it all.' It was more than Arthur in his precarious mental state could stand, and his mother, by insisting on talking of Maggie on his return, brought on 'the acutest nervous depression, formless panic, unreasoning dismay'. He had confused and terrifying dreams: 'the recollection of the interview, or the horrid screaming I heard, came into my mind with an intense terror – something seemed to crumble in my brain and clutch my heart – I thought I was going to die'.

He forced himself to visit Maggie once more. She had tried many times to kill herself; she tried strangling herself with a piece of string, and set the curtains of her room on fire. When Arthur saw her, she seemed to have 'drifted a long way on a silent tide', pale, haunted and exhausted. It was the last time he was to see her for five years. He managed to begin the new academic year at Cambridge, after making several holiday visits with moderate success, but on 2 October the deep depression returned. This time it was too bad to cope with on his own, and on the last day of the month he scrawled in his diary in pencil, 'Well, enough of this. I must enter into the battle.' He went into a Mayfair nursing-home, where he collapsed completely for three weeks.

His chief feeling was one of guilt. 'I saw my wretched, self-absorbed, indulgent life, chance after chance to be noble and good, thrown away . . . my future as, at the best, a broken and invalided shadow; and the present absolutely horrible.' He was prescribed change and travel with friends: he went to Aldeburgh where 'the sights and sounds of life fill me with horror, envy, dismay'. He went to Rome and Florence, to Buckingham Palace to receive the CVO for his editing of Queen Victoria's letters, back to Magdalene, but it was all of no use. In the middle of January 1908 he was admitted to the home of a Dr Caldicott at Hampstead, where he was to be cared for with other mentally ill patients. He was under supervision, but was allowed to go for dreary walks across the Heath and in the nearby streets. He looked constantly for messages and omens in street signs and shop windows, and was much upset by a piece of paper blown against his foot, with DOWN printed on it. Whenever he had a good day, the next day was sure to be one of unrelieved gloom. He had suicidal impulses; on the train to Tremans, 'I prayed to have courage to end my life. It seemed to me so easy to lean out and let myself be struck senseless by some bridge or signal post . . . but I knew I had not the physical courage.' On 28 July he wrote 'I was to all intents and purposes mad this morning'.

In despair he tried hypnotism at two guineas a time, but 'it was like trying to put out a fire with a drop of scent'. Nevertheless, there were fewer black days, and for some time he had 'a real sense of returning to life out of my hideous cage of suffering'. But in the summer of 1909, he was plunged to 'the nadir of wretchedness' again. He went to Harrogate, which he found 'like *Hell*', but during September he was undoubtedly getting better. He had some further sessions of hypnotism, and at last the nightmare was over.

Yet even when he was well, he was impelled to write about his illness, because he felt strongly that the 'wild beast' was merely waiting to spring out on him again. *The Altar Fire* is a study of a psychotic episode; 'the book deliberately gives a picture of a diseased spirit', says the preface. But once again it is allegedly the journal of a 'friend' who suffers from depression. The plot is melodramatic, about an author who loses fame, money, wife and both children, but all this merely serves as an excuse for long descriptions of Arthur's recent illness: 'My mind works like a mill with no corn to grind'; 'I cannot work, I cannot think. Nothing to bear, except a blank purposelessness which eats the heart out of me.' 'Can I not amuse myself with books, pictures, talk? No, because it is all a purposeless passing of dreary hours.' 'My nerveless brain seems losing its hold, slipping off into some dark confusion of sense.' 'I am often sleepless, or my sleep is filled with vivid, horrible, intolerable dreams. I wake early in the clutch of fear . . . I have all sorts of unmanning sensations, dizzinesses, tremors; I have that dreadful sensation that my consciousness of things and people around me are [sic] slipping away from me, and that only by a strong effort can one retain one's hold on them.'

He even dared to put before Edwardian readers, at a time when suicide was a crime, his idea that it would be 'better to end it . . . Better to let your dear ones suffer the worst . . . than sink into a broken and shadowed life of separation and restraint . . . I thought with what an utter joy I should feel the pang, the faintness of death creep over me.' Once he visited Wellington, and, looking at the scenes where his childhood had been passed, 'I prayed to die, so separated from life and hope did I seem.' He reflected on the unhappy weeks at Tremans, when, although he knew himself to be 'so prickly . . . so futile, so fractious', nothing that anyone could do could relieve his tortured nerves. 'I feel that trivial things, words, actions, looks, are noted, commented upon, held to be significant. If I am silent, I must be depressed; if I talk and smile, I am making an effort to overcome my depression. . . . It adds to the strain by imposing upon me a sort of vigilance, a constant effort to behave normally.' 'It would be better and easier for me if she [his mother] ignored my unhappiness altogether; sympathy and compassion only plunged me deeper into gloom.' We may be sure, however, that he would have been no better pleased if his misery had been ignored: 'A man is often not ill-pleased that his moods should be felt by his circle, and regards it as rather an insult that other people should be joyful when he is ill-at-ease.' Although he could not do without company, it was for him 'little short of torture' to conform to the rules of any household not his own.

When he was depressed he thought continually that his illness was a punishment from God. 'All the little amusements and idle businesses that were so dear to me, He probably disapproved of them all, and was only satisfied when I was safe at my lessons, or immured in church.' (Arthur's God, in his weakened state of mind,

bears an evident resemblance to Edward Benson.) Later, he decided that his illness was caused by his attempt to live alone;
Hinton Hall had been 'a profound mistake', and he gave it up, and
returned to the Old Lodge at Magdalene. Some of his friendships
had withered under the strain of his prolonged depressions; and in
any case, as the novelist Mary Cholmondeley wrote of him, 'he
regarded as friendship a degree of intimacy which most men and
all women regard as acquaintanceship'. There were new acquaintances to make and new undergraduates to adore, but he had
become aware that he was somehow on the fringes of life, not
involved in it. 'He saw that he was condemned to pass through
life, a smiling and courteous spectator of beauty and delight, but
that, through a real and vital deficiency of soul, he could have no
share in the inner and holier mysteries.' Still, however wistful he
felt at being excluded from real life, he would not at all have cared
for any closer involvement. The figure he loved to think of was that
of Ariel – light, sexless, content only to gaze, and to flit away when
tired of gazing. Ariel, he said, 'cannot quite get hold of human
relationships. They want each other, and Ariel wants no-one.
There is some secret about it all which he cannot penetrate.'

Arthur's life seemed now to be running as serenely as it ever
could, with his increasingly irritable and touchy temperament.
Like his mother, he was compelled to toil to be all things to all men.
His friend and former pupil Percy Lubbock said that when he met
people, he 'had to win their favour, to conciliate and attach them as
fast as he might'. Then, when they responded, thinking he was
offering friendship, he would rebuff them. His diary entries are
often corrosive: 'It might be supposed that his friends were
harassing company, in a life that would be happier without them.'
But Arthur could not do without the companions with whom he so
continually quarrelled and disagreed, and, since he saw himself as
fundamentally a timid, gentle, courteous man, he could not
understand why he so often became involved in unpleasant
incidents.

In the years after his breakdown he was still trying to come to
terms with, or at least to understand, his illness. In *Thy Rod and Thy
Staff*, published in 1912, he wrote openly and in his own person
about it:

In the winter of 1909 I recovered from an illness which had lasted
over two years. . . . It was the most dreadful and afflicting illness

which it is possible to have, both for the sufferer and for all about him. Neurasthenia, hypochondria, melancholia – hideous names for hideous things – it was one of these. The symptoms are persistent sleeplessness, perpetual dejection, amounting at times to an intolerable mental anguish. . . . The worst hour of my whole illness came to me [in the nursing-home] . . . feeling myself deserted by God and man, condemned to suffer a pain of which each minute seemed an eternity, in which dread, disgust, repugnance, dreariness seemed all entwined in one sickening draught. There lies the mystery of this strange affliction – that no one knows what to do for one, or how to help. Even the wisest and kindliest doctor can but listen, as it were, at the door of the torture-chamber, and hear the groans of the racked spirit within.

The feelings of three years ago were still vivid to him:

One of my worst fears during much of my illness was that of a sudden collapse of my mental faculties. There were times when I could only sit helpless, with the horror rising and growing upon me, overwhelming everything with an agony that brimmed my being. What if it all boiled up like a devil's cauldron, and left me raving and frenzied? There were times when I felt that if anyone came upon me suddenly, I could hardly have phrased an intelligible phrase; yet if it ever did so happen, I found I could always respond, close the lid, so to speak, of the throbbing and seething vessel, and talk almost as usual. Yet the fear was so strong, that I carried about with me all that time an envelope of directions as to what was to be done in the case of a collapse.

When he had to face a social gathering:

I used out of very shame . . . to galvanise myself into a sort of horrid merriment. The dark tide flowed on beneath in its sore and aching channels. No-one else could see the acute and intolerable reaction which used to follow such a strain, or how, the excitement over, the suffering resumed its sway over the exhausted self with an insupportable agony.

It is strange that at a period when, as Arthur himself said in a later book, 'most people are ashamed of insanity, because it shocked them and could not be spoken about or alluded to', he should so openly have discussed his own illness. Perhaps he was enlightened enough to see, and to say, that it was a 'a mere disease like other diseases'; perhaps he did not class his own experiences as those of insanity, preferring its origin to be in more ordinary causes, 'a perfectly natural penalty for excessive brainwork or excessive stimulation'. In his next book he said that he never got attacks of depression when he had plenty of work to do. But he knew, though he fought against the knowledge, that the excessive brainwork and stimulation were forerunners and symptoms, not causes, of his illness, and although its effects were emotional, its source was in the brain. Severe headaches always preceded and foretold an attack, and where the pain concentrated itself, 'that very portion of the brain is itself tortured, so that it pours back the sensation of suffering upon all impressions alike'.

From the over-stimulated brain came the horrible nightmares that warned him of an attack. He was, like his father, a frequent and vivid dreamer; over four hundred dreams are recorded in his diary, many of them about his father, who dominated his son's sleep as he had dominated his waking life. Arthur related some of his dreams in his books, but never the nightmares – the tramp washing a deformed child in a well, the rotting offal being stuffed into a dog's head, the repulsive insects found under the coverlet of a bed, the dangling head with the ghastly substance dripping from it. He often had dreams induced by guilt, in which he was tried and sometimes sentenced to death for crimes of which he was ignorant.

In 1914 the Great War broke out, and in October Hugh died. He had been drinking heavily for some time, and some of his acquaintances had found his behaviour manic and irrational long before his death. Arthur threw together a hurried and scrappy book about his brother. In 1915 a wealthy American lady who admired Arthur's books handed over to him £40,000 to use as he liked. In November he was offered the Mastership of Magdalene College, Cambridge.

Arthur was wild with excitement at his new status. He could now apply for a doctor's degree *jure dignitatis*. 'I am almost exactly the age that papa was when he went to Canterbury', he wrote; he had done something at last to justify himself in his father's eyes. He loved his new position, he loved dressing up for the ceremonial occasions of the University, he loved authority and autocracy. When Maggie died in May 1916, he felt it to be a heavenly release for her and for him; he had felt her shadowed life as a continual strain. It was perhaps not very wise to begin immediately sorting through her letters and papers for one of his hastily-written books as a memoir of his sister. He was dismayed to find himself rather unpleasantly reflected, when he was mentioned at all. He was also not best pleased to find how clearly poor disabled Maggie had seen all his faults and shortcomings.

Even before Maggie's death, Arthur had been 'drifting back into dreams', as he had done in 1905; he was sleeping badly, and in June began to feel 'highly explosive', as if he might burst or die. Like Ruskin, he saw 'strange streaks and tangles' floating before his eyes, and his head felt congested, giving him a perpetual headache. He felt sure that he was going to have 'a violent brain attack', as Ruskin did. On 4 July he had 'an access of horror and wretchedness so *awful* that I became aware that I was becoming actually insane'; the imaginative part of the brain had 'lost its escapement' and was 'whizzing away like a watch without a regulator'. Ross Todd thought he was exaggerating and prescribed rest and bromide; but Arthur's days passed in gnawing misery and torturing depression, until he did not know what to do or where to turn – 'the pain of mind is *indescribable*', 'It really does not seem consistent with continuing to exist to suffer so', he wrote. 'What would I not give to die and leave this place of torment! I am in hell, if ever a man was. Is there no way out?' After an attack of depression which 'struck the pen from my hand', it was clear to him that he was very ill, and he entered St Michael's Nursing Home at Ascot, 'stupefied with misery'; there are no more diary entries until January 1918.

There he lay heavily sedated for weeks. He lost weight because he refused to eat, convinced that he had ruined his solicitor. He was harassed by continual delusions, that his servants were starving because he had locked them in, that he was bankrupt and that his lack of money would eventually lead to the defeat of the Allies and a German occupation of Britain. Even the visit of two bank managers failed to convince him of his solvency. He was convinced that he emitted a disgusting smell, that the nurses talked about it and that the other patients avoided him to the extent of not being able to walk past the door of his room. He had horrible accesses of guilt: 'I have always been *worthless*'. Even when he could write again, his diary entries record continual unbearable mental agony; 'I seem to have the monster close on me,

watching me relentlessly.' A late entry shows his conviction that
he is on the verge of 'some hideous collapse', and on 15 June the
entries ceased, and we know almost nothing of him for two years,
except that three days after that entry his mother died at Tremans.
    As far as we know she had not visited him at Ascot. She was
after all in her late seventies, lame and deaf; but she had written to
him, and some of her letters make one wonder whether she was
not thrown off balance by Arthur's illness. One of her letters, dated
26 November 1917, suggests that she felt some guilt or responsibility for her children's disabilities:

> Arthur, dearest ever and ever, your dear letter all the dearer
> because not only does my heart embrace you all the closer for
> your misery, but because I lay claim, so to say, being your
> mother, to a certain responsibility in it all ... and again I say *I am
> your Mother* – and I know the beast from within – the other day I
> had the most ridiculous fit of *Remorse* – which really felt like Hell
> – it was quite absurd. And *I am your Mother*. I am not going to
> burden myself with any ridiculous responsibility for this.

But whatever Mary Benson's part in Arthur's misery had been, he
was involved in a tangled emotional relationship with her, and her
sudden death must have shattered him.
    Early in 1920, Arthur's doctors feared he was becoming too
dependent on the routines of the nursing-home, and forced him,
against his will, to make visits with his brother Fred. Every time
that Fred left him, he would burst into tears, convinced that they
would never see each other again; 'He clung to his malady', wrote
Fred, 'in the tragic manner of neurasthenics.' In October his
doctors decided that he must be induced to take up normal life
again, and insisted that he should go to stay in Norfolk with Fred
and relays of other friends, saying that he must learn to do without
constant medical attention. Arthur was furious. He had had 1,862
days of absolute misery, he wrote. 'Here I sit, devouring my soul,
with no one to consult and feeling insanity slowly closing in upon
me. It is simply incredible to me that two experts should leave a
man in this condition simply to sink or swim.' He was, he
screamed, 'in the nethermost pit'. But, kicking and protesting and
apparently struggling to get back in, he was gradually dragged out
of the pit. On 12 April 1922 he cancelled the power of attorney he
had been compelled to sign in 1917, and took up his position as
Master of Magdalene again. Until he died on 17 June 1925,

although he returned to his frenetic way of life, he had no more depression.

But he really had been in the nethermost pit this time, and had felt the hot breath of Hell scorching him. The experience had been too searing for him to wish to remember it, much less to write about it. He made translations from the Greek, he wrote a few strange washy plotless novels, and, like Ruskin, wrote his best books, about his own past, his family and friends. He also wrote an extraordinarily frank book about his mother, so far unpublished.

Arthur's logorrhea was partly inherited perhaps; all Bensons scribbled as if possessed as soon as they could hold a pencil, and both he and Fred left quantities of unpublished typescripts when they died. Arthur's publisher (who subsequently committed suicide not, one hopes, because of the mountains of Benson typescript continually pouring upon him) had to restrain him from publishing more than three books a year. But it seems clear that Arthur's compulsive writing was in part at least caused by his psychosis, and was in some way necessary to him, as an attempt to clear the overloaded circuits of his brain. Because of this, it was a huge relief and pleasure to him, although he was well aware that 'with this intense impulse to write, I ought to have contrived to make myself into a better writer, and it might be thought that there is something either grotesque or pathetic in so much emotional enjoyment resulting in so slender a performance'.

It would be pathetic, if Arthur's writing had been in any sense a construct of art; but it was partly only a wiping of the tapes, and perhaps to some extent an attempt to come to terms with the abnormal conditions under which his life must be lived, with the 'wild beast' always waiting to spring. He was continually thinking of metaphors or parables to explain his predicament to himself; he saw himself as a child living in a beautiful garden with a tender and loving guardian, but sometimes the guardian would fall upon the child, inexplicably beating, wounding and scarring him. He did not, like Ruskin, see himself as absolutely in the right and the world absolutely in the wrong; he thought that he must have made some kind of mistake in his approach to life: 'I have sported with life as though it were a pretty plaything; and I find it turn upon me like a wild beast, gaunt, hungry, angry. I am terrified by its evil motions, I sicken at its odour.'

With all his privileges, all his talents, wealth and status, Arthur Benson had found life terrifying, even though he distanced himself from any emotional involvement; he saw it always through a glass, or like one looking from a mountain-top to the world beneath. It *is* both 'grotesque and pathetic' that heavy, blundering, overbearing Arthur should take as his ideal figure the delicate, light, sexless Ariel, flitting here and there as a spectator of human life; the same figure that was later to hold the imagination of Sylvia Plath.

Case Description

It is clear from his writings and from what we know of his life that A. C. Benson's breakdowns were of a serious nature, leading to his seeking medical help on many occasions and several stays in private nursing homes for the mentally ill. Although certainly reactive to circumstances (e.g. the death of his favourite sister), the family history of insanity indicates a strong endogenous, biological component, a fact recognised by Benson himself when he wrote of it as 'a definite brain-malady in which the emotional centres are affected'.

The symptoms in all three of his breakdowns were those of major depression, for which he rates positively on almost all of the SADS-L items. His diaries are full of phrases recording his hopelessness: 'the torture chamber that I call my life'; 'the nethermost pit'; 'utterly crushed with misery and despair.' They also describe his frequent suicidal feelings, as in: 'I prayed to die, so separated from life and hope did I seem.' In his third, and worst, breakdown his loss of interest in life was such that he could not even keep his diary, normally for him the highlight of his day. At this time he also showed serious weight loss (so much so that his friends said he was a shadow of his former self), as well as symptoms of a delusional nature: he believed that people were shunning him, 'talking about me with horror and disgust' and that he 'emitted a horrible smell ... and that everyone in the house knew it and could hardly pass my room, and that everything I touched was infected by it.' Guilt beyond the ordinary is also evident in his belief that he had spent all his money and of the terrible consequences that would follow: that he (and his mother and the Bishop of Wakefield) would be 'criminally prosecuted for malversation of funds. That all the Magdalene dons would be ruined ... that it would ruin Cambridge ... cause a rupture of

Anglo-American relations, and that the Germans would win the war.'

Running through Benson's mental state there was also an element of restlessness, hyperactivity and irritability, characteristics which cause Newsome to refer to Benson as 'manic-depressive'. However, this is probably a misinterpretation of the *agitation* often seen in major depression. At no point did Benson show the elated mood or other indications of clinical mania and, although sometimes giving the impression to others that he was manic, these were often occasions when he was extremely depressed and on which he says 'I used out of very shame . . . to galvanise myself into a sort of horrid merriment'.

9

Shadows on the Brain

Virginia Woolf (1882–1941)

There could hardly be two people more unlike than A. C. Benson and Virginia Woolf; he would not have understood her writing, and she despised his, saying that he had a mind of 'foggy dew'; but there were certain points of contact between them. Benson's last romantic love, Dadie Rylands, helped Leonard and Virginia Woolf at the Hogarth Press, and A. C. and Virginia had the same consultant, Dr Savage, in their breakdowns. Virginia's childhood, like Arthur's, was full of unresolved tensions and oppositions. Her family life was full of contradictions; her father took Holy Orders although he was not a Christian, and her mother preferred what would now be called social work to looking after her own children. Leslie Stephen, Virginia's father, had married one of Thackeray's daughters, whose mother had been insane for most of her married life, and had by her a daughter Laura who was called 'retarded', but who may have been psychotic, and spent all her life in an institution after her father died. Leslie Stephen's nephew, his brother's son, also became insane. A. C. Benson knew him well at Eton and Cambridge. He was wildly extravagant, starting a periodical with insufficient backing and driving about all day in hansom cabs in a state of wild euphoria, leaving somebody else to pay the driver. Virginia Woolf remembered him pursuing her half-sister Stella with unwelcome attentions. In 1890 he improved slightly, but in 1891 he became acutely psychotic, running about naked in Cambridge, and had to be put under medical care. He died in 1892.

Leslie Stephen himself was rather abnormal. He called himself 'skinless', because of his nervously irritable response to emotional stimuli; he was an insomniac who had 'fits of the horrors', and was prone to delusions of financial insecurity. After his first wife died he married a young widow with three children, who then had by him another four, Vanessa and Thoby intentionally, and Virginia and Adrian after they hoped their family was complete. Virginia hardly ever remembered being alone with her mother, who was perpetually out nursing and helping others, or soothing and placating her husband. Though endlessly kind to those in trouble, she was sharp with her own children, impatient with stupidity, especially not sparing her eldest daughter Stella, who was beautiful and gentle but so slow-witted that she thought she had a 'stoppage' in her brain. Virginia did not speak until she was three, but had what the family called 'purple rages' in which she used her nails on her siblings and on the nursery walls, and was able to create an atmosphere of gloom and discontent around herself. Perhaps she had hallucinations at an early age; when she was six or seven she saw a hideous animal face looking over her shoulder as she looked in a mirror, which left her even in adult life unwilling to powder her nose or be measured for new clothes in front of a mirror. It was at this stage that her half-brother Gerald Duckworth began to molest her, and even towards the end of her life she remembered the horror and disgust with which she felt him exploring her genitals.

In 1895 her mother died, worn out by conflicting demands and her self-assumed burdens. Even on her death-bed she told Virginia to hold herself straight; Virginia responded by laughing behind her hands, once her mother was dead – her nurses thought she was crying. She felt nothing whatever, she said, and often felt the same afterwards in moments of crisis. But she made Stella nervous by seeing a man who wasn't there sitting on her mother's bed, and soon after she had her first breakdown. Her pulse raced, she heard voices, she was wildly excited at one time and depressed at another, was full of morbid self-criticism and guilty because she was being a burden to the family. Two factors besides the death of her mother may have contributed to this. Her other half-brother George, under the guise of comforting the two girls, had taken to coming into their bedroom and hugging and embracing them in an explicitly sexual way, which made Virginia freeze with distaste; this contributed to her sexual frigidity in later life. Also her father seemed to become almost demented with grief at the loss of his second wife, unrestrainedly groaning, weeping, howling and calling for continual sympathy from his children. Virginia, who deeply loved and hated her father, said that his excessive emotional demands accounted for many of the 'wrong things' in her life. Her breakdown continued for many months. She was afraid to meet people, afraid to go out on the streets, which she thought were murderous, since she had seen many accidents there (only some of which were real). Her doctor prescribed four hours outdoors every day, which was a great burden on relatives and friends, since she could not go out unaccompanied.

In 1896 her half-sister Stella, who had taken her mother's place with her father and somehow managed to hold the family together, married, and died the next year. This was the beginning of what Virginia was to call 'the seven unhappy years', from the memory of which she always shrank – 'Why should our lives have been so tortured and so fretted?' Apart from the family's own sorrow at Stella's death, Vanessa now had to run the household for a father virtually deranged. He was not only impossibly exigeant in every way, but became absolutely tyrannical about money. Every request for necessary funds for housekeeping purposes led to scenes of 'bellowing fury', 'savage and sinister', in which he would beat his breast and shriek aloud before signing even the smallest cheque. This exacerbated Virginia's nerves, but when her father began to go deaf and then developed cancer, she could not help pitying him; 'emotions were pumped out of me'. He had a long slow death, like the death of the mother in *The Years*, and when he at last died in February 1904 Virginia was both relieved and remorseful to an extent that frightened her and made her think there was something wrong with her. She blamed her mother for offering up her children as a sacrifice to her father, 'leaving a legacy of dependence on his part that was terrible'. She and Vanessa saw their life as a struggle to get some kind of footing in a battle where they were continually being undermined. The illness that followed her father's death was, she said, the result of 'all these emotions and complications'.

By May she hardly knew what she was doing; voices in her head urged her to wild acts, and, thinking they came from over-eating, she refused to eat. She was sent to a friend's house in Welwyn to be cared for by three nurses. She heard birds singing in Greek and the voice of Edward VII cursing obscenely in the azaleas outside the window, through which she jumped, intending to kill herself; but the window was near the ground, and she was unharmed. Three years later she was to describe this illness in *The Voyage Out*, but not under its own name; insanity was not a socially acceptable disease. J. K. Stephen's final raving madness was delicately called by A. C. Benson 'an acute attack of brain disturbance'; Rachel, the character who reflects Virginia's own experience, has a tropical fever and consequent delirium; even in 1939, Virginia rejected a version of *A Sketch of the Past* in which she had actually mentioned her first breakdown.

Rachel's illness begins, as Virginia's always did, with a terrible headache; then words began to have other meanings than their usual ones and started trains of thought which brought up unpleasant visual images. When she tried to repeat verses the adjectives got into the wrong places. Her sleep became 'transparent', and through it she saw sights that terrified her. The nurse playing patience became an old woman playing patience in a tunnel under the river, and this multiplied into many little deformed women in archways in the tunnel through which Rachel found herself struggling. Time was distorted, hours sped in minutes and minutes took hours to pass. All landmarks were obliterated, and the familiar world seemed far away. 'Red hot quick sights' flashed before her eyes, and it was enormously important that she should grasp their meaning, but she was never quick enough to catch the single point that would explain everything; just as the crisis was about to happen, something would slip in her brain, and she would have to start all over again. Then she sank to the bottom of the sea, sometimes seeing light and sometimes darkness, while every now and then someone would turn her over.

Virginia did not recover until early September, when she wrote that she was still cross and 'tempersome'. She still had headaches and insomnia, but felt as though a dead part of herself were coming to life. It was not until January 1905 that she was discharged by Dr Savage as cured. By this time Vanessa had moved the family to Bloomsbury; Laura was put in an institution, George married soon after, and the four young Stephens were free. But in November of that year Thoby died. Virginia was devastated by his death and twenty years later still felt that death would be a return to him. Vanessa, pining for consolation, married in February 1907, which must have been another shock for Virginia, who had almost a lover-like admiration for and a childlike dependence on her sister. She wrote a letter to Vanessa at this time which makes one wonder whether she had fully recovered from her breakdown: 'We [three apes and a wombat, signifying Virginia herself] have wooed you ... in the hope that thus enchanted you would condescend one day to marry us. . . . We entreat that you keep us still for your lovers.'

Virginia and Adrian set up a rather random kind of housekeeping together, in which the walls were flecked with butter thrown at each other during arguments, and the carpet stained by Virginia's completely untrained dog. Adrian was a strange character, a very slow developer, whom an analyst was to call in 1923 'a tragedy'. Virginia was pretty strange too at this time, always in difficulty with her clothes (especially with her knickers, which were apt to slide down at inappropriate times), her behaviour very volatile, her imagination, says Quentin Bell, having an accelerator but no brakes. She wrote to Vanessa every day when they did not see each other, and her letters are often quite wild. She spoke of herself as 'hooting and copulating' because Vanessa had not written, and of thinking of herself with child by a grasshopper. Perhaps these letters were mere fantasy, but it is very peculiar fantasy.

By March 1910 her headaches (like rats gnawing at the base of her neck, she said) had begun again, with their accompanying insomnia and nervous irritability, and refusal to eat. Vanessa was pregnant and could not look after her, so she went into a nursing-home at Twickenham, 'a kind of polite madhouse for female lunatics', she called it. Lying in bed in a darkened room with letters and visitors carefully restricted cannot have been enlivening, but Virginia was a difficult patient. Sometimes she was depressed, sometimes euphoric, and always rather paranoid, in that she thought Vanessa was plotting with the nurses against her. She broke the rules, was furious at attempts to keep her in order, and threatened suicide: 'My God! what a mercy to be done with it! I feel my brains, like a pear, to see if it's ripe.'

Through 1911 she had headaches and depressions, and when in January 1912 Leonard Woolf wanted to marry her the emotional pressures forced her back to Twickenham. Again she had periods of elation when she felt 'a great mastery over the world'. She wrote a wild letter to Leonard, saying that the lunatics had elected her King, and she was about to summon a conclave and make a pronouncement about Christianity. Quentin Bell comments on how little Leonard can have known what he was taking on; the family in public took Virginia's illnesses very lightly, saying, 'Oh, the old Goat's off her head again', and it must have been a shock to him when, after less than a year of marriage, she was back at Twickenham. She became paranoid about Leonard's part in her confinement, then guilty about her suspicions. She left the nursing-home with some veronal for her sleeplessness, but she was still tense and anxious, and thought people were laughing and pointing at her in the streets. Ordinary things assumed terrible and sinister forms, as they did for Ruskin and Maggie Benson. Nearly a month after she had left the nursing-home, she took 100 grains of veronal and nearly died. When she became conscious again, her symptoms had not abated. It took a year before she was fully recovered; this was September 1914.

Five months later she had a bad headache, and Leonard prescribed rest, no visitors, veronal; but one morning she began to talk to her mother, and rapidly became excited and incoherent. She had grandiose fantasies, deciding that she would write all Mrs Humphrey Ward's novels and all Beatrice Webb's diaries. Soon she was raving, and became violent towards her husband, who hardly ever saw her for the next two months. Her nurses found her an impossible patient, and it seemed that she would have to be certified and go into an asylum. Each attack seemed worse than the one before, and her friends thought it unlikely that she would recover from her two years' madness. Her whole character seemed to have deteriorated; she hurled the most malicious and cutting insults at her visitors, said Vanessa, 'and they are so clever that they always hurt'.

It was not until nearly ten years later that she could bring herself in *Mrs. Dalloway* to write about her madness, and then, she said, writing about it made her mind 'squirt' out so badly that she could hardly face it. In this book, as in *The Voyage Out*, there must be a respectable reason for the character's insanity: Septimus is shell-shocked, which after the Great War would make his madness sympathetic to readers. He shows all the symptoms of psychosis. He has grandiose ideas of himself, as the greatest of mankind, the inaugurator of a new religion, the Lord who will renew society and wipe out sin and death, the One who has been specially chosen to learn the truth before all the rest of mankind, who must deliver 'the greatest message in the world'. He is paranoid, can see people's thoughts and the lies they are making up about him, their mocking hands and faces. He has hallucinations of an old woman's face in a fern, of dogs becoming human, of looking over a sofa edge down into the sea. He has delusions, that flowers are growing through his flesh, that trees are alive, that his body has been macerated by heat till only the nerves are left. He hears voices, some telling him to kill the Cabinet, some the voices of sparrows singing in Greek. He has disordered perceptions; a single word keeps splitting and dividing, the sound of a motor horn divides into smooth columns.

Although he does not want to die, he feels doomed, and while talking and laughing thinks, 'Now we will kill ourselves.' Yet his suicide will be an attempt at communication. Like Virginia, he has been ordered solitude and rest; like her, he goes into a nursing-home weighing seven stones and comes out weighing twelve; like her, in spite of a loving spouse, he will kill himself. It is one of the most powerful expositions of madness in fiction, so powerful that it gave Virginia a 'violent mental tremor' while she was writing it. The character of Rhoda in a later book, *The Waves*, was also based on herself – a woman for whom solid objects fall apart, perceptions are distorted, and whose humanity is in some way cold and de-humanised. That Virginia thought her illnesses affected her for the worse is shown by Rhoda's deterioration when the six friends of *The Waves* meet in middle age. 'You can't think what a legacy insanity leaves behind', she wrote to a friend. ' – how the spectres come out on a sleepless night.'

Meanwhile, after a very slow convalescence, the last nurse left in November 1915. Leonard's doctor gave him a certificate of unfit-ness which prevented him from being called up for the armed forces, and Virginia's recovery was certainly due to her husband's meticulous care. Though some of her friends may have thought him too fussy, even tyrannical, in curtailing her visits and other activities, without him she would not have been able to lead the halfway normal, if restricted, life that she led until her final breakdown. In 1918 she began to keep a diary which, though never as copious as Arthur Benson's, was to give her the same sort of relief; she could write in it when she could write and read nothing else, and from it we can see the fluctuations of her mental health, and what she called her 'dismal suppressed contorted life'. She had great and many enjoyments, but she felt herself always on the edge of the abyss, and there are few years in which there are not some gloomy and depressed entries.

From 1921 to 1922 she was continually beset by what Leonard called 'the shadow across the brain'. She wrote to a friend in 1927 that every ten years she felt 'such agony of different sorts' that she tried to kill herself, and would have been glad if 'by stepping on one flagstone rather than another I could have been annihilated where I stood'. But her diary shows that she had this kind of experience oftener than every ten years. In 1926 she had 'a whole nervous breakdown in miniature'; life became insipid, she was lethargic and exhausted, the landscape assumed abnormal proportions to her eye. She had rapid mood changes and accesses of horror on waking, like Arthur Benson, in which she felt a wave of terror swelling about her heart. She could not face it, and wished she were dead. In 1929 she called herself 'a born melancholic', in 1933 she was in 'black misery', gloom and pain constricting her heart. In 1935 she felt her head 'all nerves', and was conscious that one false move might lead to 'all that familiar misery' of madness; in 1936 she had an 'almost catastrophic' episode in which January found her head 'full' and racing with ideas. Later she became depressed, restless, insomniac and liable to 'mornings of torture'. 'I have never been so near the precipice . . . since 1913.' In 1937 she had months of 'sterile misery', and the sight of roaring water made her feel that it was all she could do not to throw herself in. But she also felt the fascination of what she called her 'dips into the underworld'; they held excitement for her as well as terrors, and could make life on the surface seem dull in comparison.

With the outbreak of war in 1939, the Woolfs lived mainly in the country. They knew that if the German invasion of Britain were successful, Leonard as a Jew, and his wife, could expect a concentration camp or death. Adrian gave them a lethal dose of morphine, to be used if necessary, and the question of suicide was continually discussed throughout the summer of 1940. Whether this seemed to Virginia a licence to kill herself will never now be known. In the autumn she had a long period when her life seemed serene and she was able to finish her last book rapidly and effortlessly, but in January 1941 she fell into 'a trough of despair' and began to get irritable and nervous. Leonard persuaded her to see a doctor, but she refused to admit that there was anything wrong, and would not submit to his usual rest cure. On 28 March she wrote letters to the people she loved best, Leonard and Vanessa, saying that she was hearing voices, couldn't concentrate, was going mad and this time wouldn't recover. Recognising what a burden she would be to them in wartime, she drowned herself in the River Ouse.

She had been a complex personality. There was 'too much ego' in her cosmos, she said, and indeed she remained immature in some ways all her life. She longed to enter the child's world of fantasy, but could not resist imposing her own fantasies on the child; her niece Angelica Garnett found her often frightening and demanding in her need for affection. She was often over-fantastical in her dealings with adults too, making up preposterous personalities for them and then spreading malicious gossip about the fictional personae. This led some of her friends to call her untrustworthy – indeed her husband said that in some pages of her diary there was not a word of truth; but this may have been not so much that she was untruthful as that her 'reality' was different from that of other people. Her alter ego, Septimus, had to look gradually at real things, because otherwise they might turn into something deformed or terrible. Perhaps she had to make her own reality, and perhaps this was in a sense the source of all her writing.

Virginia said that nothing was real to her until she wrote it down (and this may be why so many of our authors kept a journal or other record; how did they know what they lived till they saw what they said?) Sometimes writing could keep her above the depths she feared and was drawn to; writing was, she said, 'the great solace and scourge'. But sometimes she saw the depths themselves as the source of her creativity. 'I can reach a state where I seem to be making things happen as if I were there', she said, and this almost delusional ability may be what Margery Kempe was using when she took part in the life of the Holy Family. If the novel had been invented, she might have written a religious best-seller. Virginia Woolf also claimed, as Rimbaud and Dylan Thomas did, to apprehend modes of thought and feeling as if they were pictorial shapes, and thought that these visual imprints might be what made her write. Like Dickens and other authors, she had a sensation of being dictated to. When she was writing *The Waves*, 'my pen seemed to stumble after my own voice, or, almost, after some sort of speaker, as when I was mad.' She felt that the 'curious interludes' when she was living abnormally were fertilising, and, ultimately, fruitful.

But in the end, although her psychosis may have given her the ability to create, it took away her life. Her family history was bad; her cousin, her father, her half-sister, all showed signs of abnormality. Vanessa had long periods of disabling lethargy, and reacted to bereavement with her father's total lack of restraint; her daughter had at least one long depressive breakdown. 'What I lack in profusion', Virginia said, 'is natural happiness'.

Antonia White (1899–1980)

In 1922 when Arthur Benson in Cambridge was climbing out of the 'nethermost pit' of his five years' psychosis, and Virginia Woolf in Richmond was struggling to put on paper her account of her own madness, the twenty-three-year-old Eirene Botting was certified as a lunatic and admitted to the Hospital of St Mary of Bethlehem, once known as Bedlam.

Her childhood had been in some ways not unlike those of Benson and Woolf, although she had no siblings to share the pressures of a home where the parents differed radically, and in every possible way. Her father, Cecil Botting, a schoolmaster, required absolute obedience and a high standard of personal and academic performance from his only child; he was immensely ambitious for her, taught her Latin and Greek at an early age and gave her a lifelong dread of making mistakes. She feared his continual fault-finding and his anger paralysed her with terror, but she also longed for his approval. His feelings for her may have been ambiguous since she remembered him showing excitement and pleasure at the prospect of smacking her bare buttocks, and described some of his behaviour in her adolescence as 'lover-like'.

Cecil was obsessively tidy, meticulously neat and punctual, his life organised in every respect; his wife Christine was untidy, vague and unpunctual, her life and her living-space always in chaos. She was much given to fantasy, seeing herself as possessing great charm and remarkable abilities; in fact she spent her time shopping, playing bridge, trying on clothes and playing the piano in a desultory way. She thought herself the most adaptable and far-sighted of women, but was in fact unreasonable, self-centred and hypochondriac. She attempted suicide when six months pregnant, and after her husband's death her behaviour became rather abnormal; she spent a great deal of her time in bed, dirty, in unwashed clothes and indulging in sexual fantasies. She did not, Eirene said, so much neglect her daughter as remain 'sublimely unaware' of the child's physical and emotional needs, leaving her to play in a sunless, fireless nursery or to hang about the basement kitchen with the servants. Her busy father was almost certainly unaware of his daughter's uncared-for state.

Two such disparate personalities as Cecil and Christine naturally found marriage difficult, and his rage at her careless extravagance led to fearful scenes between them. Money came to assume extreme importance in their daughter's life; like her father, she saw it as a source of security and power, but like her mother she frittered it away and was constantly in debt. She never loved her mother much, and even came to despise her, but she thought of her father as God.

In his mid-thirties Cecil Botting became a convert to the Roman Catholic faith, and his daughter was baptised into the Church at the age of seven. Two years later she was sent as a boarder to the Sacred Heart convent school in Roehampton, where the nuns continued the regime of fault-finding and criticism in an attempt to make her perfect, which had been begun by her father. Her own account of her schooldays in *Frost in May* gives a saccharine picture both of her parents' relationship and of her own experiences, which left her with a terror of committing mortal sin, and a longing to be among the young aristocrats who formed a large part of the school.

When she was 15 she began to write a novel in secret which was found by the nuns and she subsequently left the convent; she thought she had been expelled, but later found that her father had wished her to leave and had seized on this pretext to send her as a day-girl to St Paul's Girls' School in London. But the shock of the discovery and the terrible scene he made when summoned to the convent, in which he said that he wished to God that he had never had a daughter whose mind was such a 'sink of filth and impurity', paralysed her emotionally for much of her life. She carried over too from her childhood and adolescence many other traumas; a fear of skating or bicycling – indeed of any activity which could lead to a fall (based, she said, on her terror of falling into mortal sin); a fear of looking into mirrors lest her reflection should pull her through to the other side; a fear of turning into an animal when her pubic hair began to grow; fantasies of saving or consoling tortured or mutilated friends and a permanent preoccupation with and anxiety about money. This led her at the age of 14 to earn money by writing advertising copy, and to leave school at 17 to become first a governess, then a clerk. By the time she was 18 she had a contract to write copy for beauty products earning £250 a year, and had had some short stories accepted under the name 'Antonia White', which she would use from now on. She entered the Academy of Dramatic Art in 1919 but abandoned her course and went on tour with a small company, although admitting that she was never a good actress. In April 1921 she married an impotent alcoholic; the only thing she and her husband had in common was a love of the theatre and a passion for playing with toy soldiers.

The Sugar House, published in 1952, and the unpublished *Julian Tye,* written perhaps in the 1960s, reveal something of this disastrous marriage. Antonia and her husband were rapidly in debt, unable to deny themselves any luxuries yet existing solely on her small income. She became quarrelsome and unreasonable, with rapid mood-changes, from elation to despair, and would wander about the house in a dressing-gown, unwashed, inert, apathetic, isolating herself from any companionship and sometimes unable to write even a letter. She attempted to keep a journal, but when she looked at it later many of the entries were almost illegible, or when deciphered, so incoherent that they might have been 'written by a lunatic': some of the entries were even in mirror-writing. She began to eat compulsively, stuffing herself with anything she found lying around the house. After eighteen months the marriage was annulled, and she returned to her parents' house once again emotionally paralysed. But her emotions rapidly recovered; she was soon in love with an army officer with whom she claimed to have intense telepathic communications, but in fact she was already manic. She had been having violent headaches, but now she lost a stone in weight in three weeks, saw huge significance in trivial words and objects, and was convinced that she would be able to make her father an allowance of £1,000 a year, and that she was about to write a book of genius. Her account of her madness in *Beyond the Glass* (written in 1953–4 'as though possessed') describes her sense that her reflection in the mirror was a different person who wanted to take her over, and from whom she could not escape; her feeling that she had found the secret of life – that sleep and food were unnecessary in a state of consciousness so heightened that reality became overwhelming and memory only intermittent. She could never remember why her 'exquisite sense of timeless happiness' should lead her to attempt suicide by walking into the Thames, from which her lover rescued her.

The following evening, numb and drowsy, she became aware that evil spirits were watching her, her mother and the lodger were talking in code, and electric currents were causing her chair to rock. A few days later, violent, paranoid and deluded, believing her father to be the devil in disguise, she was committed to the Hospital of St Mary of Bethlehem. Her parents were told that she might develop a chronic form of mania, and from November 1922 until the spring of 1923 she was in the grip of delusions and hallucinations, vividly described in 'The House of Clouds', which, like *Beyond the Glass* she asserted was a veracious account of her madness. The writing partly assuaged the 'haunting' of the spectre of insanity, which she felt to be always afterwards lying in wait for her.

While in hospital she was frequently violent and under restraint, forcibly fed, in a padded cell. She had nightmares, which merged into daily life; often she heard voices in the corridor persuading visitors to dress as nurses, so that Antonia would think that she was in a hospital; but she knew that these people were really the mothers of sons killed in the Great War, and she was forced to experience one by one the terrible and often lingering deaths their sons had died. Then 'for years she was not even a human being, she was a horse', and was beaten and ridden to death, after which she was resurrected as a magic horse which had the power to gallop across the sky. Even when she saw her own hands and feet, she knew that she was in reality a horse. When the nurses deluged her with water (a form of treatment still at that time used for psychotics), she accepted this as preparation for the hunt, since she saw in the mirror only the face of a stag or a horse. Sometimes she was a salmon rubbing off her scales on the rubber floor; sometimes a sailor trapped in a scalding boiler-room; when she recognised herself, it was only to be tied down so that a ship could be launched over her body, cracking all her bones and splitting her skull. She was born and reborn continually as a flower, a dog or an imp, but her most enduring fantasy was that she was the Lord of the World, who could call up storms, drive ships off course and hold the whole world under a spell. What she could not do, however she raved and prayed, was to sleep. Time became uncertain; days would flash by like minutes, while it took months to lift a spoon from a plate to her mouth. Occasionally she came back to reality, though she did not know her name, nor her sex, and would beat on the door of her cell until her hands were swollen. If she looked out of the window, the landscape was unreal, a mere paper cut-out; but the clouds and the leaves sent her messages.

Gradually she began to remember her name and parts of her past history, and discovered that her father had been visiting her regularly, though her mother never accompanied him. By August of 1923 she was allowed to go home with him, though still under medical supervision. In a few months she was in trouble again, pregnant by a friend of her father's whose advances she had not thought it worth while to resist. Though still nominally a Catholic, she felt no guilt about having an abortion, for which her father lent her the money; he afterwards reimbursed himself from £500 given by her former father-in-law for medical expenses.

Antonia soon began to earn money again by copywriting, and in the spring of 1925 married a homosexual friend, who was to become a loved and respected father-figure for much of her life, though once again the marriage was not consummated. In spite of being frigid and terrified of sexual intercourse, she had several extra-marital affairs. Her unfinished novel provisionally titled *Clara IV* shows that she sometimes behaved so irrationally at this time that she feared she might become insane again.

In August 1929 she gave birth to a daughter by a young university lecturer, and shortly afterwards her second marriage was annulled. Antonia seemed to have very little maternal feeling for her child, and left it with a nurse at her father's house; later it was sent to a children's home. Three months afterwards Cecil Botting died, and Antonia felt only relief; shortly afterwards she became the mistress of a fellow-copywriter. After months of indecision as to whether she should marry him or the father of her daughter, she decided in his favour and married him in November 1930. Her father-in-law-to-be insisted on being given a certificate stating that her madness was not hereditary. The same doctor who had formerly told her family that she might be suffering from chronic mania now dismissed her breakdown as the result of emotional stress. In fact her new husband had reason to be aware of her mental and emotional instability, since she had not only written 'The House of Clouds' for him, but had already begun to behave with the destructiveness with which, she admitted, she made her own and her lovers' lives 'a perfect hell of torment'.

Her second daughter was born in July 1931. Antonia hated pregnancy and childbirth and felt that her daughters had robbed her of 'something vital'. She was already wishing that she had married her former lover, and both children were cared for by nurses while she worked full-time at an advertising agency. In spite of her own and her husband's earnings, they soon became embroiled in the familiar money troubles, which were increased by Antonia's irrational extravagance, as when she spent money given for her husband's medical expenses in lavish gifts for him. But with his help and encouragement she did manage to complete a novel, *Frost in May*; it had some success, but she was paralysed by the thought of writing the next book. Even reviewing for *Time and Tide* proved too great a burden, although the money was urgently needed.

In July 1934, still on the edge of a breakdown, she went on holiday to Brittany with her husband. The discovery that he was in love with another woman led to her 'complete disintegration' and another suicide attempt. She had nightmares so full of horror that her teeth chattered at the mere recollection, and although she could do no serious writing, she filled notebooks with interminable discussions about herself, her husband and his lover. At the end of March 1935 she moved out of their home and into a long period of depression. Her headaches and nightmares returned, and she made several attempts to kill herself. Often she stayed in bed all day, hardly able to write her one weekly article for the *Daily Mirror*. Sessions with a psychologist and a hypnotherapist did not help and, in desperation, feeing that 'the beast' was taking her over, she began a Freudian analysis which would last for four years.

For the tax year 1934–35 she earned only a little over £400, and in November she lost the job by which she had earned even that sum. In 1937, when her mental state had improved, she found another job in an advertising agency which should have brought her £1,000 a year, but she soon found it 'disgusting'; she was bored by regular work, and after an euphoric beginning to every new situation, would arrive later and later, waste time, do her work inadequately or not at all, and do everything possible to provoke dismissal. She said herself that whenever she felt secure in a relationship or a job, she would deliberately begin to break it up. Without an allowance from her second husband of £15 a month, and whatever financial help her hard-pressed third husband could manage, she would have found it difficult to survive.

From 1936 onwards she became, says one of her daughters, sexually promiscuous. She was never without a lover or lovers, some of them much younger than herself. Her analyst pointed out that all her lovers were homosexual, impotent or sadistic; he might have added that many of them, and many of the dominating women she sought out as friends, were psychotic. Among these were Djuna Barnes, the author of *Nightwood* with its schizophrenic heroine, Emily Coleman, who wrote about her own breakdown in *The Snow Shutter*, and Benedicta de Bezer, who was later to die in an asylum.

In 1938 Antonia began divorce proceedings, and found herself suddenly freed from her writer's block; she was able to begin work on her short story, 'The Moment of Truth', about the disastrous holiday at the beginning of her breakdown, and also wrote 21,000 words in her notebooks about her current lover. By the autumn her analysis had finished, and her notebook was filled with execrations against her father, in a huge unrecognisable handwriting. Shortly afterwards she had a second abortion, and not long after that was reconverted to Catholicism, though her faith often wavered, and her daughters felt that she used religion largely as a weapon against her enemies.

The first signs of another breakdown appeared in 1944. Antonia fell passionately in love with a very unbalanced artist, Benedicta de Bezer, also a Catholic, and with Antonia's elder daughter spent days in haunting churches, saying the daily Offices and weeping before crucifixes, all three often in delusional or hallucinatory states. The relationship lasted less than three months, but Benedicta's place as 'dominating woman' was taken by Dorothy Kingsmill, the wife of the writer Hugh Kingsmill; she was a strong believer in reincarnation and the occult and held astral communication with an Indian holy man, who was soon communicating with Antonia too. She, meanwhile, was subject to changes of mood from elation to despair, often feeling suicidal, often spending whole days in bed in a 'semi-cataleptic' state, 'dreaming against' her once-favoured elder daughter, to whom she now became inexplicably hostile. At Christmas she broke away from Dorothy, who later called her a tragic incurable case, whom it was dangerous to try to help since she was not mad enough to be permanently hospitalised but was always on the edge of insanity.

Mrs Kingsmill did help Antonia a great deal, however, in that she forced, or encouraged, her to write again. *The Lost Traveller* (in part a wish-fulfilment story) was the result of continuous effort, by Dorothy and another woman friend, who telephoned Antonia every day for a progress report, without which the novel would never have been finished. Its publication should have solved Antonia's money problems, but she was soon in debt again, and by Christmas of 1952 she was feeling suicidal once more, having turned her eldest daughter out of her flat and quarrelled with many of her friends (even with her long-suffering second husband), often over money. But she managed to complete several translations from the French, and to write two short books about her cats, and, in spite of the confusion of her life at this period, she wrote her last novel, *Beyond the Glass*, an account of her first breakdown, which she finished with remarkable speed; she said that she wrote 'the asylum part' as though she were possessed.

She was never to complete another novel; for the remainder of her writing life she struggled with an unfinished autobiography and a fifth semi-autobiographical novel. Her last years were as difficult as the rest of her life, but there were to be no more major breakdowns. She had constant money problems, moved house often, had fluctuating relationships with her daughters and was often depressed. Both her daughters have left records of the final years of her life, with their increasing physical disabilities which led to her admission to hospital, from which her impossible behaviour caused her to be sent home. She died soon after her eighty-first birthday in a Sussex nursing-home.

Antonia White's very strange relationship with her children was probably due both to the poor mothering she had herself received and to her own psychotic behaviour and reactions. Her elder daughter appears to have been simply farmed out to a children's home until Antonia's third husband brought her to live with the family when she was two. The children lived in rooms apart from their mother, and were not expected to visit her part of the house without an invitation. They were fearful of her – as indeed she was of them: but they had more reason to be afraid. Their mother's uncertain temper, her concern with herself to the exclusion of her children's needs or rights, her fierce rages, made her a formidable parent. The elder daughter remembers that the children hated their mother, and had fantasies of murdering and burying her. As they grew through their disturbed and difficult childhood, their mother, alternately rejecting and spoiling them, always domineering, always interfering, so overshadowed their lives that both found it imperative to escape from her. By their own accounts, both daughters have had severe psychological disturbances in adult life.

How Antonia's psychosis affected her writing is unclear. She was certainly not a natural writer like Woolf or Plath, but probably began to write short stories mainly for money. Most of what she wrote was about herself, though usually in a novelettish style; by far the best things she wrote were the descriptions of her own breakdowns. These have a truth and immediacy lacking in the rest of her work. Her most interesting book is probably the series of letters written about her reconversion to a fellow-Catholic, Peter

Thorpe, with whom she fell in love by letter, only to fall out of love when she met him. The book, *The Hound and the Falcon*, presents an abbreviated autobiography in a combination of truth, dishonesty and lack of insight extremely characteristic of its author. By the time she wrote the letters, lauding and upholding the Christian religion, Antonia's own faith was almost non-existent, and such discrepancies occur throughout the book. She did not, for example, tell her correspondent that she was living with a former lover, who had once again become her present lover; she did not tell him of her disturbed relations with her children, but said that she 'adored' them. She drew an entirely false picture of their response to Catholicism. But she was as honest as she knew how to be about her psychosis. She saw herself in 1941 as having reached a kind of equilibrium, after 'an unconscious struggle' of nearly fifteen years and 'a very conscious one' of five, against 'a very bad enemy' in herself, which even now was only held at a distance and had at times driven her to the edge of a terrifying abyss. There was no doubt that it was insanity, but it was not hereditary, and was, she said, diagnosed after her first breakdown as having been brain-fever. However, the breakdown after her separation from her first husband was 'a very serious form of insanity', which would almost certainly be permanent. It showed itself first as exhaustion and irritability, then came delusions and attempts at suicide, one nearly successful, then depressions so deep that it was painful even to remember them so long afterwards. She was still, in 1941, she said, susceptible to rapid mood changes; and 'sudden irrational attachments' and 'a disposition to spend money I haven't got' were warnings that 'the beast' had drawn nearer. She described her 'fearful' and 'horrible' depressions as 'ashes in the mouth and mud in the mind', 'the wheels grinding in a vacuum'. She called herself 'a barbarian and a lunatic', and said that being a schizophrenic, she could never maintain a consistent attitude, nor manage without the continual reassurance which she desperately needed but which destroyed her independence. She admitted that sex was a terrifying guilt-ridden ordeal for her, but did not admit her sexual promiscuity.

In the unfinished fifth novel, the heroine, who is Antonia herself, shows signs of other psychotic traits. She has the extreme sensitivity of hearing, as when a ship's siren vibrates through her ears like a dentist's drill, the disintegration of personality which forces her to obey the repellent and humiliating orders of the alien force which has replaced her former self, the compulsion to make scenes, the almost instantaneous mood changes, the unreasonable anger. Her voluminous notebooks, in which, like Virginia Woolf, she could write at great length when she could do no work on her books, were evidently as necessary to her, and as much a part of her life, as were those of Ruskin, Benson, Woolf and Plath to them. Yet Antonia White still felt that madness could lead her into a world that, though terrible, had a greater and more wonderful intensity than the real world, from which she felt herself separated, 'gasping for air inside a bell-jar'.

Sylvia Plath (1932–63)

Psychotics often describe themselves as being cut off from the rest of the world as though they were mere spectators of life. Arthur Benson felt he was watching the world from a high mountain, Antonia White watched it as though at a play, or from inside a bell jar. This phrase was to be made famous by Sylvia Plath, who used *The Bell Jar* as the title of her novel about her own breakdown and suicide attempt, and who became a cult figure after she killed herself at the age of thirty. There is no evidence that Plath read White's work, although many of the authors she liked best, and who influenced her own work, were, as it happened, psychotic. She was immensely struck by the poems and lectures of Robert Lowell and Anne Sexton, who use their writing to explore their own experience of mental illness, hitherto a 'private and taboo' subject; her own life and poetry were clearly influenced by Virginia Woolf. She said, 'Her novels make mine possible', and when she tried to kill herself in 1953 she felt that she was duplicating Woolf's suicide, 'only I couldn't drown'.

There was a history of psychosis in the Plath family; Sylvia's paternal grandmother was hospitalised more than once, and an aunt and cousin were depressives. Otto Plath, her father, was born, she said, 'in the black depressive heart' of Prussia, and even when he had emigrated to America he remained Prussian in temperament, a severe and rigid disciplinarian who expected his second wife, Sylvia's mother, and his two children to be submissive and well-behaved and, in the case of the two children, to achieve the highest possible grades in school. His emphasis was always on achievement; he himself had become a Professor of entomology, and though he worked a great deal at home, when he demanded complete silence from the children, and rarely played with them, they were expected to 'perform' for him when they were allowed into his presence. Otto and his wife Aurelia were profoundly different in age, outlook and temperament.

When Sylvia was three, her brother Warren was born; sickly and delicate, he took up a great deal of his mother's time and attention. Sylvia was consumed with jealousy; later she would pinch Warren to make him cry, so that his father would reprove him – Sylvia never cried. She stayed much of the time with her maternal grandparents, who adored her, so that her life veered between uncritical love and attention there and neglect and severe criticism at home. She was given to outbursts of rage, and frequently tried to run away, but her father's approval, which she craved, could only be won by excellence, and after she went to school she turned into a high achiever. She thought of her father as a colossus, and his approval was therefore necessary to survival.

In 1936 Otto Plath became convinced that he had cancer, but refused to have medical attention. Increasing pain forced him to withdraw more and more from the life of the family. In October 1940, when he had to have his right leg amputated, it appeared that this condition was due to diabetes, and would have been treatable if taken earlier, but he died of an embolism a month later. His daughter was devastated; she did not see her dead father, nor go to his funeral, and vowed never to speak to God again. She said later that all her happiness ended with his death, and much of her later work, including her journals, attempts to explain or come to terms with her violent and anguished feelings for him. The story 'Among the Bumblebees' describes the sensations of strength and superiority his presence gave her, so that she could 'face the doomsday of the world' with him, and her feelings of rage and betrayal at his infidelity with her mother and 'Lady Death'. Almost certainly, her childish feelings were partly sexual, and her later lovers were all thought of as father-figures. David Holbrook finds strong oral and genital feelings for her father in 'The Colossus' and in other poems, especially in 'Daddy'. She saw him as a boy in a youthful photograph, 'a boy of seventeen whom I love terribly', and all her life felt the pain of his loss: 'Father, it hurts, O father . . . they took away from me.' She hated him as 'an ogre' and 'a bastard', but was later to assert that her suicide attempt was an effort to get back to the father she loved and hated so obsessively.

Since Otto Plath distrusted insurance salesmen as much as doctors, he had made no financial provision for his family, who were now dependent on Aurelia Plath's earnings. She who had been forced to submit to her husband in everything was now forced to make her living in the aggressive outside world, and this she did with some success. Sylvia, though she had never such strong feelings for her mother as for her father, was determined, having lost one parent, not to lose the other, and insisted that her mother sign a promise never to remarry; some years later she prevented her from taking a better but more time-consuming job. Sylvia began to resent her financial and emotional dependence, and was to write angry poems, dreading that her mother would come to be dependent on her, like 'an old hag child'. In fact a college friend was to say that Mrs Plath lived her own life through Sylvia, refusing to let her grow up and deluging her when she was away with 'a barrage' of letters, which Sylvia religiously answered but which she found a heavy burden. Indeed if we compare her letters to her mother, full of strained exuberance and fictitious happiness, with the dooms and despairs of simultaneous journal entries, we see that Sylvia did actually treat her mother as a child who must be spared all pain and anxiety. *The Bell Jar* was written under a pseudonym so that the mother to whom it showed such immense hostility should not be hurt. If the daughter sometimes felt impulses to 'twist the life out of the fragile throat' of the mother, she also felt 'a strong murderous impulse' emanating from that mother, which she said was another reason why she had to kill herself. The huge weight of forcing herself to be happy and successful was owed to her mother because of Aurelia's sacrifice – 'a sacrifice I hate.'

Under the burden of these complex emotions Sylvia moved into adolescence. She was never popular at school in spite of her good looks and high academic achievements. Her high-school teacher found her manipulative, her fellow-students thought her affected; she was intensely competitive, strained and unable to relax, acting and over-reacting in every situation. She made rapid friendships then became quickly disillusioned, was unadaptable and demanding. She was already taking sleeping-pills regularly and finding writing a necessity to discharge emotions she could not control. Her menstrual periods were, and always were to be, irregular, with stoppages of up to five months; when they appeared, she suffered from cramps, headaches and general misery.

In 1950 Sylvia entered Smith College; most of the students came from wealthy families, while she, on a scholarship, had to be extremely careful with money. She felt bewildered and under pressure, and sometimes thought that she was going insane. In the vacations she had to work, and in her third year was forced to do housework in part exchange for her room and board, besides carrying a heavy academic workload. She was on the edge of breakdown, suffering from insomnia, loss of identity and guilt about her life, which she felt to be dark and meaningless; such friendships as she managed to make were ruined by her sudden inexplicable rages and her need to be 'kept going like an intricate clock'. Feeling herself close to breaking-point, she wrote to her mother about the possibility of suicide, but for whatever reason her distress was ignored. In the summer of 1953 she was selected to stay in New York as guest editor of the magazine *Mademoiselle,* a great honour, but one which made her feel overworked and weary, as though, she said, her mind were split open. On her last night in New York she threw all her clothes, new and old, from a high window, and went home in deep and growing depression, suffering from the insomnia so terribly described in *The Bell Jar,* and full of bizarre ideas such as that her eyes would fall out so that everyone would see the bubbling corruption behind them. Her handwriting became unrecognisable, and she could not read because the words on the page no longer made sense to her. When her mother saw that she had been gashing herself with razors she arranged for Sylvia to see a psychiatrist, who prescribed electric-shock treatment on an out-patient basis, with no preparation and no follow-up assistance. After a few days of this, Sylvia crawled underneath the family house and swallowed a quantity of sleep-ing-pills. She remained unconscious for two days and was then discovered bruised, scarred and distraught. She was taken to the locked psychiatric wing of the Massachusetts General Hospital, where she was given insulin treatments, which did not restore any wish to go on living. Olive Prouty, a wealthy novelist, paid for her removal to McLeans, an expensive private institution in Belmont. Here she had psychiatric counselling with Dr Ruth Beuscher, together with ECT, as the insulin therapy was causing her to put on weight. She had no visitors except Mrs Prouty and her old high-school English teacher, who slowly taught her to read again.

Gradually she recovered and returned to Smith, where she seems to have traded on her recent experiences, almost boasting of being a near-successful suicide; but she also said frequently that if ever she went mad again, she would certainly kill herself. Either because Dr Beuscher had encouraged her to break away from her mother's puritanical ethos, or because she was terrified of being alone at night, she took a series of lovers. She was not much more popular than she had formerly been; she was seen as a poseuse, a demanding and difficult colleague, a melodramatic loner. Academically she did well, and won a series of awards, culminating in a prestigious Fulbright Fellowship to Newnham College, Cambridge. When she sailed for England in the mid-September of 1955, she said that her whole life had exploded into a rainbow.

She found college life no easier in Cambridge than she had done at Smith. She embarrassed English and fellow-American students alike with her desperate pursuit of men and her attention-seeking behaviour. She was difficult to get on with, furious at the unintentional mishaps or carelessnesses of the other students, yet herself inconsiderate of their rights or needs. She was far from happy, but her letters home were full of spurious brightness and enthusiasm. By the spring of 1956 she was depressed and paranoid, feeling that children snowballed her because they could see the rottenness inside her, and that the student hostel bristled with hatred and suspicion. Her journals show panic about her ability to meet her academic obligations; like Dylan Thomas, she found ordinary social contacts and necessities of every day inexplicably dangerous, and could not look people in the eye for fear they would see her inward corruption. She was already having interviews with a psychiatrist when she met another student, Ted Hughes.

He was huge and authoritarian, like her father; he was the only man in the world, she said, who was her match, a god, 'rough, crude, powerful and radiant', who was to solve all her problems, in whom she was to sink her own troubled identity. They married in June 1956 and went on to Spain for the summer, but already resentments and rivalries beyond the ordinary enormous difficulties of any close personal relationships had begun to arise. Sylvia felt that she had to be perfect and self-sacrificing like her own mother, and took time from her own writing to type and place Ted's poems, but she felt the overshadowing of 'that black cloud which would annihilate my whole being with its demand for perfection'. The next summer they went to America, and she noted in her journal how her 'good self' was beginning to split off from a 'murderous self' which could no longer be ignored. She was suffering from insomnia again, 'lugubrious, black, bleak, sick', and when she did sleep, she had 'gross and oppressive' nightmares. She felt 'razor-shaped nerves', frenzies of resentment, upsurges of rage, a sense that her life was 'magically run' by two electric currents, 'joyous positive' and 'despairing negative'. Her journal throughout this summer describes episodes of panic, fury, hysteria, paralysing inertia and a feeling that her inner self was dissipating into air. Unknown to her mother or her husband, she began to see Dr Beuscher again. A short story, 'Johnny Panic and the Bible of Dreams', written about this time, expresses her sense that the world is 'run' by Panic, 'with a dog-face, devil-face, hag-face, whore-face', and that its motto was 'perfect Fear casteth out all else'. Only a few people were doomed to the 'crass fate' doctors called health and happiness. In her therapeutic sessions she expressed enormous guilt, also shown in her journals. Her husband, who shared with her an interest in occult rituals, sometimes hypnotised her so that she could sleep. In the spring of 1959 she attended Robert Lowell's poetry workshop, where she was impressed by his exploration of his own experiences of mental illness, and where she sometimes discussed the possibility of suicide with Anne Sexton, another poet who had made attempts to kill herself.

In December 1959 Sylvia and her husband sailed for England; she was pregnant. She had often in her journal equated babies with tumours, and many of her worst nightmares were about deformed children, such as the dream about giving birth to a baby with the rest of the uterus in its nose; but both parents were pleased at the birth of a daughter Frieda in 1960. Naturally enough, the nurture of the child by two writers caused immense strain, although Ted took over maternal duties in the mornings so that Sylvia could work for at least part of the day; but it was a year of difficulty and struggle. Sylvia was often aggressive and demanding, yet in her letters to her mother she represented herself as patient and put-upon. Her poems of this time show great dissatisfaction and the 'bloody private wounds' of marriage, and in spite of the fact that she said that the theme of 'The Colossus' was that of a person broken and then mended, her own moods and behaviour were often bizarre and erratic. She began to show extreme jealousy of her husband, and would often burn his notes and drafts if he came home later than she thought he should have done. She began to write her novel *The Bell Jar*, a disturbing account of her breakdown and suicide attempts in 1953.

At the end of the summer of 1961 the family moved to Devon; Sylvia was six months pregnant. The old house and garden in which they lived required a good deal of work, but initially she was pleased to be in the country, and her letters home were ecstatic. But her poems contained many images of blood, graves, 'bad' landscapes and mirrors, which she had formerly thought to be symbols of schizophrenic perception. Her son Nicholas was born in January, and all that winter she was severely depressed. Again there is a deep divide between her letters, recording the changing seasons in the peaceful Devon countryside, and her own stressful life, looking after two small children and involved in quarrels with her husband; she even found friendships burdensome and would turn visitors away with nervous aggression. When her mother arrived on a vacation that summer, Sylvia professed to be happy, but after a week or two became distraught and drove away, leaving Frieda with her grandmother. When she came back, she made a funeral pyre of all Ted's letters and her second novel and took out an insurance policy on his life which left her with only ten pounds in the world. At about this time she had what appeared to be a car accident, but the poem 'Lady Lazarus' suggests that it might have been a suicide attempt.

Her husband was by now attached to another woman; Sylvia felt betrayed, and the furious vengeful poems she wrote at this time associate him explicitly with her father, who had also betrayed her by dying. She was neither sleeping nor eating, but managed to finish her book of poems on 9 October. Two days later her husband either left her or was evicted. Her mother had to return to America, but paid for a nurse to look after the children, as Sylvia was now moving into a manic phase. She talked unceasingly and spent money lavishly on clothes and jewellery. A friend arriving in response to her frantic pleas found her erratic in behaviour, unable to stop talking and much involved in occult operations, the taking of sortes and magical rites against her husband.

In December she moved to a flat in London, writing to her mother what fun, what an adventure it all was, and how happy she felt. The tenant of the flat below hers, a Professor Thomas, thought the children unnaturally quiet, and their mother moving from hostility to uncontrollable weeping. A visiting friend found the kitchen immaculate, and wondered if anything was ever cooked or eaten there. The children at least were given boiled eggs and chicken broth, but it is doubtful whether Sylvia ate much; she became so thin and anxious that her doctor was considering admitting her to hospital, after prescribing sleeping-pills and anti-depressants which had little effect. On the evening of 10 February, Professor Thomas saw her standing in the corridor outside his flat, looking as though she were hallucinating. She looked so ill that he offered to call a doctor, but she would not allow this. The next morning, having taken a quantity of sleeping-pills, she put her head in the gas-oven and at last succeeded in what she thought of as her vocation: she killed herself.

Sylvia Plath's journals, and their schizoid contrast with letters written simultaneously, show her to be a psychotic writer, but the poems and prose meant for publication show it equally clearly. All her writing is autobiographical; she can never escape from the subject of her own impressions, her own miseries, terrors and nightmares. A major preoccupation in prose and poetry is her own inner worthlessness. This appears strongly in the short story 'Tongues of Stone' about life in a psychiatric hospital; the protagonist imagines 'the waste piling up in her, swelling her full of poisons that showed in the black darkness of her eyes when she stared into the mirror', and that the scabs on her nose which are the relics and reminders of her suicide attempt will never heal and will gradually cover her body in a leprosy that will mirror 'the backwaters of her mind'. All the poisons in her body will gather until they break out through 'the bright false bubbles' of her eyes. If this story portrays her own life as accurately as it seems to do, it is likely that she made other suicide attempts while in hospital, by trying to strangle herself, and by swallowing broken glass. The story of Lazarus, the man who was called back from the dead, exercised a permanent fascination over her, and she saw herself as Lady Lazarus, in the poem of that name: the woman who rises from the dead 'one year in every ten'. But most of her poems show her obsession with death. David Holbrook points out that in *The Bell Jar* all references to sexuality are clinical and lifeless, while all the references to death are full of hope and joy. Whatever the real reason for her suicide among the many she offered, whether it was because of her father, her mother, her own 'murderous self' or her wish to destroy her own inner corruption, it is clear that throughout her life she saw death as the way out, the release, the one certainty in her uncertain and troubled life.

Her obsession with mirrors and doubles is clearly shown both in her published work and in her journals. After her 'lost year' she wrote a thesis at Smith on Dostoyevsky's use of doubles, and was always fascinated by what she called 'the double exposure' – the effect of one scene showing through another, such as Ruskin and Woolf described. Mirrors had attracted and repelled her since as a child she had defecated over a hand-mirror. The heroine of *The Bell Jar*, looking in a mirror after her suicide attempt, sees a sexless, hideous face. In the poems mirrors can kill and talk; they reflect rooms in which tortures are taking place. The female ancestors in 'All the Dead Dears' reach 'hag hands' out of the mirror to pull in their descendant. The poems admit too their writer's fascination with magic, runes, rituals, incantations; insulin therapy is seen as the sticking of pins by witches into the wax figure of the patient.

But more than any of our writers, Sylvia Plath continually stresses the importance of writing itself to the psychotic mind. She was 'in prison' when she could not write, she could not work or eat if her imagination was 'blocked'. 'I am desperate when I am verbally repressed . . .' 'the moment I stop . . . paralysis sets in'. Writing dissipated her fury, it held her fissiparous self together, it assuaged her terror that the actual world would fold up and disappear. Words stopped the 'flux and smash', the 'deluge through the thumbhole in the dike'. Writing made other people accept her as a human being, but above all it could bring order into her confused and disordered mind. Again and again she asserted that writing was a religious act, it ordered and re-formed: 'my sickness is when . . . the physical world refuses to be ordered, re-created, arranged and selected.' But she realised the problem of all creative writers, that the 'dialogue' between living and writing was always in danger of becoming 'evasive rationalising': 'I justified the mess I'd made of life by saying I'd give it order, form, beauty.' In the end her writing did not succeed in ordering her life; her last poems were written 'in a frenzy', when she was most wretched and most disturbed by her husband's desertion and by her move to London, but these bursts of creativity did not save her from breakdown and death.

Like many psychotic writers, she felt herself separated from life by a 'transparent envelope'; even the nine years she saw as happy before her father's death 'sealed themselves off like a ship in a bottle'. The image of herself as a foetus in a glass jar was always with her. What she lacked, like her heroine and exemplar, Virginia Woolf, was natural happiness. 'To the person in the bell-jar', she wrote, '. . . the world itself is the bad dream.'

Case Descriptions

Virginia Woolf. Although there has been disagreement about the significance and causes of Virginia Woolf's insanity, that it existed is beyond dispute. Yet we cannot agree with Lyndall Gordon, that 'in view of the inadequacy of psychiatry in those early days either to diagnose or to help her, her illness will remain a mystery'. Leonard Woolf came closest when he described it as manic-depression, of which she showed all the classic features. In the 'high' states – what she herself called 'garrulous mania' – she was irritable, exuberant, restless, and voluble: 'Head bursting, head so full, racing with ideas'. At these times she felt herself to have special talents ('I feel a great mastery over the world') and in one breakdown may even have thought she was Christ. But in her depressed periods, her 'trough of despair', all this left her, 'all the devils came out; unmarried, a failure, – childless, insane, no writer'.

But obvious signs of schizophrenia, recordable on the SADS-L, were also present. Her 'manic' speech, for example, was often incomprehensible and of a schizophrenic form: 'the nouns and adverbs kept getting into the wrong place'. Even more telling, her portrayal of her fictional persona Septimus in *Mrs. Dalloway* (where she herself said she was keeping strictly to the truth of her own breakdowns) is an extremely accurate account of schizophrenia, with its delusions, paranoia and auditory hallucinations. In short, Woolf represents yet another example among our authors of the difficulty of distinguishing manic-depression from schizophrenia. She showed the symptoms of both.

Antonia White. Antonia White is unusual among our subjects because, with the permission of her daughters, we were able to inspect the case-notes relating to her first breakdown, for which she was admitted to the Bethlem Royal Hospital on 17 November 1922. She is described on admission as being in a state of 'maniacal excitement', confused, noisy, with rambling incoherent speech containing many 'clang' associations and toned with religious phraseology: she claimed at this point to be possessed by spirits and to be fighting against 'outpowers'. Her mood is referred to as 'elated' and she told the doctor that she was weeping because she was happy; just prior to admission she had tried to throw herself into the river, but had been restrained. In the early months of her stay in hospital she became increasingly restless and 'deluded', relating stories to herself, talking continuously in a 'confused jumble', and singing hymns and childish songs. Subsequently, presumably because of the lack of appropriate medication at that time (she was treated throughout with chloral hydrate and paraldehyde), she passed into a stuporose state in which it was necessary for her to be tube-fed and during which it is recorded that she 'occasionally smiles in a dull sort of way'. Recovery at first was slow and then more rapid, at the end of which time she confessed to her doctor that she had very little memory of her life during the previous two years. At the insistence of her father she was taken home on leave from the hospital and formally discharged, apparently fully recovered, on 22 August 1923.

Although rather brief, these case-notes dovetail accurately with the much richer account of the illness written from the 'patient's' viewpoint by Antonia White herself in her autobiographical novel, *Beyond the Glass* and in her short story, 'The House of Clouds'. The formal diagnosis for her first breakdown might be 'acute manic episode' (no diagnosis is given in the hospital notes) but her whole life-history indicates that she also met other diagnostic criteria for psychosis. This certainly included serious depression; summed up in her own words as 'ashes in the mouth and mud in the mind' and revealed also in her pervasive guilt, sleep disturbance, loss of energy and concentration, and her thoughts of, and attempts at, suicide. Several features of schizophrenia can also be found. These include: persecutory ideas (e.g. that her father was taking her to hospital to be experimented upon), strange bodily sensations, extraordinary visions, jumbled thought and speech, and the feeling that her personality had disintegrated, to be replaced by some alien influence whose impulses, 'however repellent and humiliating', she had to obey. Regarding auditory hallucinations, the Bethlem case-notes about her first breakdown are equivocal, recording '?' against the item; but Antonia White herself leaves us in no doubt that during that illness she was constantly plagued by the voices of imaginary figures in her head.

In summary, Antonia White again presents the diagnostician with the typical dilemma. If, for the purpose of this exercise, she is to be 'labelled', then it has to be concluded that over her lifetime she met the criteria for all forms of psychosis; leading, in SADS-L terminology, to the undifferentiated description of 'schizoaffective, with both manic and depressive features.'

Sylvia Plath. Like Antonia White, Virginia Woolf and several other of our subjects, during her short life Sylvia Plath showed, from a strictly diagnostic viewpoint, the signs of more than one form of psychotic disorder. In the affective domain, her mood was constantly unstable and, judged according to the SADS-L, she clearly meets the criteria for major depression, including, of course, her final suicide. Swings into mania were much briefer but did occur – as a 'sudden plunge upwards of ecstasy' during a depressive period. During these times she also showed signs of at least mild mania; such as hyperactivity, incessant talk, sleep disturbance, and some grandiosity of ideas ('Today I could write ten novels and vanquish the gods').

However, taking us closer to an understanding of Plath – and especially of her suicide – is her pervasive existential anxiety, which was so severe that it can only be judged schizophrenic. David Holbrook appears to agree with this, basing the whole analysis of her work on the idea; though he stops short of using the term 'schizophrenic', preferring the description 'schizoid'. Interestingly, according to Plath's biographer, Wagner-Martin, her psychiatrists 'found "no trace of psychosis" and no schizophrenia'; though, remarkably, they then proceeded to give her insulin therapy, a form of treatment to which only patients diagnosed as schizophrenic were subjected. According to our own evaluation, evidence of the schizophrenic element in Plath is to be found in several items on which she scores on the SADS-L: bizarre feelings about her own body, reports of having seen visions (in her final breakdown, of God) and paranoid ideas ('the house bristles with suspicion and frigidity'). Plath would probably now be diagnosed as suffering from a schizoaffective psychotic disorder, with predominantly depressive features.

10

Inside the Bell Jar

All of the authors we have discussed in this book were, as individuals, unique, demonstrating their creativity, and their psychosis, in various forms. In their writings, for example, they differed in the extent to which they either expressed (or, to look at it another way, attempted to conceal) their tendency to mental illness. In private diaries there is often no disguise; in poetry or prose meant for publication the disguise varies. Hoccleve is a recognisable participant in his dialogues; Benson is as evidently the hero – or at least the major character – in his novels. Woolf's novels might appear to be pure fiction, but the qualities of her personal madness reverberate in many of her characters; while the novels of White and Plath are barely concealed autobiography. When we turn to style rather than content, we may compare the clarity with which Benson described his daily agonies, the manic over-inclusiveness of Ruskin, Woolf's evocative and exquisitely constructed, but loosely associated, vignettes of consciousness, and the impenetrable structure but ever-expanding thought of Smart's *Jubilate Agno*.

Some of the differences we observe undoubtedly reflect variations in intellectual and temperamental qualities that persist independently of time and place: others were certainly coloured by the age and circumstances in which each author lived. But, individual as they were, our authors nevertheless had many features in common and, while always mindful of their differences, we shall in this final chapter concentrate on their similarities, from which we may find that there are some general conclusions to be drawn about their creativity and their psychoses.

We must, however, issue a caveat. Ours was not, in the conventional sense, a scientific study. We had no 'control group' with which our set of authors was systematically compared, and our sample was very small. It was also highly selected; though here two points are worth noting. First, our choice of subjects, while not random, was at least rather arbitrary: many other authors could have been included or substituted for those we studied had we extended our enquiry to writers in other European languages. Secondly, the similarities we shall particularise could not have been anticipated at the outset and were certainly not criteria for selection.

Set against the 'unscientific' nature of our study we need to state – for students of psychology at least – one overriding fact. Academic psychology can scarcely claim to have much advanced our understanding of the kind of questions we are trying to address here, using, that is, the narrowly focused laboratory techniques to which this discipline has felt it necessary to resort in its search for respectability as a natural science. This is not to decry entirely the value of such procedures. Indeed, in Chapter 2 we saw how their use *is* beginning to throw important light on certain basic cognitive and brain processes that might underlie, say, creativity or susceptibility to schizophrenia. However, even given the value of this laboratory research, it is still ultimately necessary, armed with the knowledge it yields, to test its significance in the world of real events and real people, albeit in our case a world of traces left behind. To do so inevitably involves sacrificing scientific precision for the richness of a material which, in any case, has an interest in its own right. If our observations are tentative then at least their validity can be judged – as they are intended to be – against the background of other more rigorous research on creativity and psychosis which we have already reviewed and which we shall occasionally enlarge upon, where appropriate, in what follows.

In considering the similarities among our authors we shall not discuss any further here their resemblance from a formal 'diagnostic' viewpoint, in terms of the psychiatric symptoms that they had in common. The detailed accounts in previous chapters and the associated 'case descriptions' clearly attest to the fact that, although often differing in the exact form their mental illnesses took, all of the subjects suffered from what, in contemporary terminology, would be classified as psychotic disorder. In this chapter we shall be concerned rather with characteristics that lie outside the usual domain of diagnostic psychiatry but which, on close inspection, many of our subjects seemed to share and which, we believe, are significant for an understanding of their creative madness.

It is not coincidental that the most general common feature we discover in our authors – and one that gives insight into several other of their characteristics – is the 'skinlessness' to which

Virginia Woolf's father, Leslie Stephen, referred in himself and which, as we saw in a previous chapter, the American psychiatrist, E. J. Anthony, quotes as the overriding trait of the psychotically prone personality.[3] There is abundant evidence of this quality in our authors – from Kempe right through to Plath, who wrote: 'It's as if neither of us, or especially myself, had any skin.' Indeed, the trait seems so central to their temperaments that it is scarcely possible to comprehend the overall tenor of the subjects' psychological experiences – including their psychiatric symptoms – without referring to this vastly enhanced sensitivity of body and mind.

The authors' skinlessness was manifest in various ways, at a physical level ranging from a simple hyperawareness of sensory stimulation – such as Ruskin's oversensitivity to sounds – to nervous irritability and bodily complaints. Headaches, for example, were very common, Woolf, White, and Plath all reporting these before their breakdowns. Clare, also highly sensitive to sound, described his head as being 'stung as though nettled'; Cowper and Ruskin referred to the excessive 'pressure' on the brain and Benson to his brain being 'congested'.

A perhaps related sign – and this was extremely frequent – was an obsessive concern with, and complaints of afflictions to the eyes. One form this took – that of intermittent 'visual sensations' – spans the centuries in a remarkable way. Kempe described it as seeing 'white specks by night and day'; Cowper as 'a frequent flashing like that of fire before my eyes'; Ruskin as 'swimming strings and eels'; Benson as 'strange streaks and tangles'; and Woolf as 'red hot quick sights'. The eyes as a psychological focus also emerge in other ways. Plath complained that her eyeballs were 'killing' her, swelling as though about to burst. Hoccleve, on the other hand, was made aware by onlookers that his eyes were in constant motion; an indication, incidentally, that finds a modern equivalent in reports that eye movements indeed sometimes *are* abnormal in psychosis and suggestions that an index of this might be a potentially useful genetic marker for the disorder.[15]

In view of the above it is not surprising that several of our authors – Hoccleve, Cowper, and Ruskin – were neurotically preoccupied with their eyesight, Ruskin having a lifelong obsession that he would go blind. Yet in no case is there evidence that their vision was less than normal. What is the reason for this channelling of anxiety into the eyes? One mundane explanation is that it was a perfectly natural, understandable concern, given that as writers they were dedicated to words and books and that, in earlier times at least, they would be pursuing their craft in poor light. This, however, could not apply to the illiterate Kempe and, in any case, more modern examples can be found of a similar preoccupation with the eyes. For example, David Jones, artist and writer, was so obsessed with going blind that he stopped work entirely in his sixties, only to start again and then continuing right into his seventies.

As another, and we believe more likely, explanation of this syndrome we would draw attention to the universal significance of the eye in representations of insanity, particularly in the visual arts.[10] Thus, in paintings of and by the mad the eyes are frequently the dominant feature, portrayed as overly large, distorted, wild, or frighteningly paranoid. Perhaps in the author this same tension is expressed in a different medium, as when Plath wrote in her journal:

I am afraid. I am not solid, but hollow. I feel behind my eyes a numb, paralysed cavern, a pit of hell, a mimicking nothingness.

At a more psychological level, the skinlessness of our authors is also revealed in their great imaginativeness, their capacity for responding easily to the contents of what in Freudian terminology would be referred to as primary process thought – or what in an earlier chapter we described more prosaically as weakly filtered preconscious associations. This quality is both a sign of skinlessness and, as Anthony points out, a vehicle for escaping the painful consequences of events in the external world to which the skinless individual is in any case already unduly sensitive. Without their imagination the literary work of our subjects would not, of course, have been possible, but it also carried its own psychological burden, notably in the form of nightmares, mentioned by almost all of the authors, even Kempe and Hoccleve. Often these nightmares reached terrifying proportions. For Cowper, as we saw in the chapter devoted to that author, they were so bad that his friend, Mary Unwin, had to stay in his room at night to comfort him. A. C. Benson endured his (presumably) alone; but his diary – a virtual catalogue of horror – refers constantly to sleep broken by 'dreams of incredible vividness, variety and rapidity – in much affliction and depression', to waking in great agitation after 'most vehement and emphatic dreams', and to 'a moaning nightmare, most horrible, as if something rushed at me'.

Typically these nightmares seemed to presage a period of collapse into psychotic breakdown, a fact which Susan Chitty recalls about her mother, in a passage that also captures Antonia White's constant nearness to psychological disintegration:

> It was at this time that Mother started to have nightmares so frightful that even the memory of them in daylight made her teeth chatter. After one of these dreams she would wake screaming Tom's name. In many of them he was leaving her. Sometimes, after a few comforting words from him, she would sleep again. Sometimes she had to get up and make entries in her diary in the dining room. She began to write in mirror writing. On a few occasions she rushed out of the house and headed for the river. She was now close to insanity . . .[6]

A recent study of the relationships between psychosis, creativity and the tendency to suffer frightening dreams supports these observations of frequent nightmares among our own subjects.[13] The investigators carried out extensive psychiatric interviewing and psychological testing of a group of individuals who had experienced nightmares since childhood and had continued to do so, at least once a week. Several results of interest emerged. First, all of the subjects were found to have unusual occupations and lifestyles, especially in the arts and crafts and included poets, musicians, art therapists and so on. Secondly, the sample as a whole manifested a high level of psychopathology. Of thirty-eight individuals interviewed, twenty-nine were in psychotherapy, fifteen had considered (and seven attempted) suicide, and four had been hospitalised for mental illness. Formally diagnosed they covered a spectrum of psychiatric conditions, though notably these were all related to psychosis, ranging from full-blown schizophrenia through borderline disorder to schizotypal personality. Another finding was the high incidence of psychopathology in the close relatives of the individuals studied. And, finally (shades of Hoccleve), a significant proportion of the subjects showed abnormalities on an eye-tracking task, a procedure currently being widely used to investigate the idea, referred to earlier, that deviant eye-movement patterns might code genetically for the disposition to schizophrenia. The authors of this study conclude that the chronic tendency to nightmares might itself tap some risk for schizophrenia. They also make an interesting suggestion: that children suffering from persistent nightmares after the age of ten or twelve might benefit from counselling to help them bring their unusual imaginativeness under control and encourage their creative ability, hence toughening them against clinical psychosis.

The fact that our subjects reported frequent nightmares is also of interest for another reason. It has often been suggested that the psychotic experience is like that of dreaming when awake, attempts even having been made to connect the possible brain mechanisms involved in disorders like schizophrenia to the neuroanatomical circuitry and neurochemistry of dreaming sleep.[9] Certainly the wildly irrational chaotic ideas and perceptions of the psychotic state *are* like a waking nightmare and in the highly imaginative this can lead to increasingly blurred boundaries between reality and unreality, between delusional and rational thought, and between random experience and material for genuine creativity. This loosening of the edges that join the conscious to the unconscious was probably true of many of our authors. It is seen most floridly in the merging of vision and dream found in Cowper; though Hoccleve also gives a hint of it when he talks of 'Troubly dremes, drempt al in wakynge' and Clare in his plaintive line, 'Life is to me a dream that never wakes.'

There is a further common feature found in several of our authors which could be seen as another sign of their hypersensitivity and which certainly tells us something about their perceptions and interpretations of the sense data around them. We are referring to the frequency with which the subjects believed in, or reported, so-called paranormal or mystical experiences. As noted in Chapter 2, concern with and interest in such phenomena are regularly found to occur in individuals of schizotypal personality. Indeed, many of the questionnaires used in research on schizotypy in normal subjects contain items that probe the respondent's belief in and report of telepathy and other forms of extrasensory perception. Furthermore, its clinical form – schizotypal personality disorder – is actually partly defined in these terms: as the person describing admitting to a strong 'sixth sense' or of feeling the close presence of another, physically absent, individual. The quality of such experiences is such that they can clearly be seen as a muted expression of the more disintegrative feelings of alien influence often seen in full-blown schizophrenia.

It comes as no surprise therefore that, even in their sane periods, many of our authors were adherents of the so-called paranormal or felt themselves subject to the influence of mystical forces emanating from outside their usual sensory channels. In former times, of course, the possibility for such experiences was nearer the surface, firmly embedded in the social culture, and strongly coloured by religious belief and theological dogma. The difference between 'genuine' transcendental experience and religious 'psychosis' was therefore even more blurred then than it is now, though, as we saw when discussing Margery Kempe, some distinctions could be, and were, made. In retrospect, whether or not we judge her experiences to be valid from a theological viewpoint, it can be said that their Christian content was inevitable. More relevant from a psychological stance, Kempe does seem to represent the earliest example among our authors of a schizotypal individual assailed by forces construed by the subject as being of supernatural origin.

Among writers in the middle period of our enquiry such beliefs, where they occurred, naturally continued to exist in a religious context. Smart's life was ruled by them, since he believed himself to be the divine instrument of God's will, using the *sortes* at the upswing from a period of depression to confirm this. Cowper, on the other hand, felt that he was marked out for peculiar rejection and relegation to a specially ordained Hell, set aside for him by an unforgiving – though otherwise all-forgiving – God. Clare alone seems to have been untroubled by thoughts of divine intervention; but even he was not entirely immune to supernatural interpretations of experience, believing that a guardian spirit he often saw in his dreams had a real existence.

In modern times preoccupation with these same phenomena has gradually become separated from narrow theological concerns, often being elaborated outside the context of organised, culturally based religious belief. In these forms the interest has continued unabated and, among our more recent authors, was deeply ingrained in most of them. (Woolf, it appears, was an exception, but possibly only because both her father and her husband, being so vehemently *against* anything to do with the paranormal, persuaded her out of expressing any such belief overtly.) Plath, for example, considered that from an early age she had had psychic powers, including precognitive ability, and regularly reported mystical experiences of one kind or another. Ruskin had revelatory dreams and both he and Benson were constantly on the look-out for omens: Benson in street signs and shop windows, Ruskin in the Bible and many other books for messages about the object of his sexual obsession, Rose Latouche. Indeed Ruskin was beset by ideas of the most weird kind, including a conviction that the weather was managed by demons and presaged a judgment day. However, it was Rose who preoccupied him most in this respect. Thus, after her death, he used a medium to try to contact her and attempted himself to 'bring her back' by occult means. For he was convinced that he was actually in touch with Rose and received messages from her (or from St Ursula with whom in Ruskin's mind she was identified).

In Arthur Benson's case, concern with the supernatural was even a family affair, the genealogy of his insanity being also a veritable pedigree of belief in the paranormal. Thus, several of his immediate and remote relatives showed similar interests. His mother, for instance, was continually preoccupied with seances, automatic writing and other occult phenomena – an indulgence, one might suppose, that was more than a little embarrassing for the wife of an Archbishop! In addition, Arthur Benson and his brothers wrote ghost stories. The most notable example, however, was his uncle, Henry Sidgwick, from whom Arthur Benson may have partly inherited his disposition to psychosis, and who was co-founder of the Society for Psychical Research. Henry Sidgwick is also known for having organised the earliest and certainly the most extensive survey of the incidence of hallucinatory experiences in the general population.[30] A mammoth task, involving interviews with over 15,000 people, the study showed that hallucinations are actually quite common, a fact still quoted as evidence for the continuity view of psychosis in the contemporary research literature on the topic.[31] Unlike modern researchers, however, Sidgwick himself was concerned less with the relevance of his findings to the understanding of hallucinations than with their psychical significance and he argued that some of the experiences reported by the subjects surveyed were indeed veridical, in predicting future events.

Although it would be absurd to argue that there is an inevitable association between psychosis and paranormal experience – only rarely does one lead to the other – the connection in our authors, at least, seems clear; so strong is the resemblance between their overriding feeling of having a 'sixth sense' and the modes of perception and ideation that resulted in their insanity. How close these are is brought out in a passage from the writings of Antonia White, another lifelong addict of clairvoyance, the occult, and other things supernatural. Here in *Beyond the Glass*, she describes the first meeting at a party between Clara, the heroine, and the young Army officer with whom she herself, in real life, fell violently in love, precipitating her into madness:

> She felt that someone was trying to attract her attention. None of the indistinguishable faces on the far side of the piano seemed to be turned towards her. Yet she was convinced that the person was not sitting anywhere near. She did her best to ignore this plucking at her attention but it continued with a gentle, teasing persistence. Then she tried another technique. She spoke silently to the unseen intruder: 'Stop it. I don't *want* to be disturbed.' It was almost as if she heard the reply. 'I know you don't. All right. See if you *can* stop me.' It developed into a kind of game.... Sometimes she thought she had won and the other had given up. But, as soon as her mind was left blank again, she realised she had been enjoying this odd game and missed the invisible attack. The next moment, the amused inner voice (she knew by now that it was a man's) would come clearer than ever 'You may as well give in. My will is stronger than yours.'

The conclusion that reported sensations of this kind may involve – to resort to an earlier jargon – the same information processing mechanisms as those which are responsible in susceptible individuals for psychotic symptoms, raises several other questions. How far, for example, are we justified in dismissing them as *merely* irrational? Or can we allow of the possibility, like the subjects themselves, that they are genuine paranormal experiences? Is the schizotype indeed the 'sensitive' beloved of psychical researchers? We must leave the reader to judge.

Whatever the opinion on that issue, we may still ask whether this particular trait of our authors has any significance, beyond its interest as just another indication of their eccentricity. We believe that it does: that it actually gives us some further insights into the skinlessness of psychotic personalities, helping us to understand something of the quality of their social interactions with those around them. The ability to read and interpret both verbal and non-verbal signals from others forms a vital part of social communication, but the sensitivity to such cues undoubtedly varies.

Reported experience of 'telepathic' contact with another person close by – as described above by Antonia White – may well indicate a genuine hyperawareness of 'leaked' social signals which are then interpreted, rightly or wrongly, as having psychological meaning. Certainly experimental research has shown that, contrary to some popular belief, psychotic individuals *can* be more perceptive in their ability, for example, to judge the true feelings of others, a finding which coincides well with clinical impression.[21] Anyone who has interacted with psychotics will know of their uncanny capacity to respond to subtle social cues, believed to have been concealed from them. It is not surprising that they themselves sometimes think *their* minds are being read. From there it may be a slippery slope into delusional belief; for the overdeveloped social antennae of the skinless psychotic temperament, combined with great imaginativeness, can also impart a disadvantage: the propensity for misinterpretation and elaboration of falsely perceived events that are the fodder of insane thought.

Another characteristic of the psychotic personality seen in our authors, and apparently belying the extreme oversensitivity of their nervous systems, is unusual *insensitivity*. This may be described as a lack of empathy, even cruelty, and an inability to feel naturally in emotionally demanding situations. Cowper, for instance, seemed unaware of the extent to which he must have disrupted the Unwin household and, although he had been totally dependent on Mrs Unwin, never mentioned her name again after her death. Ruskin was apparently unmoved by his father's death; Woolf laughed behind her hands when her mother died, and felt 'no more than a rock' at her fiancé's first kiss. Antonia White was profoundly insensitive to her children's needs; while Kempe's utter indifference to her own children contrasts markedly with her exaggerated weeping and howling at the sight of boy babies in Rome. Sylvia Plath showed the same characteristic. Although personally devastated by her father's death, she was nevertheless capable of displaying what Holbrook refers to as a 'cold intellectual callousness', a 'certain emotional failure to know how to respond'.[14]

Far from being unusual, this conjunction of hyper-sensitivity and insensibility may even be an intrinsic feature of the psychotic personality. Thus, Strindberg, another schizophrenic author, once said of himself: 'I am as hard as ice, and yet so full of feeling that I am almost sentimental.' Quoting this remark, Kretschmer considered that it actually captured the essential quality of schizoidness. 'He alone', he wrote, 'has the key to the schizoid temperament who has recognised that the majority of schizoids are not either oversensitive or cold, but that they are oversensitive and cold at the same time, and that in quite different relative proportions.'[20]

Explanations for this 'tough vulnerability' need not necessarily be mutually exclusive. The psychotic individual may be unable to acquire the 'insincere' behaviour demanded by social courtesy: his response may then appear 'insensitive', whereas in fact it represents the true, raw feeling unadmitted by more 'normal' individuals. Perhaps the psychotic person's 'insensibility' is merely a mirror image of a greater willingness to acknowledge the Emperor's nakedness. Another explanation may be that the apparent lack of feeling acts as a protection against skinlessness, as a psychological – or even physiological – device for dealing with otherwise unbearable pain. At the extreme – as in catatonia – this extends to complete lack of physical responsiveness. In other schizophrenics it is seen as oddly inappropriate or apparent absence of affective reaction; which caused some early psychiatrists to comment that it was as though there was a pane of glass between them and their patients. Was not this the same 'semi-transparent envelope', the same 'bell jar', from within which our authors looked out on the world?

However, it would be too simplistic to regard the retreat into the bell jar as merely affording temporary relief from instants of pain occasioned by skinlessness. Our authors, like many psychotic or borderline psychotic people, were chronically unable to manage their emotions, chaotically driven by inconsistent feelings, cut-off from the stable sentiments that normally guide human relations, ambivalent towards others, and sometimes not even sure who they were. This failure to achieve psychological integration is seen in several aspects of their personalities.

One sign, which often accompanies psychosis, is to be found in their occasional antisocial, almost 'psychopathic', behaviour and in traits such as recklessness, irresponsibility, and impulsivity; characteristics that drove Kempe and Smart, for example, to prison. Money – the careful management of which has generally been seen as a symbol of conformity and self-restraint – caused many problems. White and Plath, however poor, were addicted to impulse buying, especially of clothes, and Plath's self-confessed frittering of a whole month's pay on a raincoat 'with a frivolous pink lining' chimes over the centuries with Kempe's spending on a pretty cloak the forty pence (a sizeable sum) she had been given to pay off her debts. Even wealthy authors, though protected from its worst consequences, were not immune from irrational extravagance. Ruskin squandered enormous sums on grandiose and unrealistic schemes. Benson, while chronically anxious about money until his sudden accession to wealth, was yet unable to help buying things that attracted him: after his death his brother found his rooms at Cambridge crammed with possessions – 'piled high with boxes . . . a towering cliff of them'. Woolf's husband usually managed their finances, but once on a solitary expedition she bought on impulse a house which was completely unsuitable and had to be immediately resold.

Weak impulse control and the inability to delay gratification is a sign of immaturity to be seen in one form or another in all our authors. 'We ought always to have our own way', said Ruskin furiously in protest against not being allowed to make advances to young girls. Indeed it is in their sexual relationships, sexual behaviour and sexual proclivities that we find abundant evidence of our authors' immature, unstable psychology. True, that did not always take the form of lack of self-restraint: Hoccleve and Cowper were, if anything, sexually very timid and Benson, the only one apart from Cowper who never married, was horrified of sexual relations, preferring instead platonic attachments to young men. Marriage was no more successful. Smart, after a short period with his wife, was called to celibacy by God, Ruskin never consummated his marriage, and Clare's conjugal relationship can scarcely have been helped by his lifelong delusion that he had two wives. Of the women, Kempe veered between periods of overwhelming sexual temptation and a desire for total abstinence; Plath was promiscuous; Woolf was frigid even in her one lesbian affair; and of White's three marriages two remained unconsummated and of her many lovers only one was sexually satisfactory.

What, we may ask, lay at the core of these difficulties? One answer must be that all of the subjects failed in some way – like many psychotics – to develop a sense of their own identity. Plath said quite explicitly, 'I do not know who I am, where I am going', while Clare, who was literally never quite sure who he was, wrote in his *Essay on Self-Identity*, 'a person who denies himself must either be a madman or a coward' and later pathetically sought to reassure himself by writing, 'there are two impossibilitys that can never happen – I shall never be in 3 places at once nor ever change to a woman & that ought to be some comfort.'

One outward indication of the inner turmoil that frequently accompanies the disintegrated or ill-developed ego is its expression in unrestrained anger, a feature which characterised many of our subjects. Rage was certainly a very typical emotional response by Plath, Woolf, White and Ruskin, while Benson continually had quarrels because he could not control his temper. Among earlier authors, Hoccleve became angry because of the failure of others to recognise the hand of God in his recovery; Cowper's sense of the enmity of God was only restrained by the knowledge that he was dependent upon divine Grace for any improvement; while Carkesse (an author who made only a brief appearance in this book but who was also psychotic) directed considerable rage against the injustice of his employers and the insanity of his doctors.

Sometimes in the cases we have discussed the anger stemmed, as it typically does, from the need to blame others for inadequacies in the self: both Cowper and Clare had a tendency to blame their publishers for a lack of public acclaim, Clare also feeling increasingly that his public was unreasonable in expecting him to write at all, in view of what was being done to him in hospital. This sense of self-importance can, in turn, be seen as itself a sign of the fragile ego attempting to find an identity and a surprising number of our authors displayed such need to be regarded as 'special'. Witness here Kempe as the bride of God; Smart as God's specially dedicated psalmist, the second David; Cowper as the only man in a specially created Hell, created just for him; and Ruskin as the man destined to put the world to rights. Even where this streak of arrogance is absent, the psychotic's search for an identity may be manifest in other ways: through the construction of false personae, the adoption of what clinicians call the 'as if' personality – as though this were necessary because there is no real self to be presented to the world. This can be found in Woolf, and in Benson, and again in Plath – whose outwardly lively, carefree, sociable personality belied her inner chaos and of whom it was said that she was not at all spontaneous, that actually she 'needed preparing for any experience'.[32] In Clare the same tendency is found in his taking on, at one point, the persona of Byron with whom Clare closely identified and as a result of which he wrote two poems with exactly the same titles as Byron's own: *Don Juan* and *Childe Harold*. Here, and in his early literary forgeries, we find an ominous prognostic sign of Clare's eventual almost total loss of self-identity. The incomplete sense of self we have described is most acute when the individual is alone. For it is then that the person is forced to confront himself, unsupported by the temporary feeling of certainty which being with others might give. This often motivates – in an attempt to avoid being alone – the recklessness, seeking of sensation, and promiscuity to which we referred earlier in some of our authors. Yet frantic socialising of this kind rarely suffices to bolster, and may even overwhelm, the already fragile, skinless ego which yearns to escape back into solitude. But that, in turn, is the breeding ground of fantasy, introspection, and what clinicians recognise in the borderline personality as 'depressive loneliness'. This simultaneous need to escape the self and yet escape those who threaten it has been described as the 'inner shambles' of the psychotic personality, articulated as: 'I want what I don't want. Being alone is horrible; I want to be alone.'[4] Arthur Benson expressed it in almost exactly the same way when he wrote: 'I like solitude, and it does not suit me.'

Finally, there is one highly specific, and certainly very curious, indication of the precarious sense of identity from which our subjects suffered: the fear that several of them had of mirrors. We even find some reference to this in Hoccleve who, it may be recalled, when told by others that he looked peculiar hurried back home to inspect himself in the mirror 'to see if he looked normal, but he realised he might not be a good judge of that'. But it is in our three twentieth-century female authors that we find the mirror phenomenon at its most extreme. The mirror as a theme appears frequently in Plath's writings, while Woolf, after seeing a hideous animal face in the mirror as a child, was afraid even as an adult of her own reflection. In White, we discover, it was the breaking of a mirror in a friend's house that was one of the events alerting others to the onset of her first breakdown and her admission to hospital. For by now, as Lyndall Hopkinson points out, she was constantly looking into mirrors 'to make sure she still existed'.[16] As Clara in *Beyond the Glass* (a title of course significant in itself) White explains why this ultimate confrontation of the self is so painful for the psychotic personality:

> Not since she was a child had she had this sense of another person staring back at her from the glass. In those days she had often held long conversations with the reflection. Usually the

other was friendly: a twin sister who thought and felt exactly like herself. Occasionally she became mocking, even menacing. Clara would smile placatingly and the other would return a sneering grin. Gradually the other would take charge, twisting its features into grimaces she was compelled to imitate. Clara would try to turn away but the tyrant in the looking-glass held her hypnotised. When, at last, she wrenched herself free, she was weak and giddy. For days after, she would hurry past mirrors with her eyes shut.

This worry about mirrors is not, we believe, a coincidental finding. It may be connected with the strong interest in the *Doppelganger* image so popular in Victorian literature, an interest which Plath continued in her thesis on Dostoevsky's use of doubles. However it is also of great interest from a clinical viewpoint. Although never referred to by contemporary psychiatrists, several early clinicians, particularly in the French literature, discussed the tendency for schizophrenics to be preoccupied with, and behave oddly in front of, mirrors.[1, 28] Three possible explanations, all perhaps of some interest here, were proposed for this so-called 'mirror sign'. First, that it arises from sexual difficulties and is a kind of erotic parading associated with narcissism. Secondly, that it is connected with the subject's autism, the mirror image acting as a kind of interlocutor. And thirdly, that the subject is attempting some conscious control of facial expression, arising from uneasy feelings that changes are taking place in the personality.

Another explanation of the mirror sign – stemming from some very recent revival of interest in the phenomenon – is at a different level, though not necessarily contradicting the other three accounts.[12] The suggestion is that it may be a further indication of the unusual way in which the brain hemispheres function in psychosis and in the psychotic personality. The idea here is that some of the disrupted thinking and perception found in psychosis is due to increased emotional arousal 'leaking' from the right hemisphere. But the right hemisphere is also specialised for the perceptual analysis of facial expression, a processing capacity that is known to be odd in psychotics. Combined together, these two right hemisphere peculiarities could account for the disturbing perceptions which psychotics report when they confront their own faces in a mirror. In this respect it is worth noting that, even under

The Benson Genealogy

Diagram illustrating the distribution of psychosis and related 'borderline' conditions in the Benson family.

normal circumstances, one's own mirror reflection is rather unusual: being reversed it portrays an image of oneself different from
that which others see and, as a task in social perception, presents
the hemispheres with a unique problem. If, in addition, brain
organisation itself is arranged differently – as it seems to be in
psychotic individuals – then it is not surprising that they get a
strange appreciation of their own identity when looking at themselves in a mirror.

About the possible origins of our authors' psychopathology we
may, supported by the evidence reviewed earlier, conclude that all
of our subjects carried some genetic predisposition to psychotic
disorder. The prototypical example of this, of course, is the Benson
family, whose genealogical tree speaks for itself [see diagram]. The
family was riddled with a tendency to insanity which was certainly
exacerbated by two instances of inbreeding, including a first-
cousin marriage in the third generation. Arthur Benson's parents
were also related and in his, the final, generation we see a strong
convergence of the genetic effect. Even where manifest psychosis
was not evident, personality traits associated with it, or milder
forms of borderline disorder, are discernible in many relatives.
Even E. F. Benson, probably the happiest and most stable of them
all, had depressive periods in which he felt 'a screen of glass'
between himself and the rest of the world. The Benson genealogy
also illustrates the association between insanity and intellectual
accomplishment: Arthur Benson says in *The Leaves of the Tree* that
over twelve members of the Bensons and Sidgwicks had achieved
First Class degrees at Oxford or Cambridge and that over thirty of
them had published books.

Among the remote and immediate relatives of our other authors,
from Cowper onwards, we also find abundant evidence of psychopathology, ranging from clear psychosis to the serious eccentricity
which, as some recent research has shown, is often a characteristic
of the psychotic personality.[33] Cowper himself had both a cousin
and an uncle who were severely depressive and his father was
withdrawn, unsociable and probably schizoid; as was Plath's. Plath
also had a paternal grandmother who was hospitalised several
times, as well as an aunt and a cousin who were depressive; while
Ruskin's grandfather was incurably insane. White's mother was
certainly unstable and eccentric, unable to manage money, neglect-
ful of her child, and lived much of her time in a world of fantasy;
while White's own children, by their own admission, have not

been without psychological problems. Finally, the Woolf family was by no means an exception. Virginia's eccentric father who, as we have noted, coined the term 'skinlessness' had another daughter and a granddaughter who had depressive episodes, as well as an eccentric nephew who became psychotic and died insane.

These facts of inheritance are no explanation of psychosis, but they do point to some trait or traits of vulnerability, the expression of which was shaped by the experiences and circumstances of our subjects' lives. A discussion of such factors is, regrettably, beyond the scope of this book, but we can make some general observations for future study. Even to attempt to disentangle, for any of our subjects, the relative influence on their behaviour of genetic and environmental factors is difficult: it would require a different research strategy from our own.

Yet the reason we cannot answer that question from our data has some interest in its own right. With the exception of Clare, all of the authors on whom we have information were brought up in families where at least one parent manifested either serious eccentricity or actual psychosis. One important consequence of this is the 'synergistic' effect of individuals, sharing similar genetic traits, interacting with and reinforcing one another's psychoticism. Even if – as in the case of parent and child – the effect operates predominantly in one direction, it may do so in several ways: through the parental role model for social, sexual and other behaviour and, as in our present examples, helping to promote the irrationality of thought and skinlessness of already oversensitive individuals. We cannot escape the conclusion that many of our authors – Ruskin, Benson, Woolf, White and Plath, for example – were caught up in this vicious web of family pathology.

Whether or not a shared psychotic temperament was evident, there were other signs of stress or psychological trauma. In several cases – Benson, Plath, and White – the parents were of radically different temperaments, necessarily placing strain on the growing, and already vulnerable, child. In a few instances – Ruskin, Benson, and Plath – this might have been further exaggerated by the fact that the parents were very disparate in age. Also particularly traumatic in some cases was the early parental loss that was evident in a surprisingly high proportion of our authors. Thus, Plath lost her father when she was eleven, Smart when he was nine; while Cowper and Woolf lost their mothers, the former in early childhood, the latter in puberty. Yet in other cases it was the *presence*, rather than the absence, of one or other parent that was significant; summed up in the dramatic statement with which Susan Chitty opens her book about Antonia White: 'The trouble with my mother was her father'. It seems that our skinless authors could not win.

Only Clare stands out from these trends: his parents seem to have been very caring and his family situation happy, albeit beset by extreme poverty. However, Clare's very exceptionalness does illustrate one further, particular, point. That is, that certain forms of psychosis – currently labelled 'chronic schizophrenia' – seem to have an insidious course, almost proceeding independently of environmental influence and deteriorating into psychological withdrawal. Clare's illness certainly seems to have had this quality, if we follow it from his dreamy, solitary boyhood, through his gradually lost grip on reality, to his final days sitting on a window-seat looking vacantly into the garden of his Northampton asylum. It was there that Clare wrote the last, and some say the noblest, of his poems, in which he captures for us several of the themes – of personal dissolution, self-preoccupation, despair, and overwrought imagination – which we have seen, even in the less afflicted, can run through the psychotic experience:

> I am – yet what I am, none cares, or knows;
>   My friends forsake me like a memory lost: –
> I am the self-consumer of my woes: –
>   They rise and vanish in oblivion's host,
> Like shadows in life's frenzied stifled throes: –
> And yet I am, and live – like vapours tost
>
> Into the nothingness of scorn and noise, –
>   Into the living sea of waking dreams,
> Where there is neither sense of life or joys,
>   But the vast shipwreck of my life's esteems;
> Even the dearest, that I love the best
> Are strange – nay, rather stranger than the rest.
>
> I long for scenes, where man hath never trod
>   A place where woman never smiled or wept
> There to abide with my Creator, God;
>   And sleep as I in childhood, sweetly slept,
> Untroubling, and untroubled where I lie,
> The grass below – above the vaulted sky.

Clare's words bring us to consideration of the extent to which our authors show in their writings evidence of the psychoses from which they suffered, and how their experience of mental illness shaped their work. Again we have space only to draw some general conclusions, identifying certain features that may help to define the 'psychotic voice.' In the course of doing so we may also be able to answer some other questions about the creativity of our authors, in the light of the ideas discussed at the beginning of this book. Can they, for example, all be judged creative for the same reason? Was their creativity an intrinsic part of their tendency to insanity? Would they have been capable of even greater creativity without their struggle against psychosis?

Our subjects, while a small and extreme sample, do seem to confirm the conclusion that there is a genuine association between creativity and insanity. Yet we noted earlier the difficulty of finding an unambiguous definition of 'creativity', including its occasional confusion with 'intelligence', which is a necessary but not sufficient prerequisite for creative performance. All of our authors were undoubtedly intelligent or highly intelligent, though we have formal evidence of this for only two of them: Plath whose IQ, tested at junior high school, was found to be 160; and Cowper whose IQ Cox, in her biographical analysis of famous historical figures, estimated to be between 135 and 140.[7, 32]

Eminence, the other commonly used yardstick of creativeness, is more problematical. It is difficult to say whether Ruskin, Benson or Woolf would ever have attained publication without wealth or, in Woolf's case, her husband's Press; or whether Ruskin would have reached his undoubted eminence without the drive and arrogant certainty of the manic personality. Nevertheless, all three of these did possess what we may begin to identify as at the core of creativity – imaginativeness.

All of our authors, irrespective of time, place, or circumstances, acquired traits or the impact of mental illness, possessed this one quality in abundance; though it was expressed in different ways, from Kempe's raw energy (which might in another century have made her a Marie Corelli or a Patience Strong) to Arthur Benson's veritable deluge of typescript. That the quality was intimately connected with their tendency to psychosis is not, we believe, in doubt and it is possible that *all* creativity requires some such stimulus. Nevertheless, we may ask whether there is anything very particularly 'psychotic' about the work of our own subjects, acting either to disrupt or facilitate it.

One characteristic we commonly find in our subjects – and understandable from what we know of how the psychotic mind works – is their difficulty in putting a shape to their ideas. A prime example is Smart's *Jubilate Agno* on which Russell Brain commented:

> To attempt to describe the *Jubilate Agno* is like trying to depict the features of the vast and fantastic landscape of a dream, for there is something dream-like in its multiplicity of details, either unrelated to each other or related by the irrational logic of the unconscious mind.[5]

Although in its sheer impenetrability the *Jubilate* is an extreme case, a similar spreading or fissiparous form was natural to many of our authors who, although by no means short of material, often had problems organising it. This is especially evident where friends or editors did not cut or compress what they wrote and some of the most illuminating examples of the unrestrained 'psychotic voice' are to be found in diaries and letters, which allow the writer to express his or her thoughts and feelings completely untramelled by the prospect of publication. Here the material pours out in a formless mass. Although few authors can equal Benson's four million words, both Ruskin's and Woolf's diaries take up several volumes, and White's – as yet unpublished – required many notebooks. (We do not know how much of Plath's journals of her short life have been censored or destroyed.)

It is not only the quantity, but also the manner of presentation, that is psychologically revealing. Style is sometimes loose and disorganised, occasionally taking on the form typically found in psychotic communication. This is especially true of Ruskin, the following example, taken from his *Brantwood Diary*, being one of numerous similar passages:

> The devil put a verse into my head just now – 'let us not be desirous of *Vain Glory*' – I am *NOT* oh, Devil, I want useful Glory – 'provoking one another' – oh Devil – cunning Devil – do you think I want to provoke Beata Vigri and little Ophelia then? – I will – pro – voke Somebody else, God willing "today" and to

purpose. And Bishop Laertes, – you had as lief take your fingers from my throat – the Devil will not take my soul, yet a while – Also – look you – and also looking other [things may be at your throat before long (deleted)]. Thou pray'st not well – even by your own account the Devil will not answer you therefore and least said soonest mended – for – if up when the scuffle comes – foils should be Sheffield whettles – it is dangerous work – Laertes – "very" – as Mr Jingle said.

Besides its incomprehensibility we see here detailed peculiarities of association, grammar and meaning that have commonly been identified in formal analytic studies of psychotic language.[2] These features include derailed, tangential and pressured thought, obscure logicality of theme, word approximations, persistent repetition of ideas and constant failure to follow a chain of thought to a manifest conclusion.

Almost as disjointed and showing similar 'psychotic' qualities of loosely associated thought is the following passage from Sylvia Plath's journal (12 January 1953):

We're nearer to spring than we were in september, i heard a bird sing in the dark of december, january, febmar, aprimay, apricots, beneath the bough. And though, there has always furthermore in addition inescapably and forever got to be a Thou. Otherwise there is no i because i am what other people interpret me as being and am nothing if there were no people. (Like the sound of the hackneyed tree falling axed by old saws in the proverbial forest.)

Naturally the author's fluctuating mental state affects the degree to which linguistic expression is disturbed. Smart, when more sane, did eventually find a form, in the *Song of David*, for the incoherent thoughts he poured out in the *Jubilate*. The entry from Ruskin's diary quoted earlier was written just before his 1898 breakdown. Benson, on the other hand, in keeping with his predominantly depressive moods, was unable to write at all in periods of severe illness, even in the diary to which he was normally so compulsively driven. Antonia White shows dramatically how the chaos of psychotic thought may burst out in private, on some stimulus such as the psychoanalysis in which she was forced to confront her feelings about her long-dead father. Lyndall

Hopkinson notes how at this period her mother's reactions show first in a changed handwriting and hints of paranoia.[16] Then, she says:

> it all comes pouring out. As if swept by a hurricane the words fall about in all directions, capitals have taken the place of the usual underlinings, letters sometimes slope backwards and forwards in the same word as they grow larger and more distanced from one another. Grammar has been swept away by the winds.

Hopkinson then gives the following example:

> Now if as seems clear from several indications I want my father's penis or a child by him e.g. a work engendered with his loving approval what am I fussing about.
> I can't have his loving approval because he is DEAD.
> I couldn't have had intercourse with him anyway because apart from morals
> (a) he didn't want it
> (b) I couldn't have endured it without mutilation. . . .
> Even [if] I've not got a penis I've not got nothing. Feel no one wants me yet I undervalue them if they do want me. . . . All the time I feel far more hate & contempt than love. Sometimes hate & contempt for myself: more for other people. Hate and envy. . . . Yes I will write backhand in spite of my father I WILL I WILL I WILL. Couldn't even write – filthy dirty beastly old man – the way I WANTED TO. Well I will. . . . You've ruined my life.

This passage illustrates well both how near the surface of awareness the contents of the unconscious mind are in the psychotic person and how easily, once these are brought into consciousness, the linguistic expression of thought is disrupted. The context in which it was written is of course significant. The procedure of psychoanalysis is deliberately designed to probe the depths of the unconscious; but, as pointed out by Carl Jung – himself a pioneer of the use of the method with psychotics – it has to be used with caution in such individuals, precisely because of their ready access to fantasy material that can overwhelm them.[17] That is particularly true of strongly emotive material which has its origins in memories of early experience. In this respect it is interesting to note that, as clearly in White's case, unconscious thoughts relating to aggression may be especially important; a conclusion supported by the results of recent studies examining the effect on psychotics of stimulating psychodynamically relevant fantasies.[24] The method used there involved subliminal activation of salient emotional complexes and demonstrated that evoking aggressive fantasies was particularly likely to exacerbate psychotic symptoms, including a disorganisation of thought.

Turning to the published work of our authors, the more gross signs we have just described are naturally often less manifest, for a variety of reasons: editorial revision, temporary self-imposed discipline, somewhat greater objectivity of content and the constraint of literary form. In the last of these respects poets often have an advantage, since they are constrained (or used to be, when *vers libre* was not the only poetic form) by the rules and the shapes of the couplet, the sonnet, the hexameter. Where other kinds of form were imposed from without our authors did well; as, for instance, in translation, a task to which several of our authors like Antonia White resorted when other forms of literary expression were beyond them. Compare here, too, the difference between the structured thought of Cowper's translation of Milton's Latin poems with the huge formless bulk of his own *The Task*.

The writer of fiction may attempt to impose a weak form by describing the events of a day, a year, or a certain arbitrary span of time, as in *To the Lighthouse, Frost in May*, or *Ulysses*; but even then the author rarely attains the tightly-knit and intricate structure of plot and sub-plot that we see in Trollope or George Eliot. Virginia Woolf is perhaps a good illustration here. It has sometimes been said that her genius as a writer lay in her breaking away from the traditional form of the novel in her use of the 'stream of consciousness' style. While this is perfectly legitimate as a *literary* comment, we would venture to suggest that it is only possible fully to understand her style by taking account of its origins in her psychology as a psychotic writer, with the tendency to tangential thought and difficulty in maintaining theme that that implies. In other words, it seems probable to us that ultimately this was the only way she *could* write, some progression towards her eventual style being seen if we compare Woolf's later works with her first novel, *The Voyage Out*: there we see a more traditional structure, but even then some hints of the innovations of style that subsequently emerge in her writings.

The overall impression we get of Woolf is of the continual

struggle, by an extremely talented individual, to seek a form and organisation for her thoughts, necessitating constant polishing and repolishing against intrusions of unwanted material and resulting eventually in passages which, individually, are beautifully constructed but loosely connected together. This is confirmed by what we know of her method of working, described by Louie Mayer, her housekeeper for over thirty years.[27] She writes:

> There was one thing I found rather strange on my first day. The floors in Monks House were very thin, the bathroom was directly above the kitchen, and when Mrs Woolf was having her bath before breakfast, I could hear her talking to herself. On and on she went, talk, talk, talk: asking questions and giving herself the answers. I thought there must be two or three people up there with her. When Mr Woolf saw that I looked startled, he told me Mrs Woolf always said out loud the sentences she had written during the night. She needed to know if they sounded right, and the bath was a good, resonant place for trying them out.

Mayer goes on:

> When we carried the breakfast trays to Mrs Woolf's room, I noticed that she had always been working during the night. There were pencils and paper beside her bed so that when she woke up she could work, and sometimes it seemed as though she had had very little sleep. These pieces of paper, some of them containing the same sentence written over and over again, would be in heaps about the room. They were on the chairs, on the tables, and sometimes even on the floor. It was one of Mrs Woolf's habits, when she was working, to leave her writing about in these little heaps of paper. I would find them about the rest of the house too: in the sitting room and dining room on tables and mantelpieces.

In addition to their difficulty in organising their thoughts – or as a reflection of it – all of our authors show in their work another, very prominent, feature: an intense preoccupation with the self, or what Kretschmer called the 'extreme subjectivity' of psychotic personalities, for whom the world is only what affects themselves. In their personal records this is revealed as extreme emotional reactions and oversensitivity, including concentration upon even the tiniest physical ailment which is blown up out of all proportion: as, for example, in Benson's almost irritating daily scrutiny of his own condition. Only Clare among our authors kept a journal that is not especially subjective, more a kind of nature notebook, interspersed with some short accounts of books or reviews; but then he intended, he says, 'only to give my opinion of things I may read or see'. It is in his letters that he reveals his real preoccupations.

The published works of our authors reveal the same subjectivity. For Kempe the world exists only as it affects her: even God does what Margery wants. Cowper's genius sometimes distracts the reader from the subjectivity of his writing; but as Norman Nicholson says, 'we can always hear the voice of the poet himself. . . . To those who love Cowper, his poetry is a biography.'[26] Clare is the ever-present onlooker in his poems, recalling the natural scene, and turning to Nature or Art as a refuge from the world of pain and suffering.

Similarly in Ruskin's work we find that the true subject is not art, but Ruskin himself. Turning from his description of a painting to the painting itself one may be utterly unable to see in it what he saw: as when, in *Modern Painters* he gives grass an expression 'of thorny discontent and savageness'; or when, in *The Stones of Venice*, he describes a statue as 'huge, inhuman, monstrous, . . . – leering in bestial degradation, too foul to be . . . beheld for more than an instant.' Benson, too, saw things idiosyncratically: his many descriptions of the country scenes, gardens or buildings that he loved often end in his hurrying away from some moss-covered statue that seems unbearably wicked, or from some 'sinister little door, that gave me a discomfort that it seems impossible to express in speech'. In a similar vein, Virginia Woolf's book reviews (and indeed *The Common Reader*) seem to two of us to say more about the reviewer than the reviewed.

Our authors were equally subjective in writing fiction, striving to impose order on, or extract meaning from, the chaos of their past. All of Benson's novels are either thinly disguised autobiography or debates with himself on his own preoccupations. Woolf's illness forms a large element in *The Voyage Out*; *Jacob's Room* is a portrait of her brother; *Orlando* is a fantasy of her friendship with Vita Sackville-West; and *To the Lighthouse* is based on childhood memories. With White and Plath we are also in the realm of pure subjectivity: they write about nothing but themselves (even though White 'normalises' some things, especially the portraits of her parents). Almost all of Plath's poems are cries of agony arising from her condition: her work, she freely admitted in her journal, was 'only a naked recreation of what I felt'.

We noted earlier that insanity is often intuitively recognisable – we 'feel something wrong' – and similarly in the literature of the psychotic we frequently sense a curious atmosphere. Subjective 'skinlessness', combined with insensitivity in other ways, imparts a quality to the writing that is difficult to define. Yet we feel it when we enter, for instance, the almost claustrophobic world of many of Virginia Woolf's novels, or of Benson's diary. Perhaps what we sense is what Plath called 'sexless neurotic luminousness'.

This strange timbre of the 'psychotic voice' can be recognised if we make comparisons with some non-psychotic authors writing in the same *genre*. Looking, for example, at the diary form we find that the psychotic uses it less to record events than to explore his inner world voluminously and obsessively. Compare this with, say, Pepys. He, too, was interested in himself, but only as part of his outer world: his observations may be personal, his judgments erratic, but he can be objective and knows when he is not.

Similarly, in the novel. Comparing our three women authors with, say, Jane Austen we find a different atmosphere: one of good sense, good judgment, relish for daily life and, above all, effortless order; so that every incident, character and speech contributes to the pattern of the whole. We find a controlled imaginativeness instead of the psychotic's struggle to impose structure, and the natural happiness Woolf said her life lacked.

In the earlier literature a similar picture emerges. In Julian of Norwich and Geoffrey Chaucer we have almost exact contemporaries of Kempe and Hoccleve, working in identical *genres*. Julian, like Margery, dictated her accounts of her mystical revelations, but the difference is profound. Julian gives only the barest details about herself and her life, so that the reader may understand the circumstances in which her visions occurred. She also analyses them carefully, distinguishing the three types of vision known to theologians – corporeal, imaginative and intellectual – and sets these apart from a dream that occurred later. She also shows by many small touches that the natural bent of her mind was sceptical, rather than credulous, her calm contemplation differing greatly from Margery's wild emotional subjective religiosity.

Comparing Hoccleve and Chaucer we see the contrast particularly in the theme of humour directed against the self – a sure sign of mental strength. Admittedly the humour of a past age is difficult to judge, yet we see even now the supreme artistic self-confidence with which Chaucer mocks himself in, say, *The Tale of Sir Thopas* or *The Hous of Fame* and what a deep gulf separates this from Hoccleve's fussy and anxious self-portrait in *Le Male Regle* or the *Complaint*. In style, too, there are notable differences. Chaucer's delicate and assured handling of the digressions for which the Wife of Bath's Prologue is famous is a far cry from the uncontrolled and obsessive digressions of the *Regement of Princes*. It is in his repeated surrender to self-indulgence and the free flow of associative thinking that Hoccleve is his most lively self.

It is important to emphasise that none of the above – indeed nothing in this book – should be taken to imply that the psychotic authors we have discussed are in any way inferior to those who would be regarded as 'sane'. The literary worth and aesthetic quality of their work must be judged on quite different criteria and in this respect all of our authors have merited their inclusion here as creative persons whose influence has, albeit to varying degree, endured. Cowper and Clare are among our greatest poets; Ruskin wielded enormous influence in his time; Woolf is considered by many critics to be a major novelist; and Plath has made her name in our modern period as a poet.

Whether – to return to a question posed earlier in this chapter – our authors would have been *more* creative had they not suffered the constant threat of mental breakdown is still problematical. In one, rather superficial, sense that must have been true, if only in relieving them of the distractions from the irrational ideas and strong emotion that formed a barrier to organised thought. In another sense the question is wrongly phrased. For their creativity *was* their madness, their madness their creativity and, agonising though it may have been for them as individuals, their work could not have taken the particular form it did – and by which we must judge it – without their lives and temperaments being what they were.

There is another way we might frame the above question and that is to ask whether our subjects' creativity would, in some cases at least, have taken a different form had their life circumstances been different. Although impossible to answer directly this does take us back full circle to the early chapters of our book, raising again several of the issues discussed there; such as the general connection between madness and creativity and the extent to which, if genuine, we can learn from it something of the nature of these two associated qualities. If we pursue our arguments there – particularly those drawing on genetic evidence – then we can surely conclude, definitely for several of our authors and probably for all, that some inherited property of their nervous systems contributed to both their vulnerability to psychosis and their capacity for flexible, original thinking.

Genes do not however code for ideas, or feelings, or behaviour. Nor, by the same token, do they inexorably determine that tendencies to psychopathology break out into the distress of mental illness: the translation only occurs through the progression that is life experience which, if malign, shapes the individual towards a caricature of his or her morbid disposition and, if favourable, may protect from its worst consequences. In this respect psychotic personalities are unique in having unusually easy access to the reservoir of their imagination. But what is found there – disturbing or uplifting – is what has been deposited there throughout life and it is here that creativity and psychosis find their true meeting-point: in what is available either to inspire as reflective originality or shatter with destructive emotion. In several of our authors – for example Antonia White – it seemed to be the latter that predominated and it could be asked whether, had her upbringing been different, her creativity might have found a calmer, less self-indulgent expression. Here we are reminded of Anthony's observation, referred to in Chapter 2, to the effect that many individuals – probably as genetically predisposed to psychosis as our own subjects – nevertheless manage to achieve a more 'healthy', outer-directed form of creative competence, perhaps because of exposure to more nurturant life circumstances.

In making the last point we are aware, of course, that it is of only theoretical interest here and that it would be futile to try to impose on the lives of the authors we have discussed speculations about 'what might have been'. More seriously, perhaps, it warns us of the danger of a too intense psychological scrutiny, divorced from an appreciation of their literary merit. Here we have tried to combine both, for we believe that neither can be understood in isolation from the other. But in the last analysis our authors were themselves, their creativity, their tendency to serious mental aberration and their experiences of life indivisible.

It is from this very conjunction that we can learn several lessons about the nature of psychosis itself, some of which might appear trivial were it not that contemporary psychiatry has been slow to learn them. One is the difficulty of clearly distinguishing discrete forms of psychosis, such as schizophrenia or manic-depression, 'categories' which it might just be possible to apply to single periods of illness but which frequently merge when, as in the case of our authors, a whole life-span is being judged.

Another conclusion concerns the timelessness of psychosis, its occurrence – in a remarkably similar form – throughout history, certainly as far back as the period covered here and almost as surely much longer than that. To non-clinical readers this observation might seem self-evident: it certainly will to those familiar with the frequent portrayal of madmen in early literature. Yet the fact is that currently in academic psychiatry there are serious proposals that disorders like schizophrenia may not have existed before the nineteenth century.[11] Interestingly, this debate has been conducted from two quite distinct points of view. One, focusing on social causes for psychosis, has tried to explain the psychological incompetence found in *chronic* schizophrenia as stemming from the demands placed on certain individuals by the industrialisation of Western societies.[29] While certainly comprehensible as an account of some secondary consequences of psychosis, this theory says nothing about the underlying form of the disorder and is therefore quite irrelevant to the issue of its recency.

The second interpretation of the alleged historical evidence for the recency of schizophrenia is quite different. It has currently become popular in *organic* psychiatry as one of a series of steps in an argument that the psychoses are merely neurological diseases of the same type as, say, Alzheimer's disease. In one version the fallacy has been compounded by grafting on to the interpretation of the (untenable) historical data the theory that schizophrenia is caused by a virus – or, more strictly, a retrovirus – thus accounting for the supposed spread of the 'disease' during the changing social conditions of the nineteenth century. Actually, there is absolutely no experimental evidence for such a causal agent in psychosis, a fact that has led some other psychiatrists to comment that the idea 'borders on the absurd'.[19] Even more absurd is the logical conclusion to which one adherent of the viral hypothesis was led when trying to incorporate into the theory the kind of evidence reviewed here, on the genetic link between creativity and psychosis.[8]

It is clear, even from the study of our ten authors, that psychosis

is more complicated than that; that neither a totally social interpretation nor a view of it as a simple neurological disease can
entirely explain the psychotic experience. Its continuity with
psychological health, as well as its occasional association with
superior mental functioning, marks it out as a much more subtle
psychobiological disorder, having a long genetic history and rooted
in the very nature of Man; a fact articulated by Karlsson whose
work we quoted in Chapter 1 and who concludes his book with the
following observation:

> In view of the convincing evidence that carriers of the proposed
> schizophrenia gene may be serving the human race as its chief
> source of creativity, society should now recognise that mental
> patients and their relatives have indeed made important con-
> tributions. Without their genes man may still live in caves.[18]

The above remark is now beginning to take on an even greater
significance that deserves a further, final comment. We are referring to the very recent emergence of the so-called 'new genetics':
the development of revolutionary techniques that will make it
possible to identify the locus on the chromosomes of actual genes
responsible for specific biological functions.[23] So far this work has
mostly concentrated on genes that code for gross biological aberrations: rare, often lethal, defects such as Duchenne muscular
dystrophy or cystic fibrosis. In principle, however, the same
techniques can be used to explore the genetic basis of normal
human characteristics and will undoubtedly lead eventually to the
writing of the envisaged 'Book of Man', mapping out the whole
human genome. Within that book will lie, if not the answer to the
mystery of psychosis, at least the secret of its genetics.

In the meantime the 'new genetics' is creating other problems
that are of considerable relevance here. Inevitably its discoveries
have led to growing public debate about the ethical implications of
applying the newly acquired knowledge to the prevention of
disease. Significantly this has now spread to the discussion of
mental disorders, following recent claims – actually much exaggerated in the media coverage and not replicated in other studies –
that specific genetic linkages have been found for psychosis, both
manic-depression and schizophrenia.[22, 25] In the wake of these
reports the possibility of 'genetic engineering' to eliminate psychosis were rapidly put up for discussion. As an example, even

before the findings for schizophrenia had been officially published the BBC broadcast a programme on the ethical consequences of the 'new genetics'. On the programme Mary Warnock, the highly respected chairperson of an earlier committee of enquiry into embryo research, was asked whether she thought it justifiable to abort foetuses known to be carrying the gene for medical conditions such as muscular dystrophy or cystic fibrosis. Following her reply to even this horrendous moral question – that it *might* be – the interviewer immediately led her on to consider whether schizophrenia might be included on the list. She gave a cautiously affirmative reply.

The above story is not related as a criticism of Mary Warnock; presumably she is no expert on mental illness. Nor is reference to it intended to underrate the importance of the ethical issue: this will continue to exist, and indeed sharpen, as new findings about the heritable influences in psychological dysfunction emerge. The point is made, rather, to illustrate how premature bracketing of psychosis with other forms of disorder (i.e. medical defect states) has already served to oversimplify, to divert attention away from the true implications of 'new genetics' research for our understanding and management of psychosis. For if those currently engaged upon writing the 'Book of Man' are to be believed, then ultimately it will be possible to select genetically, not just for freedom from lethal diseases, but also for genes that contribute to 'desirable' human traits of temperament and intellect. Then one choice that might have to be made is whether to eliminate or to nurture 'skinlessness', with its deeply paradoxical qualities of creativeness and morbidity. How, we wonder, will a future generation decide? Will it, in its search for tranquillity and freedom from pain, choose to silence the sounds from the bell jar forever?

Appendix

A. Schedule of Questions

Items relating to manic disorder

1 (a) Did you ever have a period that lasted at least a week when you felt extremely good or high – clearly different from your normal self?

(b) What about periods when you felt very irritable and easily annoyed?

2 During the most severe period:

(a) Were you more active than usual – either socially, at work, at home, sexually, or physically restless?

(b) Were you more talkative than usual or felt a pressure to keep on talking?

(c) Did your thoughts race or did you talk so fast that it was difficult for people to follow what you were saying?

(d) Did you feel you were a very important person, had special powers, plans, talents, or abilities?

(e) Did you need less sleep than usual?

(f) Did you have trouble concentrating on what was going on because your attention kept jumping to unimportant things around you?

(g) Did you do anything foolish that could have got you into trouble – like buying things, business investments, sexual indiscretions etc?

3 During the most severe period:

(a) were you so excited that it was almost impossible to hold a conversation with you?

(b) Did it cause trouble with people, with your family, with your work or other usual activity?

(c) Were you hospitalised?

Items relating to depressive disorder

4   Did you ever have a period that lasted at least a week when you were bothered by feeling depressed, sad, blue, hopeless, down in the dumps, that you didn't care any more, or didn't enjoy anything?

5   During the most severe period were you bothered by:
(a) Poor appetite or weight loss or increased appetite or weight gain?
(b) Trouble sleeping or sleeping too much?
(c) Loss of energy, being easily fatigued or feeling tired?
(d) Loss of interest or pleasure in your usual activities or sex?
(e) Feeling guilty or down on yourself?
(f) Trouble concentrating, thinking or making decisions?
(g) Thinking about death or suicide?
(h) Being unable to sit still and have to keep moving or the opposite – feeling slowed down and having trouble moving?

6   Did you attempt suicide [Actual suicide].

7   During that time did you seek help from anyone, like a doctor or minister or even a friend, or did anyone suggest you seek help. Did you take any medication?

Items relating to schizophrenic disorder

8   Has there been a time when:
(a) You heard voices or other sounds that other people couldn't hear?
(b) You had visions or saw things that were not visible to other people?
(c) You had strange smells or strange feelings in your body?
(d) You had beliefs or ideas that you later found out were not true – like people being out to get you or talking about you behind your back?
(e) People had trouble understanding what you were saying because your speech was mixed up or you didn't make sense in the way you were talking?

9   Did you ever feel your thoughts were broadcast so that other people knew what you were thinking, or feel that thoughts were put into your head that were not your own, or that thoughts were taken away from you by some external force?

10 Have you ever had the feeling that you were under the control of some force or power other than yourself, or as though you were a robot and without a will of your own, or that you were

forced to make movements or say things without your wanting to, or to think things or have impulses that were not your own?

Additional information requested
Age(s) when symptoms manifested.
Period(s) of hospitalisation.
Medication or other treatments.
Family history of similar symptoms or illnesses.
Other details thought relevant.

B. Diagnostic criteria

(Subject scores positively for items as indicated below for each disorder. Numbers in brackets refer to questions listed in Section A above.)

Manic disorder
I   High mood (1a)
     Irritability (1b)
II   At least *two* of the following:
     Activity (2a)
     Talk (2b)
     Thoughts (2c)
     Grandiosity (2d)
     Sleep (2e)
     Distractibility (2f)
     Recklessness (2g)
III Seriously impaired functioning (3a, 3b) or hospitalised (3c)

Depressive disorder
I   Hopelessness for at least one week (4)
II   At least *three* of the following:
     Appetite etc (5a)
     Sleep (5b)
     Energy (5c)
     Anhedonia (5d)
     Guilt (5e)
     Concentration (5f)
     Suicidal thought (5g)

Movement (5h)
Suicidal attempt [suicide] (6)
III   Seeks help, medication etc (7)

Schizophrenic disorder
I   Any *one* of the following:
Voices (8a)
Visions (8b)
Smells etc (8c)
Paranoid ideas (8d)
Thought jumbled (8e)
Thought broadcast (9)
Influence (10)
II   Any episode longer than two weeks.

Note: Where the criteria for more than one of the above disorders were met the descriptions 'manic-depressive' or 'schizoaffective' disorder were applied, as appropriate.

Bibliography and References

(*Note:* In chapters 1, 2 and 10 references are indicated by numbered items in the text. The bibliography for the other chapters is presented in alphabetical order of authors.)

1 Great wits and madness

1. Albert, R. S. (ed.), *Genius and Eminence* (Oxford: Pergamon, 1983).
2. Andreasen, N. J. C., 'Creativity and mental illness: prevalence rates in writers and their first-degree relatives', *American Journal of Psychiatry*, 144 (1987) 1288–92.
3. Andreasen, N. J. C. and Canter, A., 'The creative writer: psychiatric symptoms and family history', *Comprehensive Psychiatry*, 15 (1974) 123–31.
4. Andreasen, N. J. C., Tsuang, M. T. and Canter, A. 'The significance of thought disorder in diagnostic evaluations', *Comprehensive Psychiatry*, 15 (1974) 27–34.
5. Arieti, S., *Creativity* (New York: Basic Books, 1976).
6. Barron, F., 'Some studies of creativity at the Institute of Personality Assessment and Research', in G. A. Steiner (ed.) *The Creative Organisation* (Chicago: University of Chicago Press, 1971).
7. Becker, G., *The Mad Genius Controversy* (Beverly Hills: Sage, 1978).
8. Bleuler, M., *The Schizophrenic Disorders* (New Haven: Yale University Press, 1978).
9. Bowerman, W. G., *Studies in Genius* (New York: Philosophical Library, 1947).
10. Cattell, R. B. and Butcher, H. J., *The Prediction of Achievement and Creativity* (Indianapolis: Bobbs-Merrill, 1968).
11. Claridge, G., *Origins of Mental Illness* (Oxford: Blackwell, 1985).
12. Claridge, G., Canter, S. and Hume, W. I., *Personality Differences and Biological Variations: a Study of Twins* (Oxford: Pergamon, 1973).
13. Cox, C. M., *The Early Mental Traits of Three Hundred Geniuses*, Vol. III of *Genetic Studies of Genius*, (ed.) L. M. Terman (Stanford: Stanford University Press, 1926).
14. de Bono, E., *Lateral Thinking* (Harmondsworth: Penguin, 1970).
15. Ellis, H. A., *A Study of British Genius*, 2nd edition (New York: Houghton-Mifflin, 1926).
16. Götz, K. O. and Götz, K., 'Personality characteristics of professional artists', *Perceptual and Motor Skills*, 49 (1979) 327–34.
17. Götz, K. O. and Götz, K., 'Personality characteristics of successful artists', *Perceptual and Motor Skills*, 49 (1979) 919–24.
18. Heston, L. L., 'Psychiatric disorders in foster home reared children

of schizophrenic mothers', *British Journal of Psychiatry*, 112 (1966), 819–25.

19. Karlsson, J. L., 'Creative intelligence in relatives of mental patients', *Hereditas*, 100 (1984) 83–6.

20. Karlsson, J. L., *Inheritance of Creative Intelligence* (Chicago: Nelson-Hall, 1978).

21. Keefe, J. A. and Magaro, P. A., 'Creativity and schizophrenia: an equivalence of cognitive processing', *Journal of Abnormal Psychology*, 89 (1980) 390–8.

22. Lombroso, C., *The Man of Genius* (London: Walter Scott, 1891).

23. MacKinnon, D. W., 'The nature and nurture of creative talent', *American Psychologist*, 17 (1962) 484–95.

24. McConaghy, N., 'The use of an object sorting test in elucidating the hereditary factor in schizophrenia', *Journal of Neurology, Neurosurgery and Psychiatry*, 22 (1959) 243–6.

25. McConaghy, N. and Clancy, M., 'Familial relationships of allusive thinking in university students and their parents', *British Journal of Psychiatry*, 114 (1968) 1079–87.

26. McNeil, T. F., 'Prebirth and postbirth influence on the relationship between creative ability and recorded mental illness', *Journal of Personality*, 39 (1971) 391–406.

27. Payne, R. W. and Hewlett, J. H. G., 'Thought disorder in psychotic patients', in H. J. Eysenck (ed.) *Experiments in Personality*, Vol. II (London: Routledge and Kegan Paul, 1960).

28. Pickering, G., *Creative Malady* (Oxford: Oxford University Press, 1974).

29. Prentky, R. A., *Creativity and Psychopathology* (New York: Praeger, 1980).

30. Richards, R., 'Relationships between creativity and psychopathology: an evaluation and interpretation of the evidence', *Genetic Psychology Monographs*, 103 (1981) 261–324.

31. Richards, R., Kinney, D. K., Lunde, I., Benet, M. and Merzel, A. P. C.,'Creativity in manic-depressives, cyclothymes, their normal relatives, and control subjects', *Journal of Abnormal Psychology*, 97 (1988) 281–8.

32. Roe, A. A., *The Making of a Scientist* (New York: Dodd Mead, 1952).

33. Rothenberg, A., *The Emerging Goddess* (Chicago: University of Chicago Press, 1979).

34. *Schizophrenia Bulletin*, 11 (1985) No. 4 (whole issue).

35. Sternberg, R. J. (ed.), *The Nature of Creativity* (Cambridge: Cambridge University Press, 1988).

36. Storr, A., *The Dynamics of Creation* (Harmondsworth: Penguin, 1976).

37. Terman, L. M. and Oden, M. H., *The Gifted Group at Mid-life*, Vol. V of *Genetic Studies of Genius*, (ed.) L. M. Terman (Stanford: Stanford University Press, 1959).

38. Wagner-Martin, L. W., *Sylvia Plath. A Biography* (London: Chatto and Windus, 1987).

39. Watt, N. F., Anthony, E. J., Wynne, L. C. and Rolf, J. E. (eds.), *Children at Risk for Schizophrenia* (Cambridge: Cambridge University Press, 1984).

2 Wings in the Head

1. Anthony, E. J., 'Risk, vulnerability, and resilience: an overview', in E. J. Anthony and B. J. Cohler (eds.) *The Invulnerable Child* (New York: The Guilford Press, 1987).
2. Beaton, A., *Left Side Right Side* (London: Batsford, 1985).
3. Beech, A. R. and Claridge, G., 'Individual differences in negative priming: relations with schizotypal personality traits', *British Journal of Psychology*, 78 (1987) 349–56.
4. Bentall, R., Claridge, G. and Slade, P., 'The multi-dimensional nature of schizotypal traits: a factor analytic study with normal subjects', *British Journal of Clinical Psychology*, 28 (1989).
5. Birchwood, M., Hallett, S. and Preston, M., *Schizophrenia. An Integrated Approach to Research and Treatment* (London: Longman, 1988).
6. Brockington, I. F., Kendell, R. E., Wainwright, S., Hillier, V. F. and Walker, J., 'The distinction between affective psychoses and schizophrenia', *British Journal of Psychiatry*, 135 (1979) 243–8.
7. Broks, P., 'Schizotypy and hemisphere function – II. Performance asymmetry on a verbal divided visual-field task', *Personality and Individual Differences*, 5 (1984) 649–56.
8. Claridge, G., *Origins of Mental Illness* (Oxford: Blackwell, 1985.
9. Claridge, G., '"The schizophrenias as nervous types" revisited', *British Journal of Psychiatry*, 151 (1987) 735–43.
10. Claridge, G. and Broks, P., 'Schizotypy and hemisphere function – I. Theoretical considerations and the measurement of schizotypy', *Personality and Individual Differences*, 5 (1984) 633–48.
11. Claridge, G. and Hewitt, J. K., 'A biometrical study of schizotypy in a normal population', *Personality and Individual Differences*, 8 (1987) 303–12.
12. Frith, C. D., 'Consciousness, information processing and schizophrenia', *British Journal of Psychiatry*, 134 (1979) 225–35.
13. Galin, D., 'Implications for psychiatry of left and right cerebral specialisation', *Archives of General Psychiatry*, 31 (1974) 572–83.
14. Goodwin, G. M., Johnson, D. A. W. and McCreadie, R. G., 'Comments on the Northwick Park "functional" psychosis study', *British Journal of Psychiatry*, 154 (1989) 406–9.
15. Gordon, L., *Virginia Woolf. A Writer's Life* (Oxford: Oxford University Press, 1984).
16. Gray, J. A., *The Psychology of Fear and Stress* (London: Weidenfeld and Nicolson, 1971).
17. Hallett, S., Quinn, D. and Hewitt, J., 'Defective interhemispheric integration and anomalous language lateralisation in children at risk for schizophrenia', *Journal of Nervous and Mental Disease*, 174 (1986) 418–27.
18. MacDonald, N., 'Living with schizophrenia', *Canadian Medical Association Journal*, 82 (1960), 218–21.
19. Perecman, E. (ed.), *Cognitive Processing in the Right Hemisphere* (Orlando: Academic Press, 1983).
20. Scharfetter, C. and Nusperli, M., 'The group of schizophrenias, schizoaffective psychoses, and affective disorders', *Schizophrenia Bulletin*, 6 (1980) 586–91.

21. *Schizophrenia Bulletin*, 11 (1985) No. 4 (whole issue).
22. Shimkunas, A., 'Hemisphere asymmetry and schizophrenic thought disorder', in S. Schwartz (ed.) *Language and Cognition in Schizophrenia* (Hillsdale: Lawrence Erlbaum, 1978).
23. Spitzer, R. L. and Endicott, J., *Schedule for Affective Disorders and Schizophrenia – Lifetime Version* (SADS-L) (New York: New York State Psychiatric Institute, 1977).
24. Stone, M. H., *The Borderline Syndromes* (New York: McGraw Hill, 1980).
25. Strömgren, E., 'Autism', *European Journal of Psychiatry*, 1 (1987) 45–54.
26. Watt, N. F., Anthony, E. J., Wynne, L. C. and Rolf, J. E. (eds.), *Children at Risk for Schizophrenia* (Cambridge: Cambridge University Press, 1984).
27. Wexler, B. E., 'Cerebral laterality and psychiatry: a review of the literature', *American Journal of Psychiatry*, 137 (1980) 279–91.

3 Mediaeval madness: Margery Kempe, Thomas Hoccleve

Atkinson, C., *Mystic and Pilgrim* (London: Cornell University Press, 1983).
Bartholomaeus Anglicus (trans. J. Trevisa), *De Proprietatibus Rerum* (London: Wynkyn de Worde, ?1495).
Bernheimer, R., *Wild Men in the Middle Ages* (Cambridge, Harvard University Press, 1952).
Burrow, J. A., 'Autobiographical Poetry in the Middle Ages: The Case of Thomas Hoccleve. Sir Israel Gollancz Memorial Lecture, British Academy, 1982', *Proceedings of the British Academy*, LXVIII (1982) [389]–42.
Cholmely, K., *Margery Kempe, Genius and Mystic* (London: The Catholic Book Club, 1948).
Doob, P. B. R., *Nebuchadnezzar's Children. Conventions of Madness in Middle English Literature* (London: Yale University Press, 1974).
Drucker, T., 'The Malaise of Margery Kempe', *New York State Journal of Medicine*, 72 (1972) 2911–17.
Feder, L., *Madness in Literature* (Princeton: Princeton University Press, 1980).
Hoccleve, T. (ed. F. J. Furnivall and I. Gollancz, rev. J. Mitchell and A. I. Doyle), *Hoccleve's Works. The Minor Poems* (London: Oxford University Press, 1970, EETS, ES, 61, 73).
Hoccleve, T. (ed. F. J. Furnivall), *Hoccleve's Works. III. The Regement of Princes and Fourteen of Hoccleve's Minor Poems* (London: Kegan Paul, Trench, Trubner, 1897, EETS, ES, LXXII).
Hoccleve, T. (ed. M. R. Pryor), *Thomas Hoccleve's Series: An Edition of MS Durham Cosin V iii 9* (Los Angeles, University of California. Unpublished doctoral dissertation. University Microfilms Order No. 69–7257).
Julian of Norwich (ed. E. Colledge and J. Walsh), *A Book of Showings to the Anchoress Julian of Norwich* (Toronto: Political Institute of Mediaeval Studies, 1978. Studies and Texts 35), 2 vols.
Julian of Norwich (ed. R. Hudleston), *Revelations of Divine Love, Shewed to a*

Devout Ankress by Name Julian of Norwich (London: London, Burns Oates, 1952), 2nd ed.

Kempe, M. (ed. S. B. Meech and H. E. Allen), *The Book of Margery Kempe* (London: Oxford University Press, 1940, EETS, OS, 212).

Kempe, M., *The Book of Margery Kempe, a Modern Version by W. Butler-Bowden. With an Introduction by R. W. Chambers* (London and Toronto: Oxford University Press, 1954, The World's Classics 543).

Malory, Sir T. (ed. E. Vinaver), *The Works of Sir Thomas Malory* (London: Oxford University Press, 1954).

Medcalf, S., 'Inner and Outer' in S. Medcalf (ed.) The Later Middle Ages (London: Methuen, 1981).

Mitchell, J., *Thomas Hoccleve. A Study in Early Fifteenth-Century Poetic* (Urbana: University of Illinois Press, 1968).

Oates, W. E., *Religious Factors in Mental Illness* (London: George Allen and Unwin, 1957).

Petersen, D. (ed.), *A Mad People's History of Madness* (Pittsburgh: University of Pittsburgh Press, 1982).

Porter, R., *A Social History of Madness* (London: Weidenfeld and Nicolson, 1987).

4   The Powers of Night: Christopher Smart

Brain, R., *Sane Reflections on Genius* (London: Pitman, 1960).

Carkesse, J., *Lucida Intervalla* (1679), (Los Angeles: William Andrews Clarke Memorial Library, University of California, Los Angeles, 1979. The Augustan Reprint Society, 195–6, Introduction by M. V. Deporte).

Devlin, C., *Poor Kit Smart* (London: Rupert Hart-Davis, 1961).

Forrest, D. V., 'Nonsense and Sense in Schizophrenic Language', *Schizophrenia Bulletin*, 2 (1976), 286–301.

Grigson, G., *Christopher Smart* (London: Longmans, Green, 1961, Writers and Their Work, 136).

Mahony, R. and B. W. Rizzo, *Christopher Smart. An Annotated Bibliography 1743–1983* (New York, London: Garland Publishers, 1984).

Sherbo, A., *Christopher Smart, Scholar of the University* (East Lansing, Michigan, Michigan State University Press, 1967).

Skultans, V., *English Madness. Ideas on Insanity, 1580–1890* (London: Routledge and Kegan Paul, 1979).

Smart, C. (ed. K. Williamson and M. Walsh), *The Poetical Works of Christopher Smart* (Oxford: Clarendon Press, 1980–   ).

5   Buried above Ground: William Cowper

Cowper, W. (ed. H. S. Milford), *The Complete Poetical Works* (London: Oxford University Press, 1907).

Cowper, W. (ed. J. King and C. Ryskamp). *The Letters and Prose Writings of William Cowper* (Oxford: Clarendon Press, 1979–86), 5 vols.

Cowper, W. (ed. J. D. Baird and C. Ryskamp), *The Poems* (Oxford: Clarendon Press, 1980–   ).

Hayley, W. (rev. T. S. Grimshawe), *The Life and Works of William Cowper*

(London: Saunders and Ottley, 1836), 2nd ed. 8 vols.

King, J., *William Cowper. A Biography* (Durham, N.C.: Duke University Press, 1986).

Meyer, J. E. and R., 'Self-Portrayal by a Depressed Poet: A Contribution to the Clinical Biography of William Cowper', *American Journal of Psychiatry*, 144: 2 (1987), 127–32.

Nicholson, N., *William Cowper* (London: John Lehmann, 1951).

Ryskamp, C., *William Cowper of the Inner Temple, Esq. A Study of His Life and Works to the Year 1768* (Cambridge: Cambridge University Press, 1959).

Spiller, R. E. (ed.), 'A New Biographical Source for William Cowper. (The Holograph Memorandum Book, Relating Wholly to His Cousin, the Poet Cowper, and Mrs Unwin During Their Residence with Him in Norfolk, 1795–1800)', *Publications of the Modern Language Association of America*, XLII: 4 (1927), 946–62.

6   Strange Death in Life: John Clare

Blackmore, E., 'John Clare's Psychiatric Disorder and Its Influence on His Poetry', *Victorian Poetry* 24: 3 (1986), 209–28).

Chilcott, T., *A Publisher and His Circle, the Life and Work of John Taylor, Keats's Publisher* (London: Routledge and Kegan Paul, 1972).

Clare, J. (ed. E. Robinson and D. Powell), *John Clare* (Oxford: Oxford University Press, 1984).

Clare, J. (ed. E. Robinson), *John Clare's Autobiographical Writings. With Wood Engravings by John Lawrence* (Oxford: Oxford University Press, 1983).

Clare, J. (ed. E. Robinson, D. Powell and M. Grainger), *The Later Poems of John Clare 1837–1864* (Oxford: Clarendon Press, 1984), 2 vols.

Clare, J. (ed. M. Storey), *The Letters of John Clare* (Oxford: Clarendon Press, 1985).

Clare, J. (ed. A. Tibble and R. K. R. Thornton), *The Midsummer Cushion* (Ashington, Northumberland: Mid Northumberland Arts Group in Association with Carcanet Press, 1979).

Clare, J. (ed. M. Grainger), *The Natural History Prose Writings of John Clare* (Oxford: Clarendon Press, 1983).

Clare, J. (ed. E. Robinson and D. Powell), *The Parish* (New York: Harmondsworth, 1985).

Clare, J. (ed. G. Grigson), *Poems of John Clare's Madness* (London: Routledge and Kegan Paul, 1949).

Clare, J. (ed. J. W. and A. Tibble), *The Prose of John Clare* (London: Routledge and Kegan Paul, 1951).

Kris, E., *Psychoanalytic Explorations in Art* (London: Allen and Unwin, 1953).

Martin, F. (ed. E. Robinson and G. Summerfield), *The Life of John Clare* (London: Frank Cass, 1964). 2nd ed.

Tennent, T., 'Reflections on Genius', *Journal of Mental Science*, XIX (1953), 1–7.

Tibble, J. W. and A., *John Clare. A Life* (London: Cobden-Sanderson, 1932).

Tibble, J. W. and A., *John Clare: His Life and Poetry* (London: William Heinemann, 1956).

Wilson, J., *Green Shadows. The Life of John Clare* (London: Hodder and Stoughton, 1951).

7 The Storm-Cloud and the Demon: John Ruskin

Abse, J., *John Ruskin. The Passionate Moralist* (London: Quartet Books, 1980).
Benson, A. C., *Ruskin. A Study in Personality* (London: Smith, Elder, 1911).
Fellows, J., *The Failing Distance: The Autobiographical Impulse in John Ruskin* (Baltimore, Johns Hopkins University Press, 1975).
    Ruskin's Maze. Mystery and Madness in His Art (Princeton: Princeton University Press, 1981).
Hilton, T., *John Ruskin. The Early Years 1819–1859* (London: Yale University Press, 1985).
Hunt, J. D., *The Wider Sea. A Life of John Ruskin* (London: Dent, 1982).
Leon, D., *Ruskin the Great Victorian* (London: Routledge and Kegan Paul, 1949).
Lutyens, M., *The Ruskins and the Grays* (London: John Murray, 1972).
Ruskin, J. (ed. H. G. Viljoen), *The Brantwood Diary of John Ruskin, together with Selected Related Letters and Sketches of Persons Mentioned* (London: Yale University Press, 1971).
    (ed. E. T. Cook and A. Wedderburn), *The Works of John Ruskin* Vols. I–xxxix (London: George Allen, 1903–12).
Wilenski, R. H., *John Ruskin: An Introduction to Future Study of His Life and Work* (London: Faber and Faber, 1933).

8 The Beast Behind the Hedge: A. C. Benson

Askwith, B., *Two Victorian Families* (London: Chatto and Windus, 1971).
Benson, A. C., *The Altar Fire* (London: Smith, Elder, 1907).
    At Large (London: Smith, Elder, 1908).
    Beside Still Waters (London: Smith, Elder, 1907).
    Diary (Old Library, Magdalene College, Cambridge).
    (ed. P. Lubbock), *The Diary of Arthur Christopher Benson* (London: Hutchinson 1925).
    The House of Quiet. An Autobiography (London: John Murray, 1904).
    Hugh. Memoir of a Brother (London: Smith, Elder, 1915).
    The Leaves of the Tree (London: Smith, Elder, 1911).
    Life and Letters of Maggie Benson (London: John Murray, 1917).
    Life of Edward White Benson. Sometime Archbishop of Canterbury (London: Macmillan, 1899), 2 vols.
    Memoirs of Arthur Hamilton, B. A. of Trinity College, Cambridge. Extracted from His Letters and Diaries with Reminiscences of His Conversation, by His Friend Christopher Carr of the Same College (London: Kegan Paul, 1886).
    Memories and Friends (London: John Murray, 1924).
    Ruskin. A Study in Personality (London: Smith, Elder, 1911).
    The Silent Isle (London: Smith, Elder, 1910).
    The Thread of Gold (London: John Murray, 1905).
    Thy Rod and Thy Staff (London: Smith, Elder, 1912).
    The Trefoil. Wellington College, Lincoln and Truro (London: John Murray, 1923).

The Upton Letters (London: Smith, Elder, 1905).
Where No Fear Was (London: Smith, Elder, 1914).
Benson Deposit (Bodleian Library, Oxford).
Benson, E. F., *Final Edition. An Informal Biography* (London: Longmans, 1940).
Benson, E. W., *Diaries* (Library, Trinity College, Cambridge).
Newsome, D., *On the Edge of Paradise. A. C. Benson the Diarist* (London: John Murray, 1980).
Sayle, C. (ed.), *Arthur Christopher Benson As Seen by Some Friends* (London, G. Bell, 1925).

9 Shadows on the Brain: Virginia Woolf, Antonia White, Sylvia Plath

Benson, A. C., *The Leaves of the Tree* (London: Smith, Elder, 1911).
Butscher, E. (ed.), *Sylvia Plath. The Woman and the Work* (London: Peter Owen, 1979).
Chitty, S., *Now to My Mother. A Personal Memoir of Antonia White* (London: Weidenfeld and Nicholson, 1985).
Freedman, R. (ed.), *Virginia Woolf. Revaluation and Continuity. A Collection of Essays* (London: University of California Press, 1980).
Garnett, A., *Deceived with Kindness* (London: Chatto and Windus/The Hogarth Press, 1984).
Gordon, L., *Virginia Woolf. A Writer's Life* (Oxford: Oxford University Press, 1984).
Holbrook, D., *Sylvia Plath. Poetry of Existence* (London: The Athlone Press, 1988).
Hopkinson, H. T., *Of This Our Time* (London: Hutchinson, 1982).
Hopkinson, L. P., *Nothing to Forgive* (London: Eyre and Spottiswoode, 1988).
Plath, S., *Ariel* (London: Faber and Faber, 1965).
(ed. T. Hughes), *The Bell Jar* (London: Faber and Faber, 1966).
The Collected Poems (London: Faber and Faber, 1981).
The Johnny Panic and the Bible of Dreams. Short Stories, Prose and Diary Excerpts (London: Faber and Faber, 1977).
(ed. T. Hughes and F. McCullough), *The Journals of Sylvia Plath* (New York: Dial Press, 1982).
(ed. A. S. Plath), *Letters Home. Correspondence (1950–1963)* (London: Faber and Faber, 1976).
Spater, G. and I. Parsons, *A Marriage of True Minds* (London: Cape, 1977).
Trombley, S., *All That Summer She Was Mad. Virginia Woolf and Her Doctors* (London: Junction Books, 1981).
Wagner-Martin, L. *Sylvia Plath. A Biography* (London: Chatto and Windus, 1988).
White, A. (ed. S. Chitty), *As Once in May* (London: Virago, 1983).
Beyond the Glass (London: Virago, 1979).
Frost in May (London: Virago, 1978).
The Hound and the Falcon: The Story of a Reconversion to the Catholic Faith (London: Longmans, 1965).

'The House of Clouds' in *Strangers*, 45–66.
The Lost Traveller (London: Eyre and Spottiswoode, 1950).
Strangers (London: The Harvill Press, 1954).
The Sugar House (London: Eyre and Spottiswoode, 1952).
Woolf, L., *Autobiography* (London: The Hogarth Press, 1960–64), 4 vols.
Woolf, V., *Collected Essays* (London: The Hogarth Press, 1966).
(ed. A. Bell and J. Troutman), *The Diary of Virginia Woolf*, vols. I–V (London: The Hogarth Press, 1983).
Jacob's Room (London: The Hogarth Press, 1915)
(ed. Q. Bell and N. Nicholson), *The Letters of Virginia Woolf* (London: The Hogarth Press, 1975–80), 6 Vols.
(ed. J. Schulkind), *Moments of Being. Unpublished Autobiographical Writings of Virginia Woolf* (London: Sussex University Press, 1976).
Mrs. Dalloway (London: The Hogarth Press, 1925).
Night and Day (London: The Hogarth Press, 1919).
Orlando (London: The Hogarth Press, 1928).
The Voyage Out (London: The Hogarth Press, 1915).
The Waves (London: The Hogarth Press, 1931).
The Years (London: The Hogarth Press, 1937).

10   Inside the Bell Jar

(Note: For sources of literary material of authors referred to in this chapter see the bibliographies to Chapters 3–9.)

1. Abély, P., 'Le signe du miroir dans les psychoses et plus spéciale-ment dans la démence précoce', *Annales Médico-psychologiques*, 88 (1930) 28–36.
2. Andreasen, N. C., 'Thought, language and communication dis-orders', *Archives of General Psychiatry*, 36 (1979) 1315–30.
3. Anthony, E. J., 'Risk, vulnerability, and resilience: an overview', in E. J. Anthony and B. J. Cohler (eds) *The Invulnerable Child* (New York: The Guilford Press, 1987).
4. Bleuler, M., 'What is schizophrenia', *Schizophrenia Bulletin*, 10 (1984) 8–9.
5. Brain, R., *Sane Reflections on Genius* (London: Pitman, 1960).
6. Chitty, S., *Now to My Mother. A Very Personal Memoir of Antonia White* (London: Weidenfeld and Nicolson, 1985).
7. Cox, C. M., *The Early Mental Traits of Three Hundred Geniuses*, Vol. II of *Genetic Studies of Genius*, (ed.) L. M. Terman (Stanford: Stanford University Press, 1926).
8. Crow, T. J., 'A re-evaluation of the viral hypothesis: Is psychosis the result of retroviral integration at a site close to the cerebral domi-nance gene?', *British Journal of Psychiatry*, 145 (1984) 243–53.
9. Fischman, L. G., Dreams, hallucinogenic drug states, and schi-zophrenia: a psychological and biological comparison', *Schizophrenia Bulletin*, 9 (1983) 73–94.
10. Gilman, S. L., *Seeing the Insane* (New York: Wiley, 1982).
11. Hare, E., 'Schizophrenia as a recent disease', *British Journal of Psychiatry*, 153 (1988) 521–31.

12. Harrington, A., Oepen, G., Spitzer, M. and Hermle, L., 'Zur Psycho-pathologie und Neuropsychologie der Wahrnehmung von Gesich-tern', in M. Spitzer, F. A. Vehlein and G. Oepen (eds) *Psychopatholo-gy and Philosophy* (Berlin: Springer-Verlag, 1988).
13. Hartmann, E., Russ, D., van der Kolk, B., Falke, R. and Oldfield, M., 'A preliminary study of the personality of the nightmare sufferer: relationship to schizophrenia and creativity', *American Journal of Psychiatry*, 138 (1981) 794–7.
14. Holbrook, D., *Sylvia Plath. Poetry and Existence*. (London: The Athlone Press, 1976).
15. Holzman, P. S., 'Recent studies of psychophysiology in schizophre-nia', *Schizophrenia Bulletin*, 13 (1987) 49–75.
16. Hopkinson, L. P., *Nothing to Forgive. A Daughter's Life of Antonia White* (London: Chatto and Windus, 1988).
17. Jung, C. G., 'Schizophrenia', *Collected Works of C. G. Jung* (translated by R. F. C. Hull), vol. 3 (London: Routledge and Kegan Paul, 1960).
18. Karlsson, J. L., *Inheritance of Creative Intelligence* (Chicago: Nelson-Hall, 1978).
19. King, D. J. and Cooper, S. J., 'Viruses, immunity and mental disorder', *British Journal of Psychiatry*, 154 (1989) 1–7.
20. Kretschmer, E., *Physique and Character* (translated by W. J. H. Sprott) (London: Kegan, Trench and Trubner, 1925).
21. LaRusso, L., 'Sensitivity of paranoid patients to non-verbal cues'. *Journal of Abnormal Psychology*, 87 (1978) 463–71.
22. McGuffin, P., 'Major genes for affective disorder', *British Journal of Psychiatry*, 153 (1988) 591–6.
23. McKie, R., *The Genetic Jigsaw. The Story of the New Genetics* (Oxford: Oxford University Press, 1988).
24. Mendolsohn, E. and Silverman, L. H., 'Effects of stimulating psychodynamically relevant unconscious fantasies on schizophre-nic psychopathology', *Schizophrenia Bulletin*, 8 (1982) 532–47.
25. *Nature*, 336 (10 November 1988).
26. Nicholson, N., *William Cowper* (London: John Lehmann, 1951).
27. Recollections of Virginia Woolf by Louie Mayer, *Ms.*, 1 (1972) 71 ff.
28. Rosenzweig, S. and Shakow, D., 'Mirror behaviour in schizophrenic and normal individuals', *Journal of Nervous and Mental Disease*, 86 (1937), 166–74.
29. Rowe, D., *Beyond Fear* (London: Fontana, 1987).
30. Sidgwick, H. (and many others), 'Report of the census of hallucina-tions', *Proceedings of the Society for Psychical Research*, 26 (1894) 259–394.
31. Slade, P. D. and Bentall, R. P., *Sensory Deception. A Scientific Analysis of Hallucination* (London: Croom Helm, 1988).
32. Wagner-Martin, L. W., *Sylvia Plath. A Biography* (London: Chatto and Windus, 1987).
33. Weeks, D. J. (with Ward, K.), *Eccentrics. The Scientific Investigation* (Stirling: University of Stirling Press, 1988).

Index

Note: Page numbers in bold type refer to main chapter entries for authors.